Brevity 4

Other Books by

guy & rodd

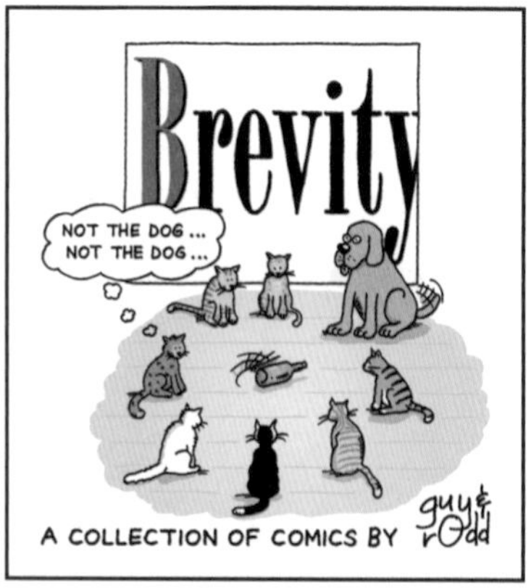

Brevity
NOT THE DOG ...
NOT THE DOG ...
A COLLECTION OF COMICS BY
guy & rodd

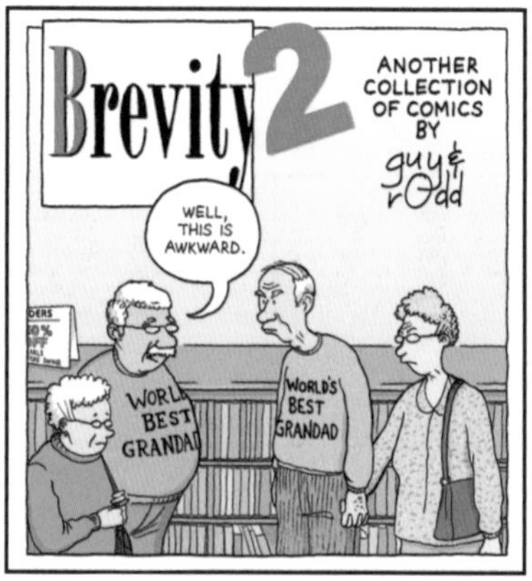

Brevity 2
ANOTHER COLLECTION OF COMICS BY
guy & rodd
WELL, THIS IS AWKWARD.
WORLD'S BEST GRANDAD
WORLD'S BEST GRANDAD

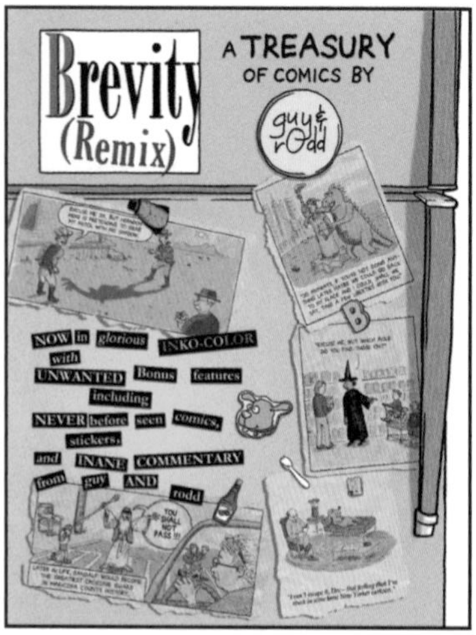

Brevity (Remix)
A TREASURY OF COMICS BY
guy & rodd
NOW in glorious INKO-COLOR with UNWANTED Bonus features including NEVER before seen comics, stickers, and INANE COMMENTARY from guy AND rodd

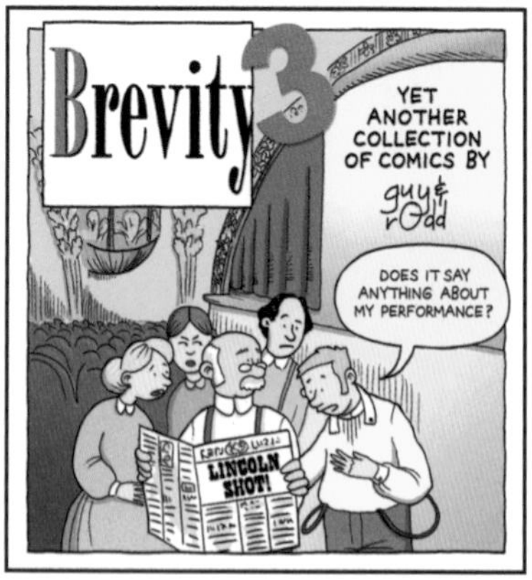

Brevity 3
YET ANOTHER COLLECTION OF COMICS BY
guy & rodd
DOES IT SAY ANYTHING ABOUT MY PERFORMANCE?
LINCOLN SHOT!

Brevity 4

ANOTHER
COLLECTION
OF
FINE COMICS
HAND SELECTED
BY

guy &
rOdd

**Andrews McMeel
Publishing, LLC**

Kansas City

Brevity is distributed by United Feature Syndicate, Inc.

09 10 11 12 13 SDB 10 9 8 7 6 5 4 3 2 1

ISBN-13: 978-0-7407-7361-7
ISBN-10: 0-7407-7361-5

Library of Congress Control Number: 2008942229

www.andrewsmcmeel.com

Guy would like to dedicate this book to his brain. Thanks for always being there, and for writing most of the jokes in this book. You are the best. I love you.

Rodd would like to dedicate this book to Kit Kat, his favorite candy bar, which paid him a small promotional fee.

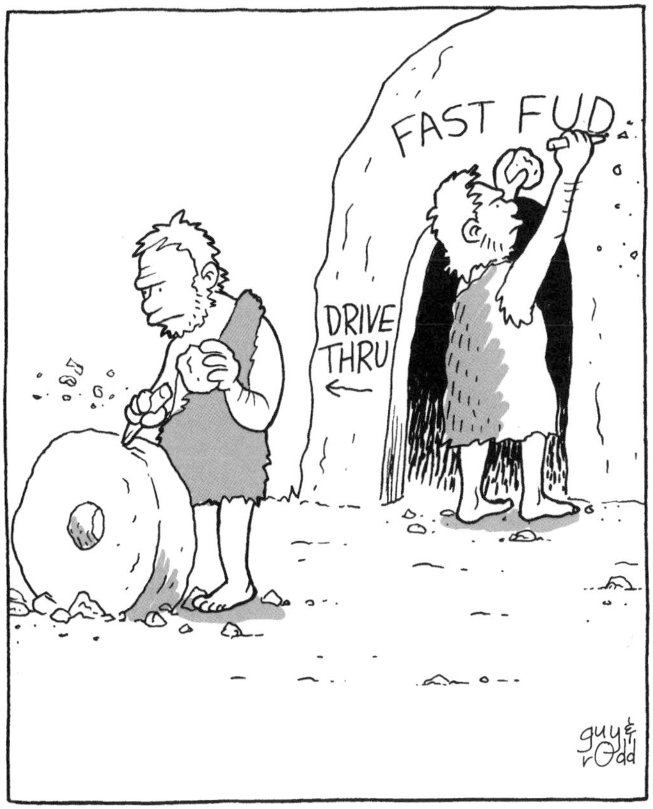
FAST FUD
DRIVE THRU
guy & rOdd

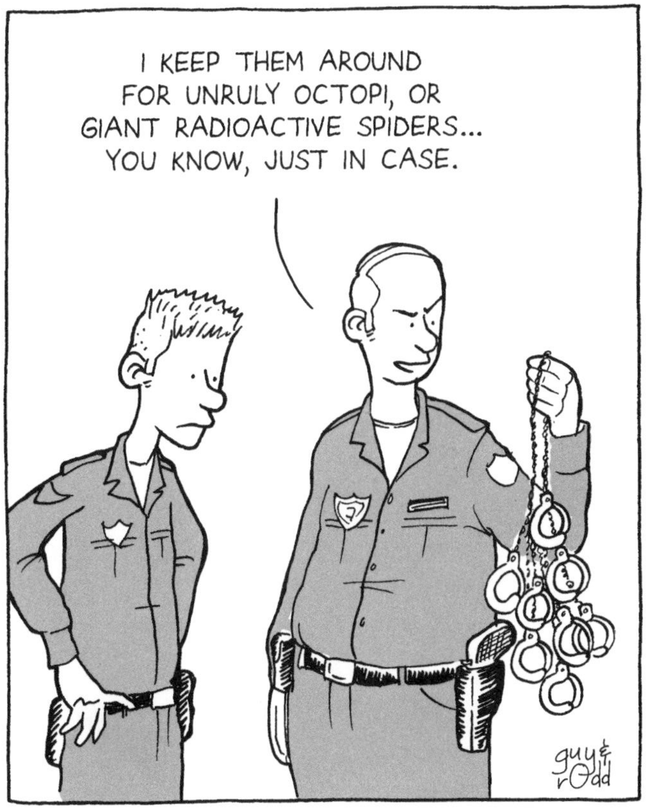
I KEEP THEM AROUND FOR UNRULY OCTOPI, OR GIANT RADIOACTIVE SPIDERS... YOU KNOW, JUST IN CASE.
guy & rOdd

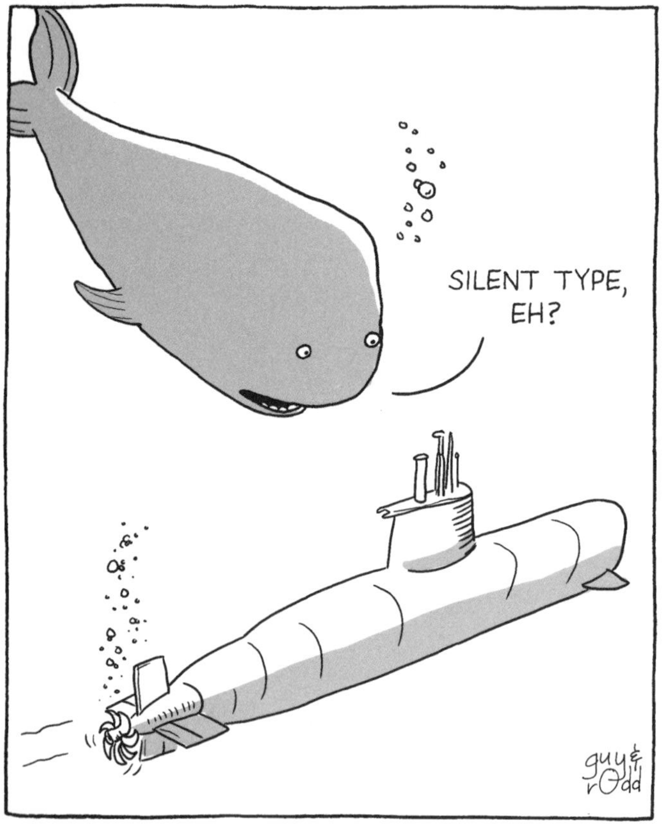
SILENT TYPE, EH?
guy & rOdd

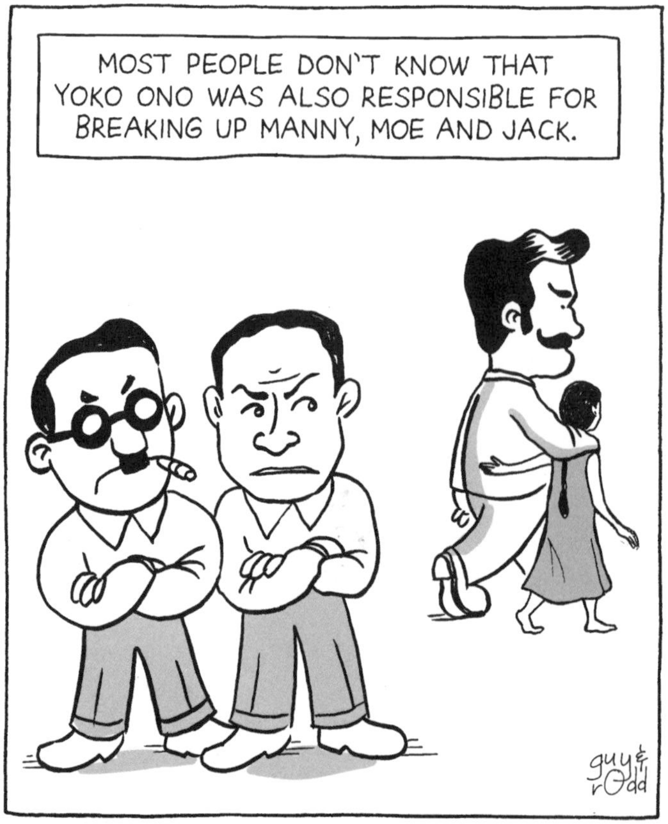
MOST PEOPLE DON'T KNOW THAT YOKO ONO WAS ALSO RESPONSIBLE FOR BREAKING UP MANNY, MOE AND JACK.
guy & rOdd

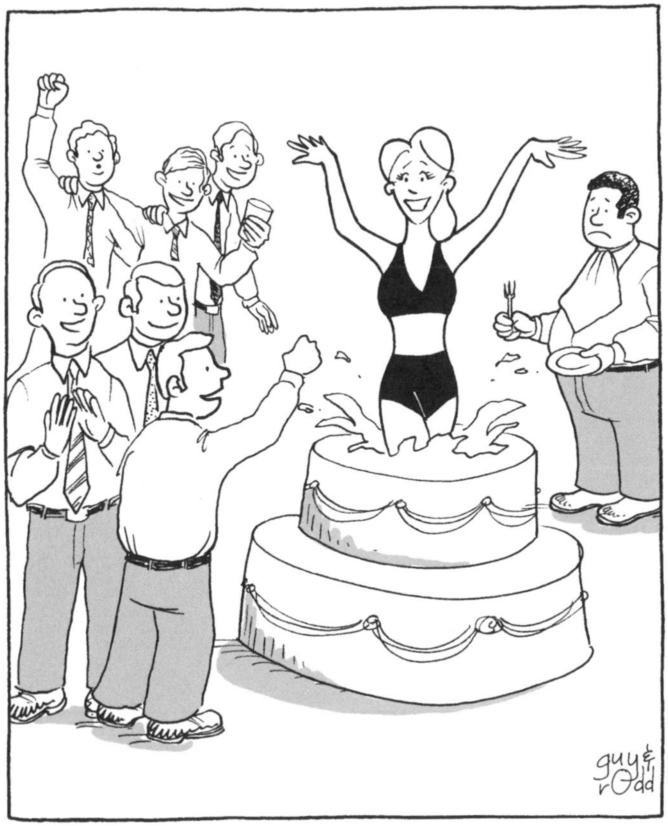
guy & rodd

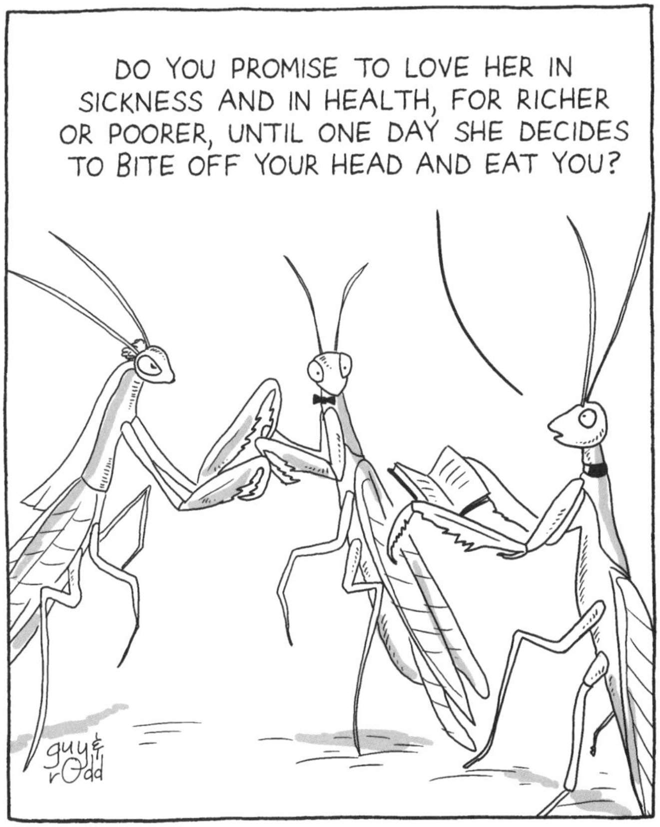
DO YOU PROMISE TO LOVE HER IN SICKNESS AND IN HEALTH, FOR RICHER OR POORER, UNTIL ONE DAY SHE DECIDES TO BITE OFF YOUR HEAD AND EAT YOU?
guy & rodd

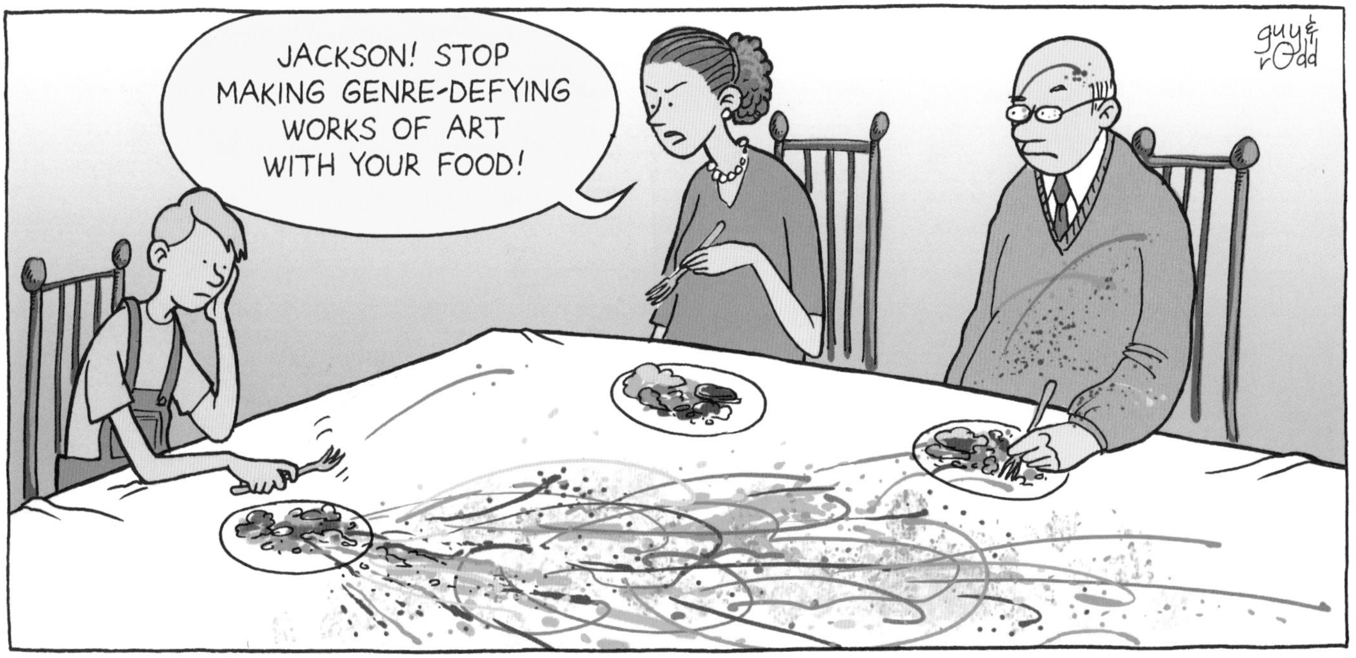
JACKSON! STOP MAKING GENRE-DEFYING WORKS OF ART WITH YOUR FOOD!
guy & rodd

GOOD-BYE GUM, YOU'VE BEEN A GREAT FRIEND THESE LAST SEVEN YEARS.

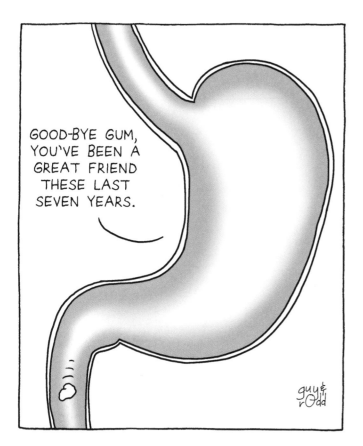

THE LION, THE WITCH
AND THE WARDROBE STYLIST

MOST PEOPLE DON'T KNOW THAT
SOUTH AMERICAN PYRAMIDS WERE
ORIGINALLY BUILT AS AN ALTAR
TO THEIR GOD, THE SLINKY.

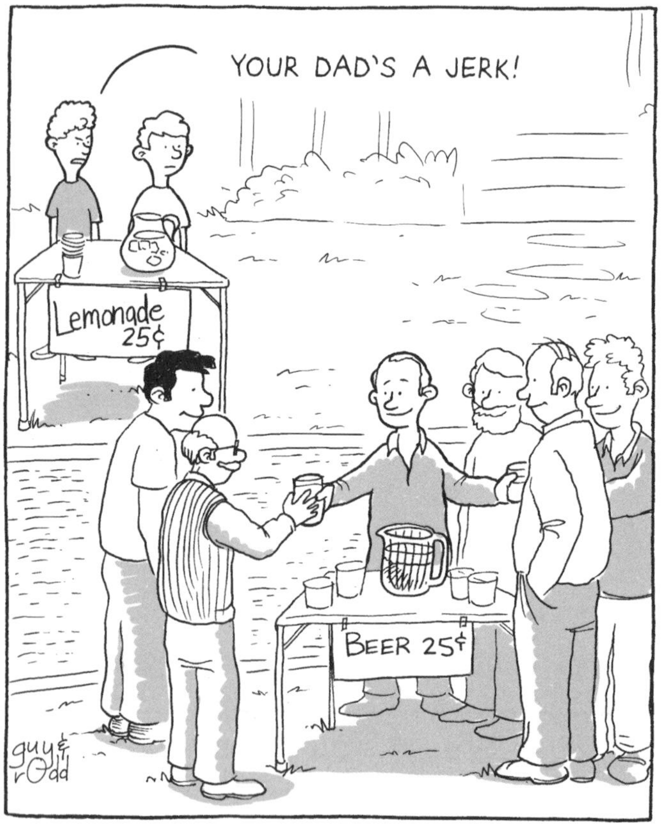
YOUR DAD'S A JERK!
Lemonade 25¢
BEER 25¢
guy & rOdd

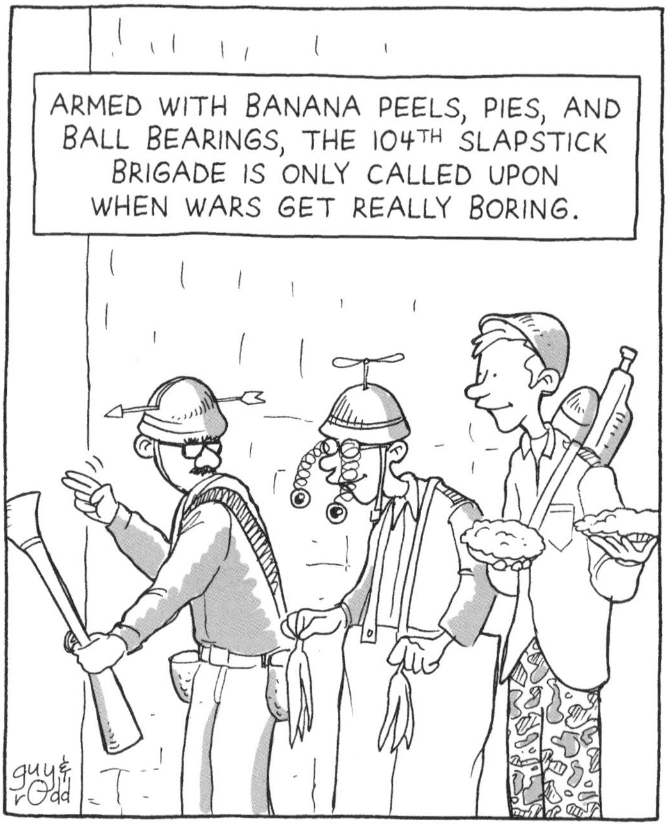
ARMED WITH BANANA PEELS, PIES, AND BALL BEARINGS, THE 104TH SLAPSTICK BRIGADE IS ONLY CALLED UPON WHEN WARS GET REALLY BORING.
guy & rOdd

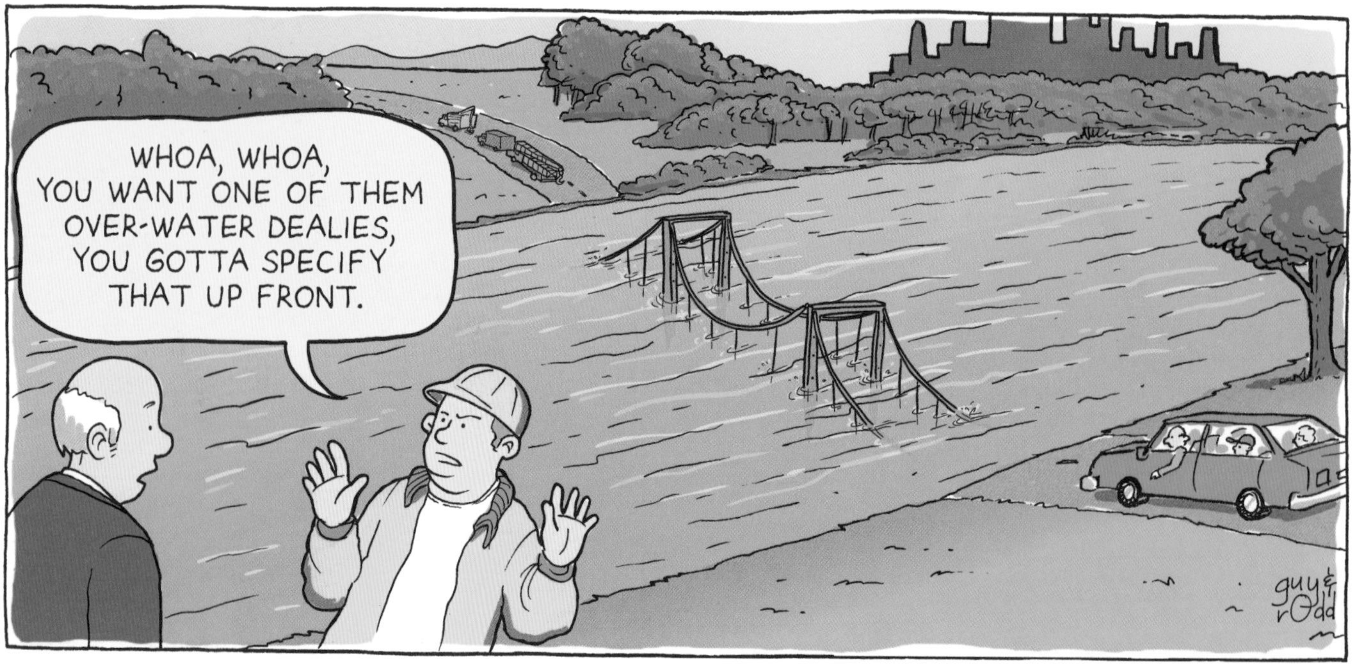
WHOA, WHOA, YOU WANT ONE OF THEM OVER-WATER DEALIES, YOU GOTTA SPECIFY THAT UP FRONT.
guy & rOdd

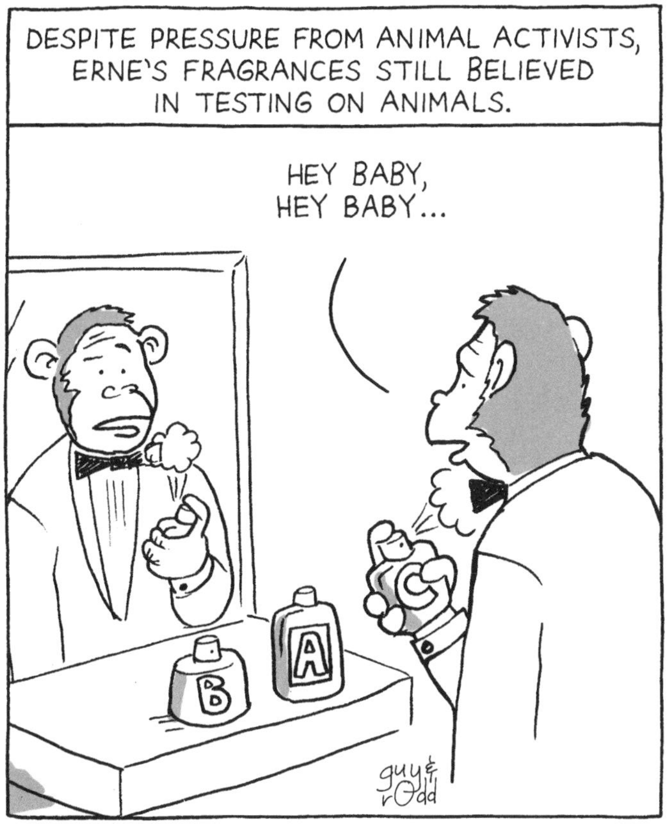
DESPITE PRESSURE FROM ANIMAL ACTIVISTS, ERNE'S FRAGRANCES STILL BELIEVED IN TESTING ON ANIMALS.
HEY BABY, HEY BABY...
guy & rOdd

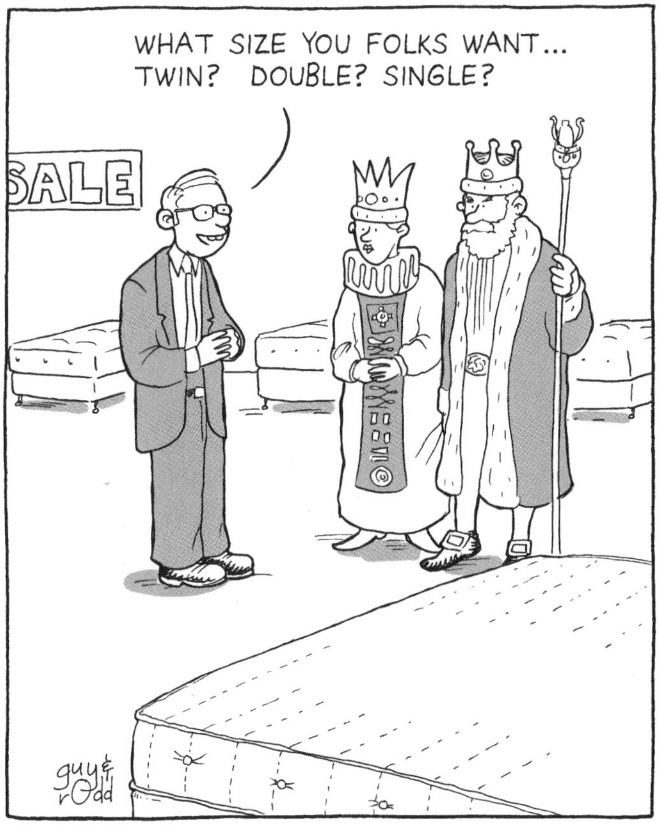
WHAT SIZE YOU FOLKS WANT... TWIN? DOUBLE? SINGLE?
SALE
guy & rOdd

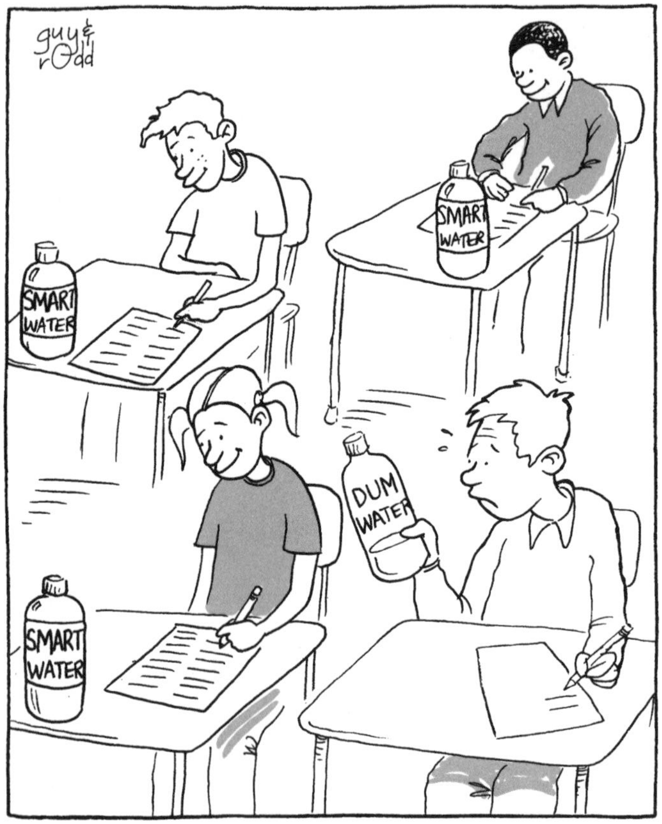
guy & rodd
SMART WATER
SMART WATER
SMART WATER
DUM WATER

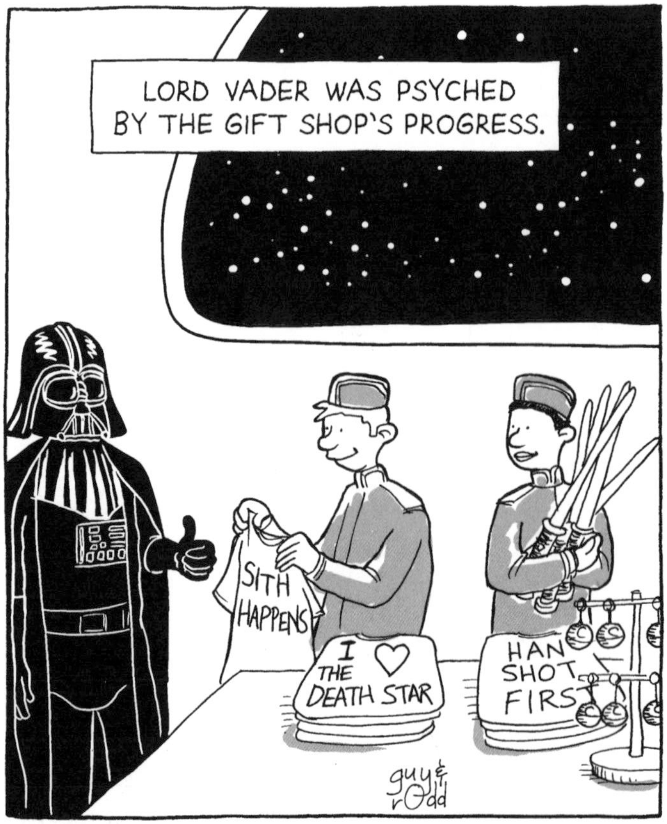
LORD VADER WAS PSYCHED BY THE GIFT SHOP'S PROGRESS.
SITH HAPPENS
I ♡ THE DEATH STAR
HAN SHOT FIRST
guy & rodd

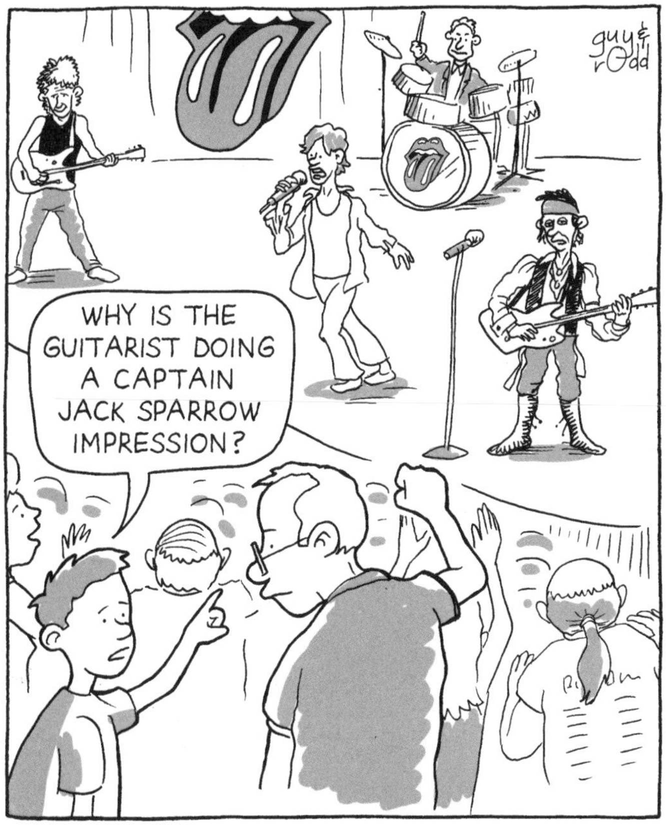
WHY IS THE GUITARIST DOING A CAPTAIN JACK SPARROW IMPRESSION?
guy & rOdd

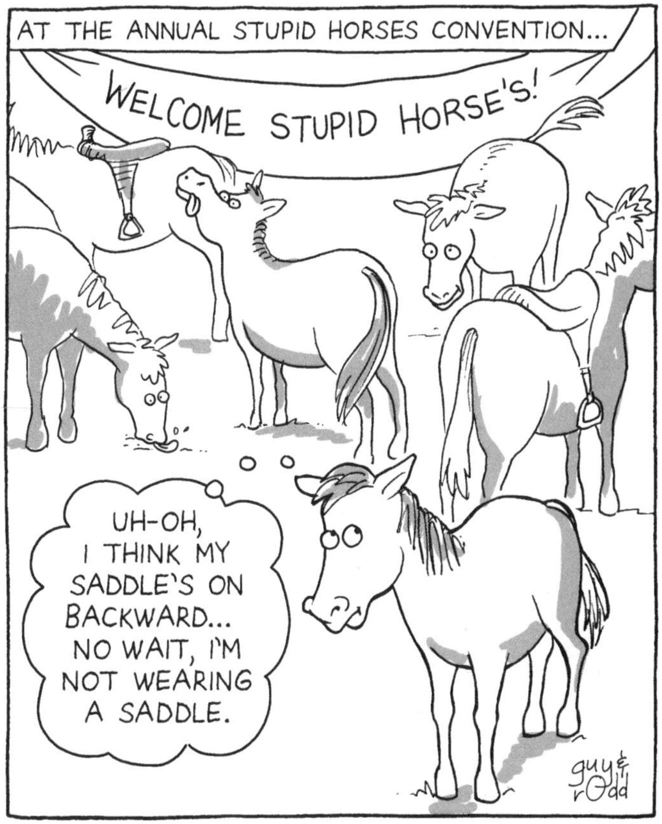
AT THE ANNUAL STUPID HORSES CONVENTION...
WELCOME STUPID HORSE'S!
UH-OH, I THINK MY SADDLE'S ON BACKWARD... NO WAIT, I'M NOT WEARING A SADDLE.
guy & rOdd

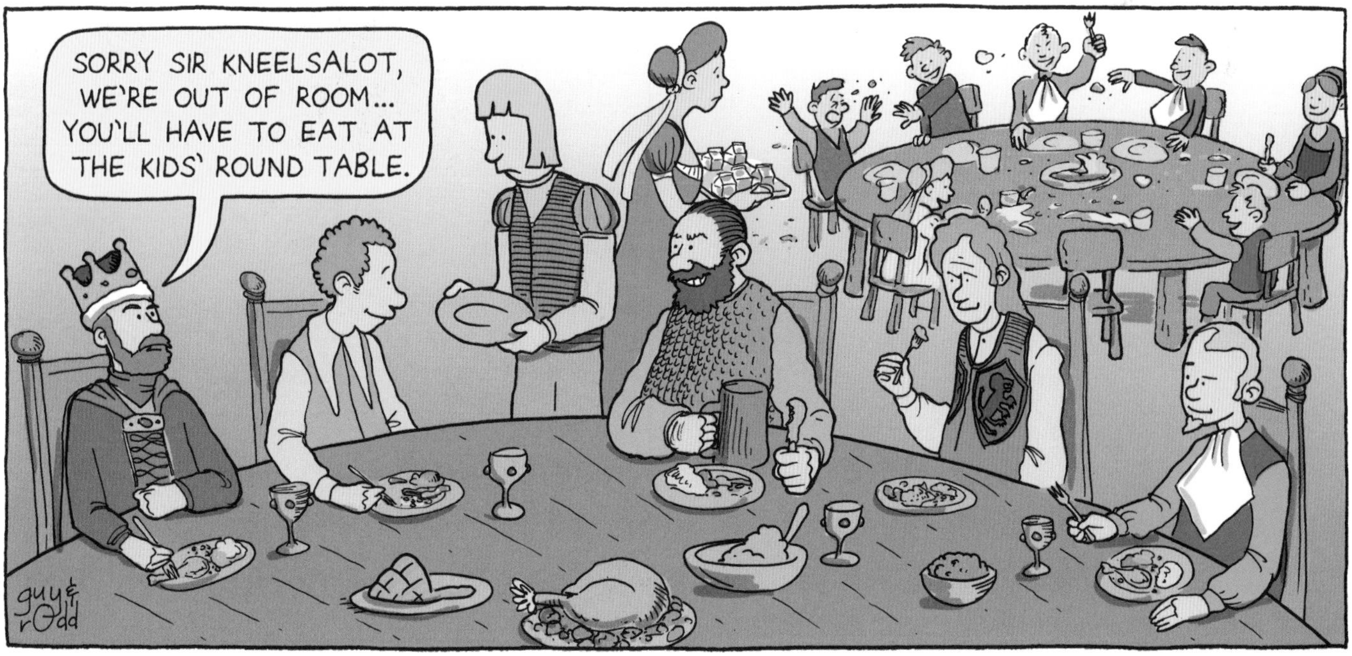
SORRY SIR KNEELSALOT, WE'RE OUT OF ROOM... YOU'LL HAVE TO EAT AT THE KIDS' ROUND TABLE.
guy & rOdd

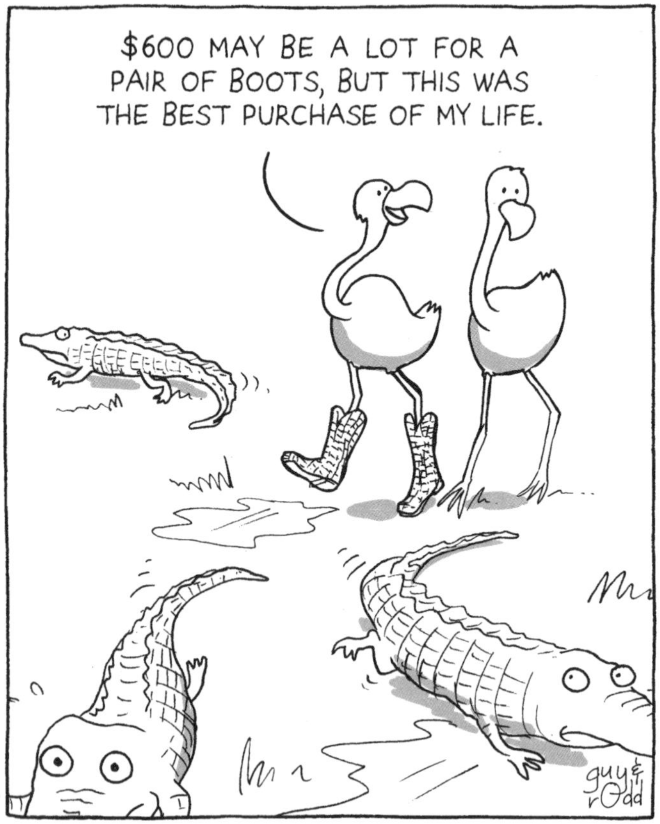
$600 MAY BE A LOT FOR A PAIR OF BOOTS, BUT THIS WAS THE BEST PURCHASE OF MY LIFE.
guy & rOdd

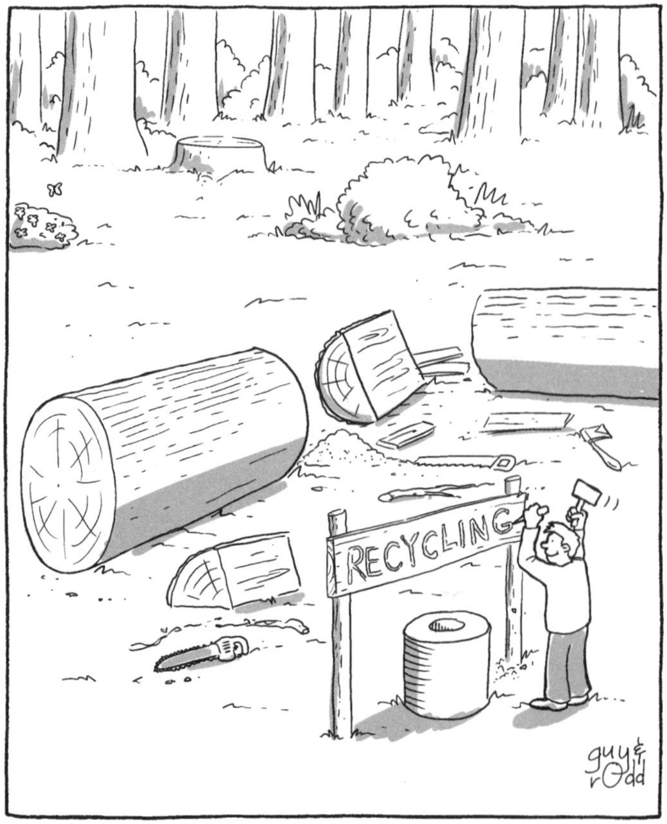
RECYCLING
guy & rOdd

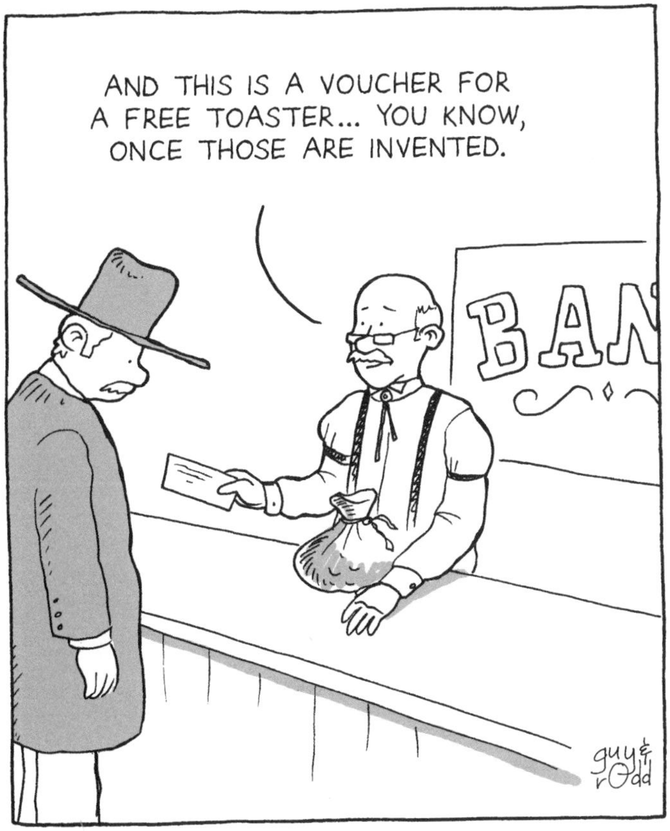
AND THIS IS A VOUCHER FOR A FREE TOASTER... YOU KNOW, ONCE THOSE ARE INVENTED.
BAN
guy & rOdd

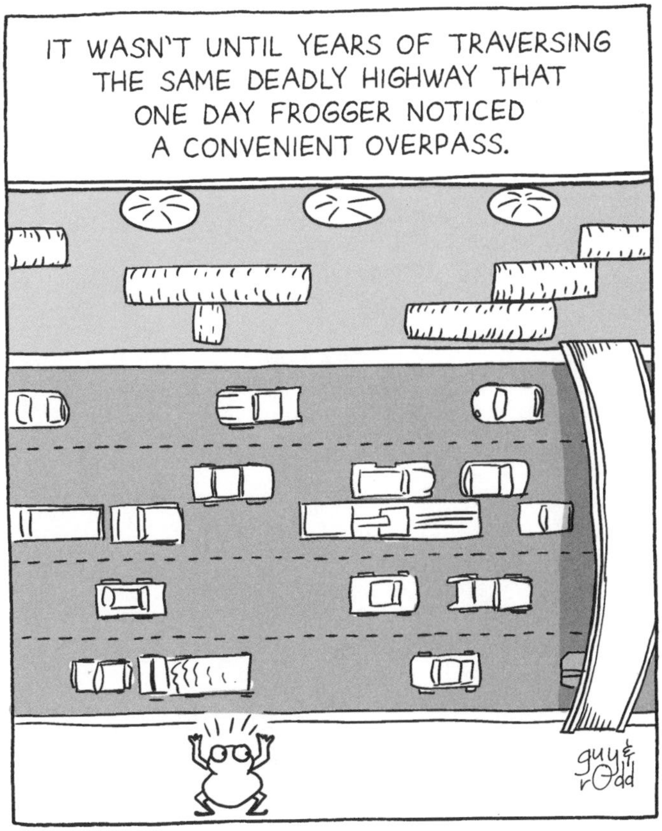
IT WASN'T UNTIL YEARS OF TRAVERSING THE SAME DEADLY HIGHWAY THAT ONE DAY FROGGER NOTICED A CONVENIENT OVERPASS.
guy & rOdd

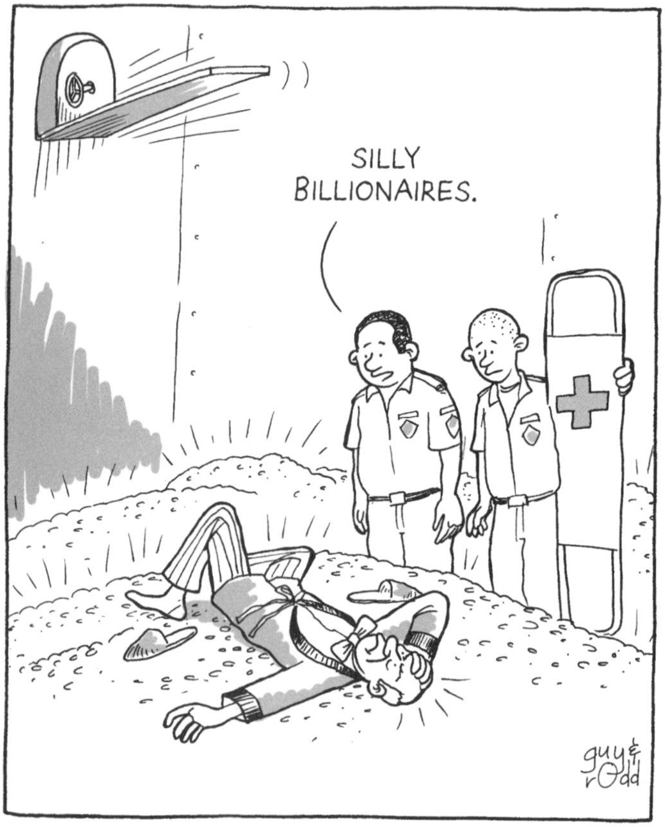
SILLY BILLIONAIRES.
guy & rOdd

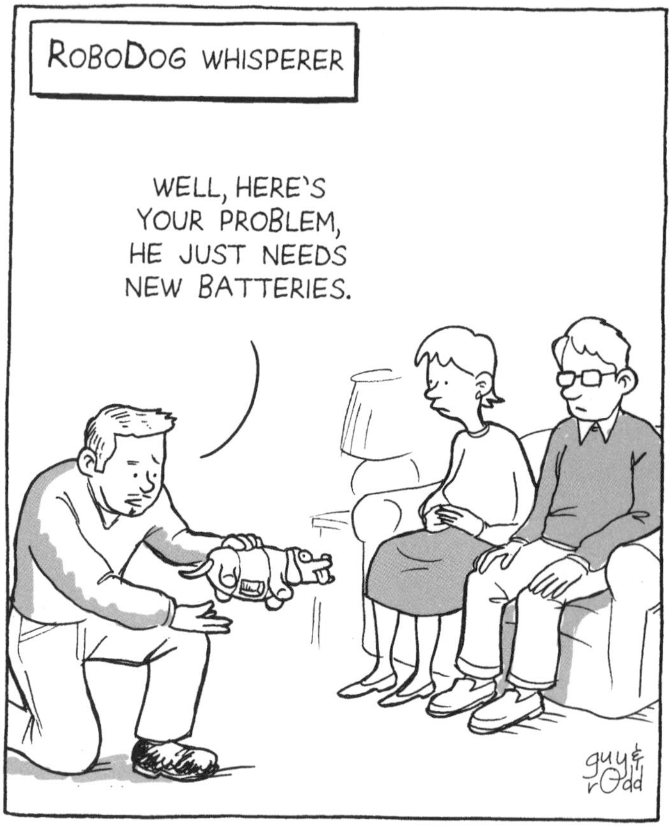
ROBODOG WHISPERER
WELL, HERE'S YOUR PROBLEM, HE JUST NEEDS NEW BATTERIES.
guy & rOdd

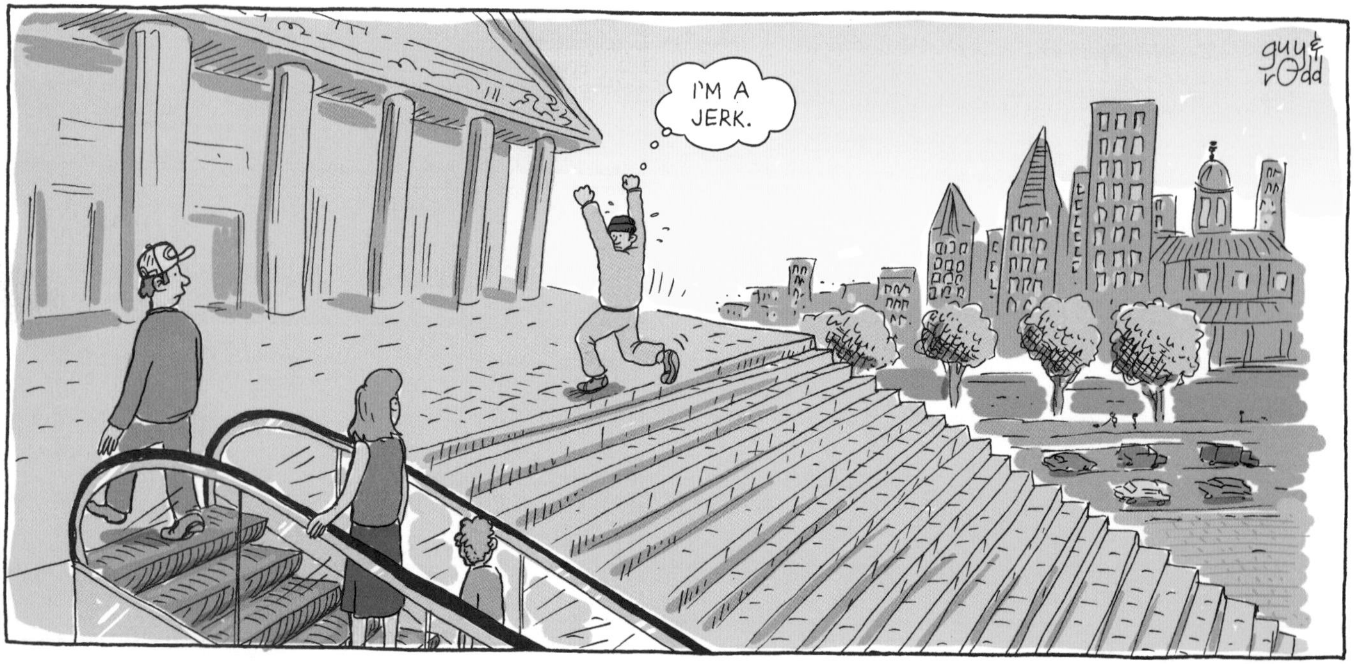
guy & rOdd
I'M A JERK.

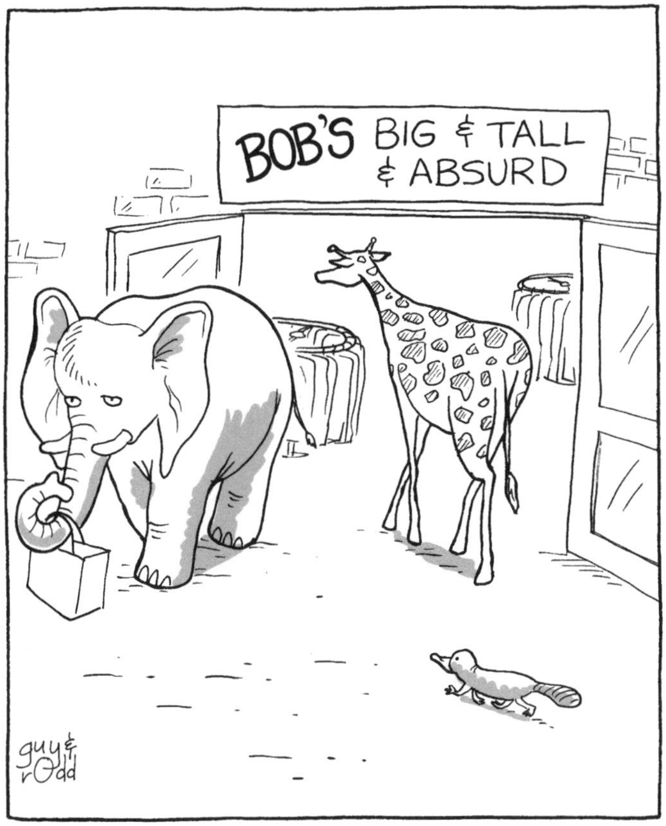
BOB'S BIG & TALL & ABSURD
guy & rOdd

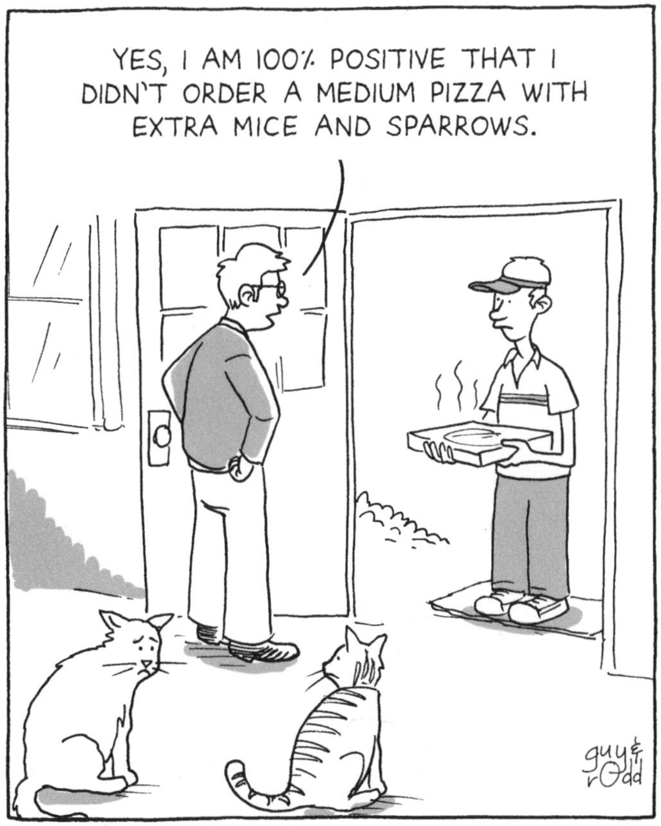
YES, I AM 100% POSITIVE THAT I DIDN'T ORDER A MEDIUM PIZZA WITH EXTRA MICE AND SPARROWS.
guy & rOdd

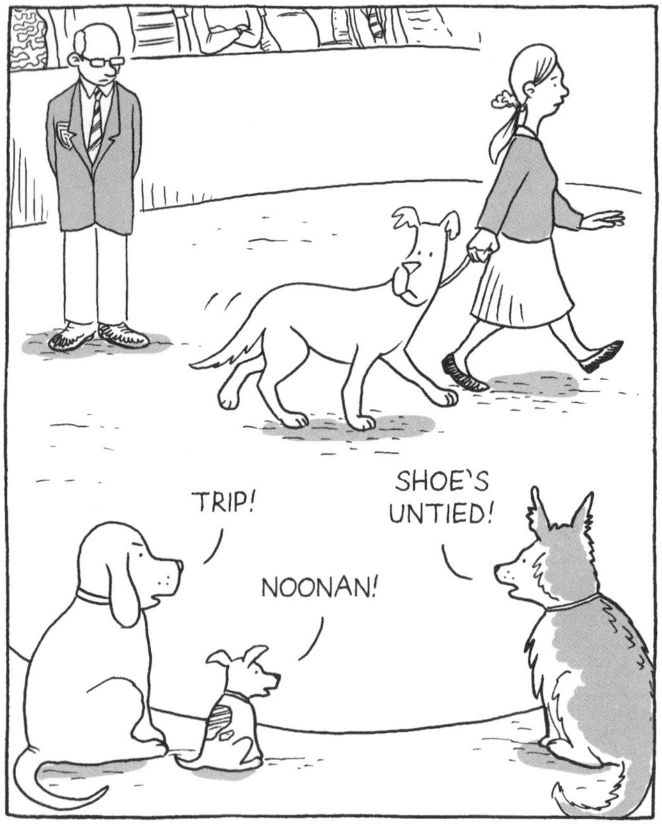
TRIP!
NOONAN!
SHOE'S UNTIED!

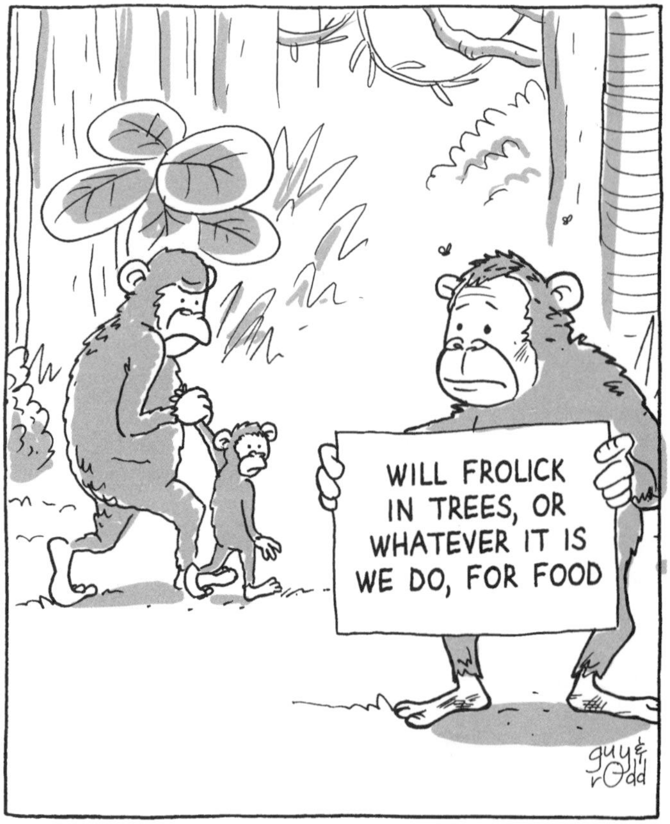
WILL FROLICK IN TREES, OR WHATEVER IT IS WE DO, FOR FOOD
guy & rodd

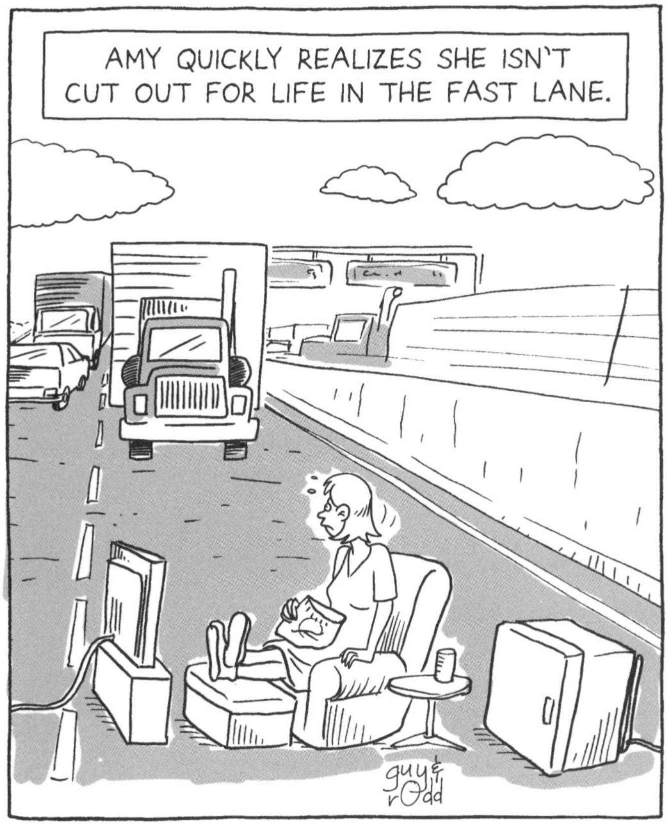
AMY QUICKLY REALIZES SHE ISN'T CUT OUT FOR LIFE IN THE FAST LANE.
guy & rOdd

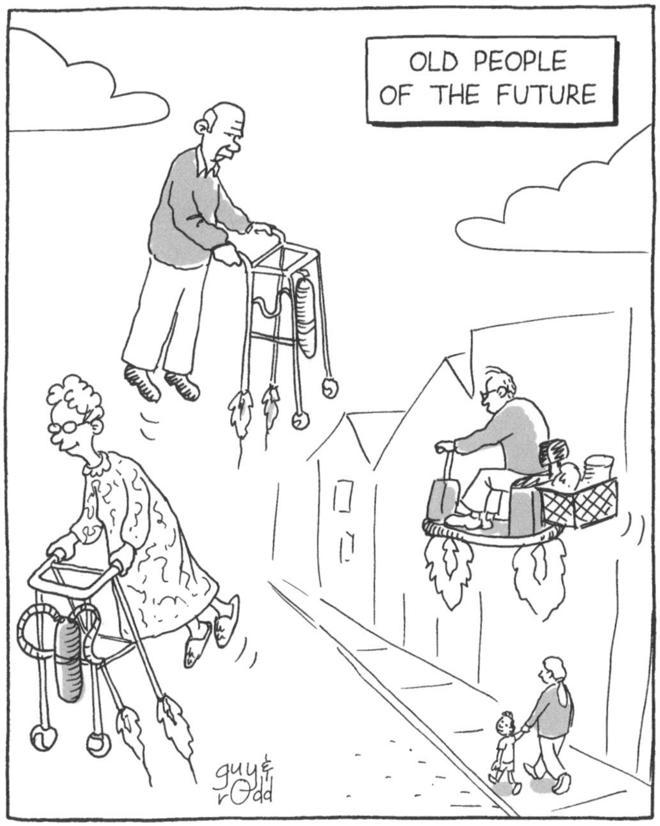
OLD PEOPLE OF THE FUTURE
guy & rOdd

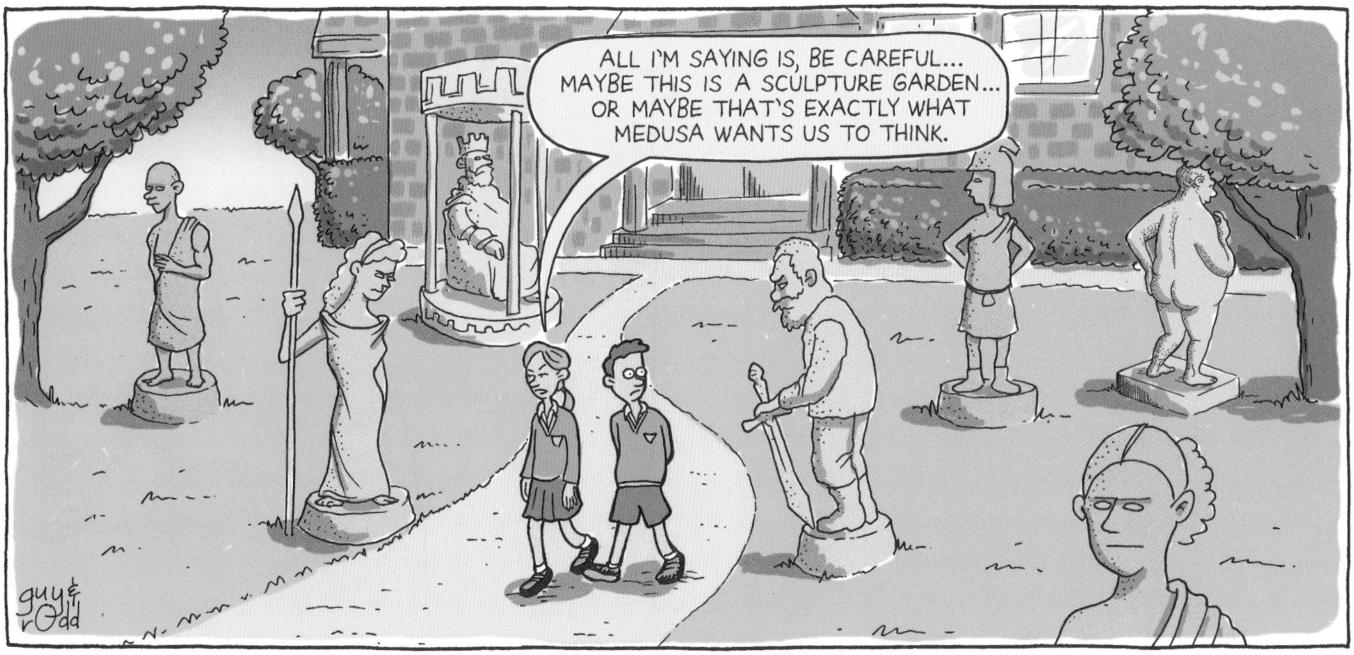
ALL I'M SAYING IS, BE CAREFUL... MAYBE THIS IS A SCULPTURE GARDEN... OR MAYBE THAT'S EXACTLY WHAT MEDUSA WANTS US TO THINK.
guy & rOdd

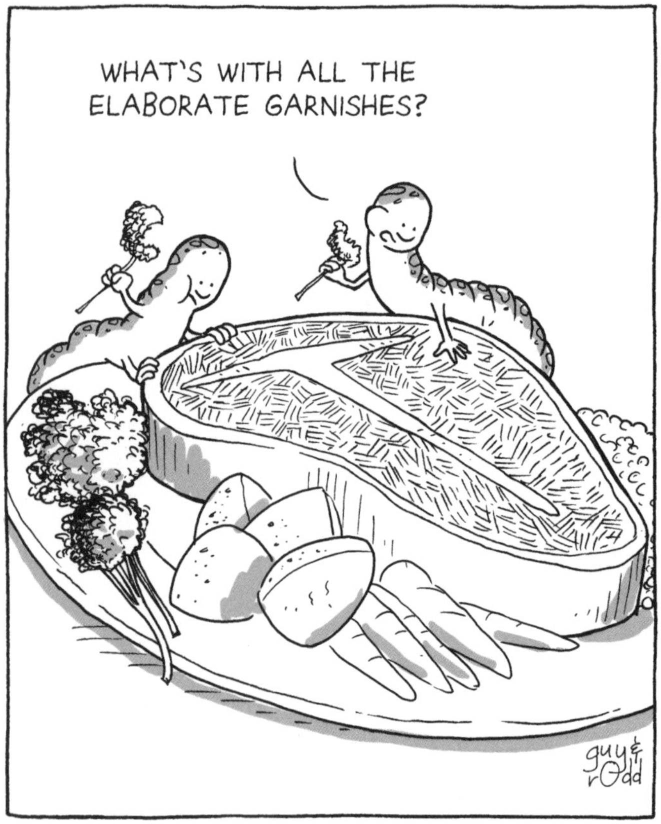
WHAT'S WITH ALL THE ELABORATE GARNISHES?
guy & rOdd

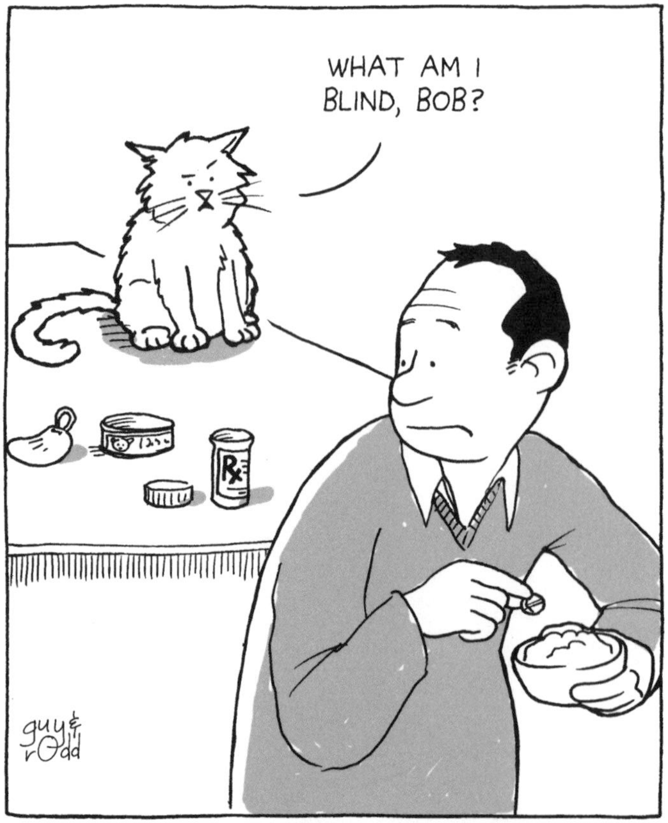
WHAT AM I BLIND, BOB?
Rx
guy & rOdd

YOU AREN'T HERE
YOU AREN'T HERE
YOU AREN'T HERE
YOU AREN'T HERE
YOU AREN'T HERE
YOU AREN'T HERE
YOU AREN'T HERE
YOU AREN'T HERE
YOU AREN'T HERE
YOU AREN'T HERE
YOU AREN'T HERE
YOU AREN'T HERE
YOU AREN'T HERE
YOU AREN'T HERE
YOU AREN'T HERE
YOU AREN'T HERE
YOU AREN'T HERE
1
2
3
4
12
15
20
21
22
23
24
30
31
32
33
51
52
53
54
55
56
57
58
59
60
62
63
64
guy & rOdd

Guy: you are awesome at video games!
Dear Guy- you have really nice legs!
Dear Guy: you are sooo cool!
Call me this Summer! Love Candace
guy & rOdd

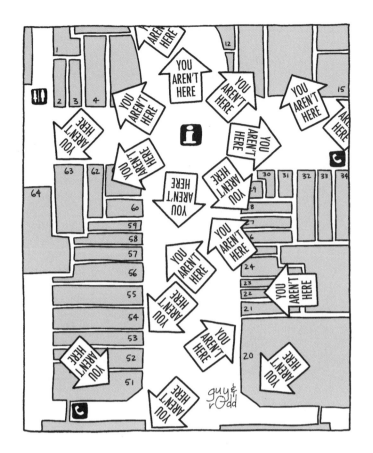

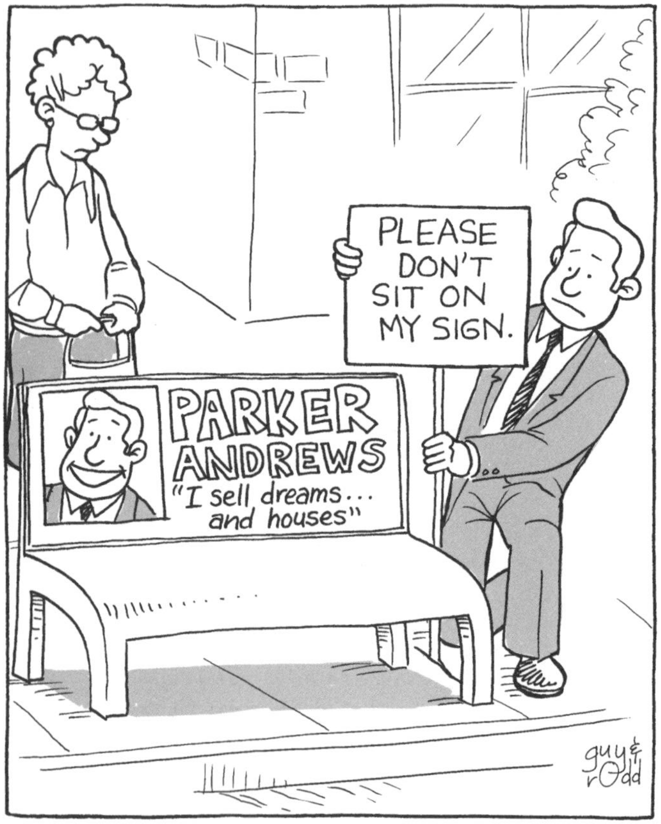
PLEASE DON'T SIT ON MY SIGN.
PARKER ANDREWS
"I sell dreams... and houses"
guy & rOdd

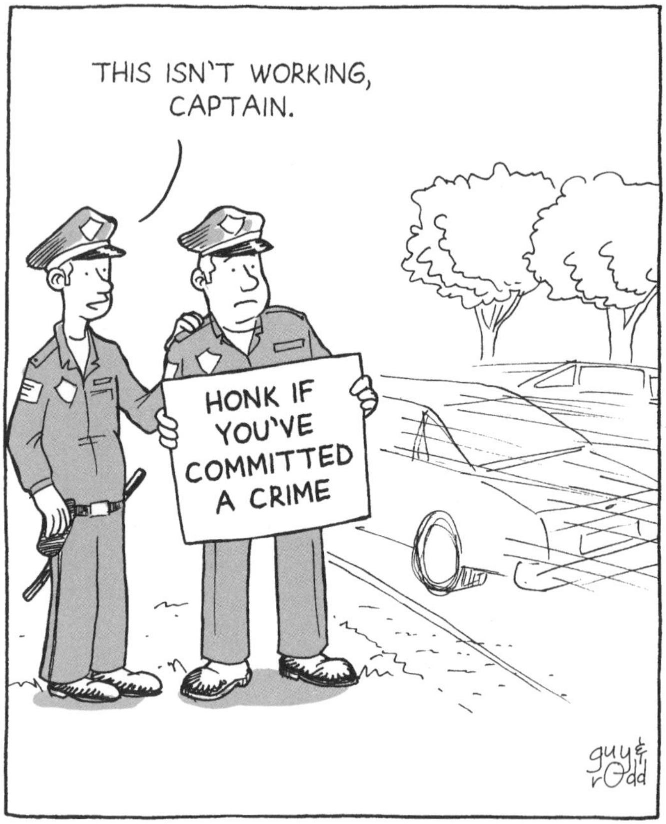
THIS ISN'T WORKING, CAPTAIN.
HONK IF YOU'VE COMMITTED A CRIME
guy & rOdd

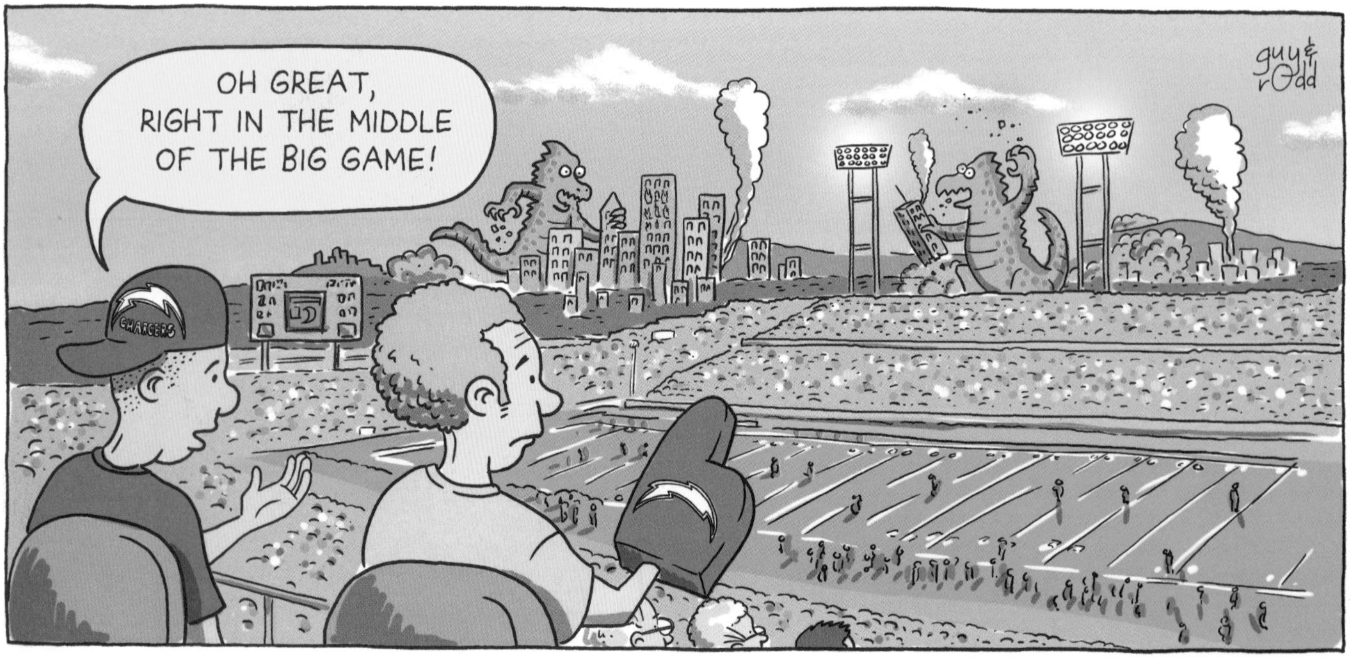
guy & rOdd
OH GREAT, RIGHT IN THE MIDDLE OF THE BIG GAME!
CHARGERS

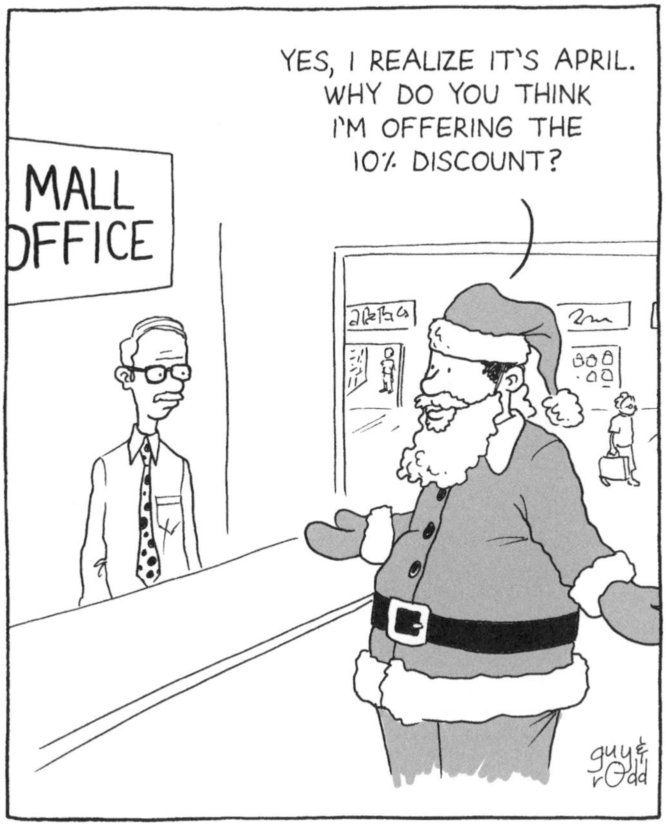
YES, I REALIZE IT'S APRIL. WHY DO YOU THINK I'M OFFERING THE 10% DISCOUNT?
MALL OFFICE
guy & rOdd

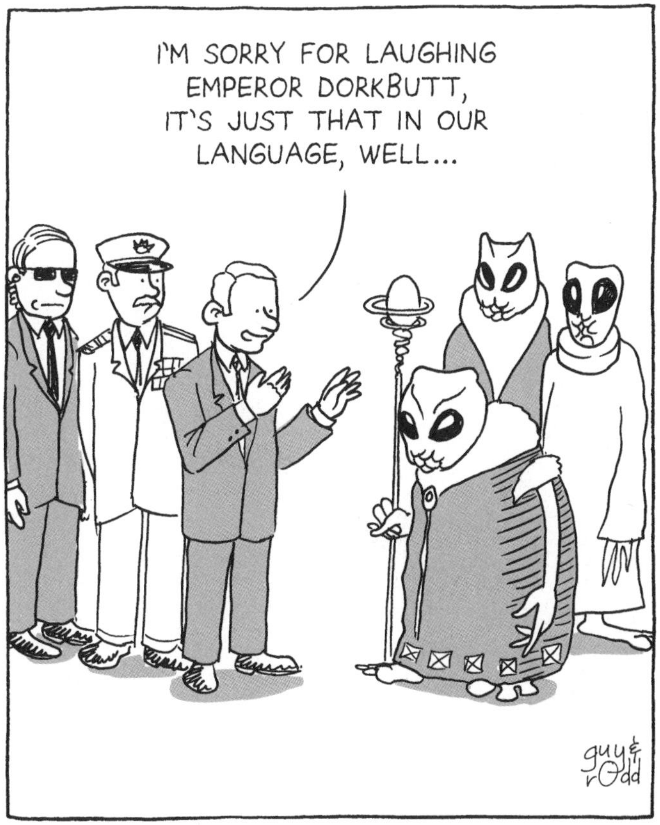
I'M SORRY FOR LAUGHING EMPEROR DORKBUTT, IT'S JUST THAT IN OUR LANGUAGE, WELL...
guy & rOdd

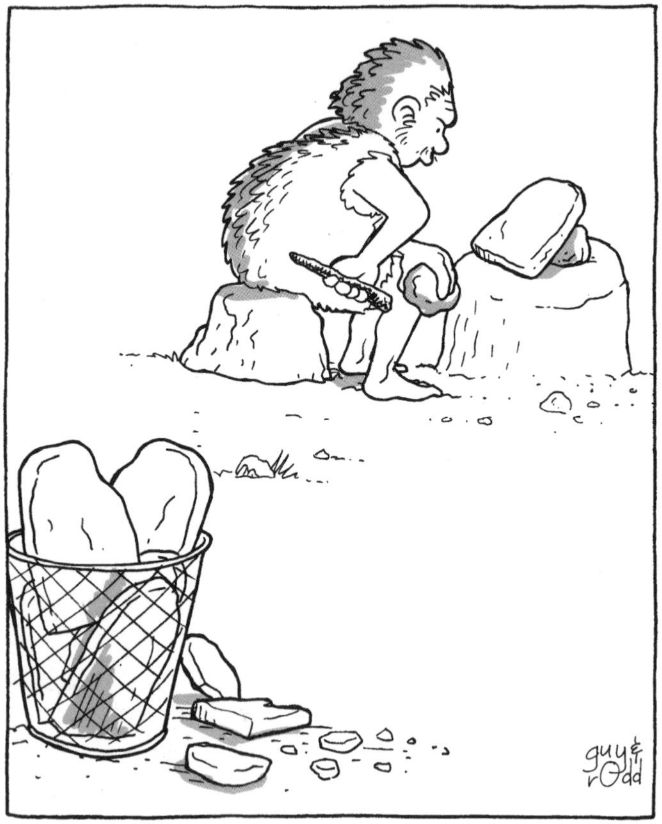
guy &
rOdd

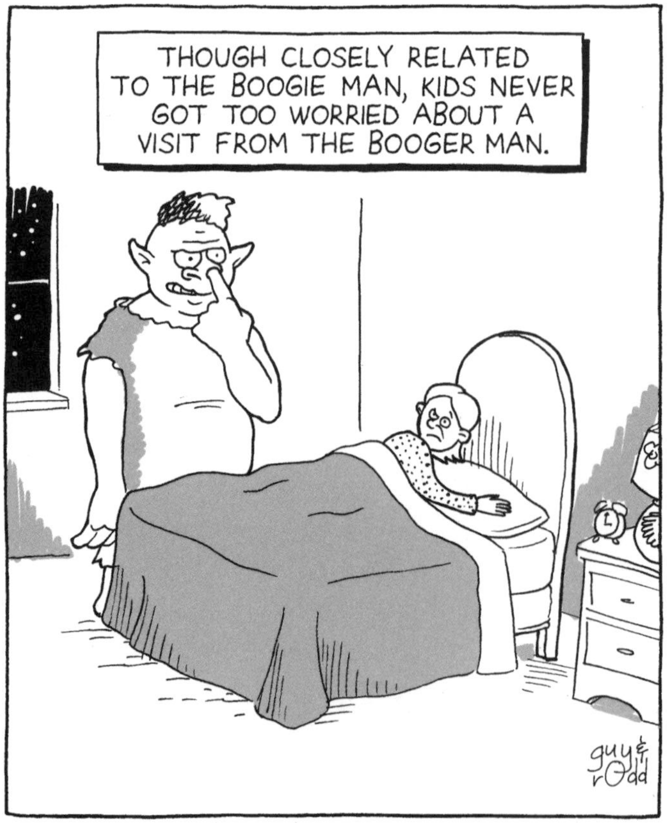
THOUGH CLOSELY RELATED TO THE BOOGIE MAN, KIDS NEVER GOT TOO WORRIED ABOUT A VISIT FROM THE BOOGER MAN.
guy &
rOdd

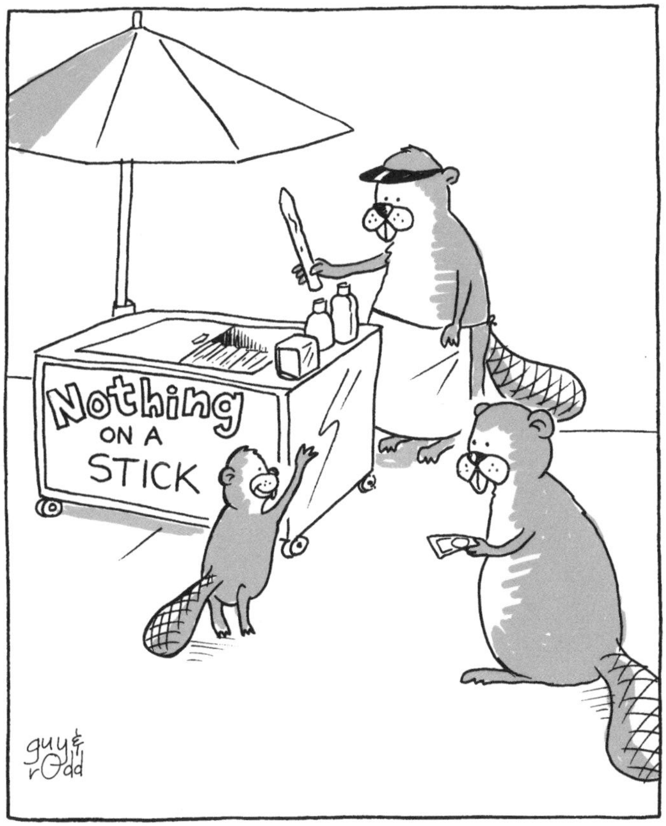
Nothing
ON A
STICK
guy & rodd

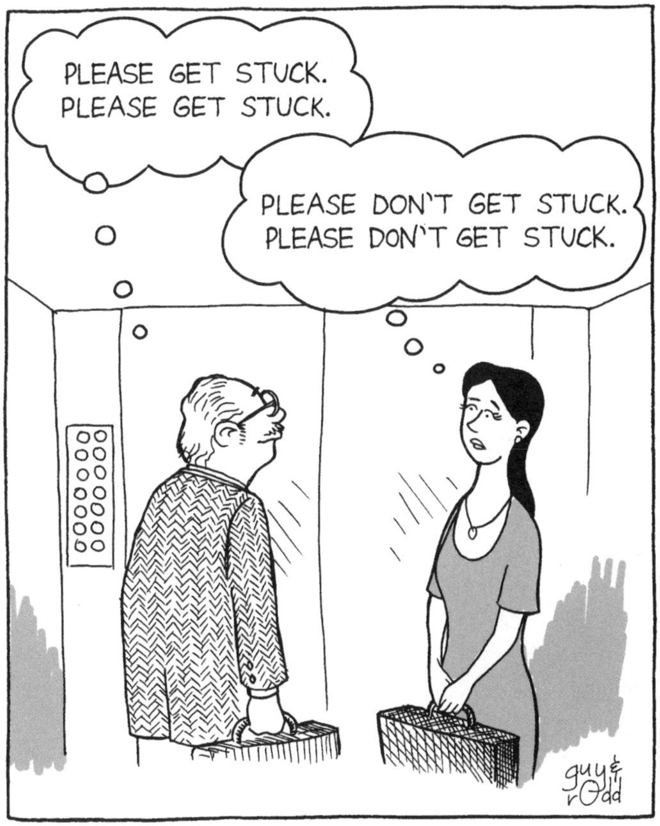
PLEASE GET STUCK.
PLEASE GET STUCK.
PLEASE DON'T GET STUCK.
PLEASE DON'T GET STUCK.
guy & rodd

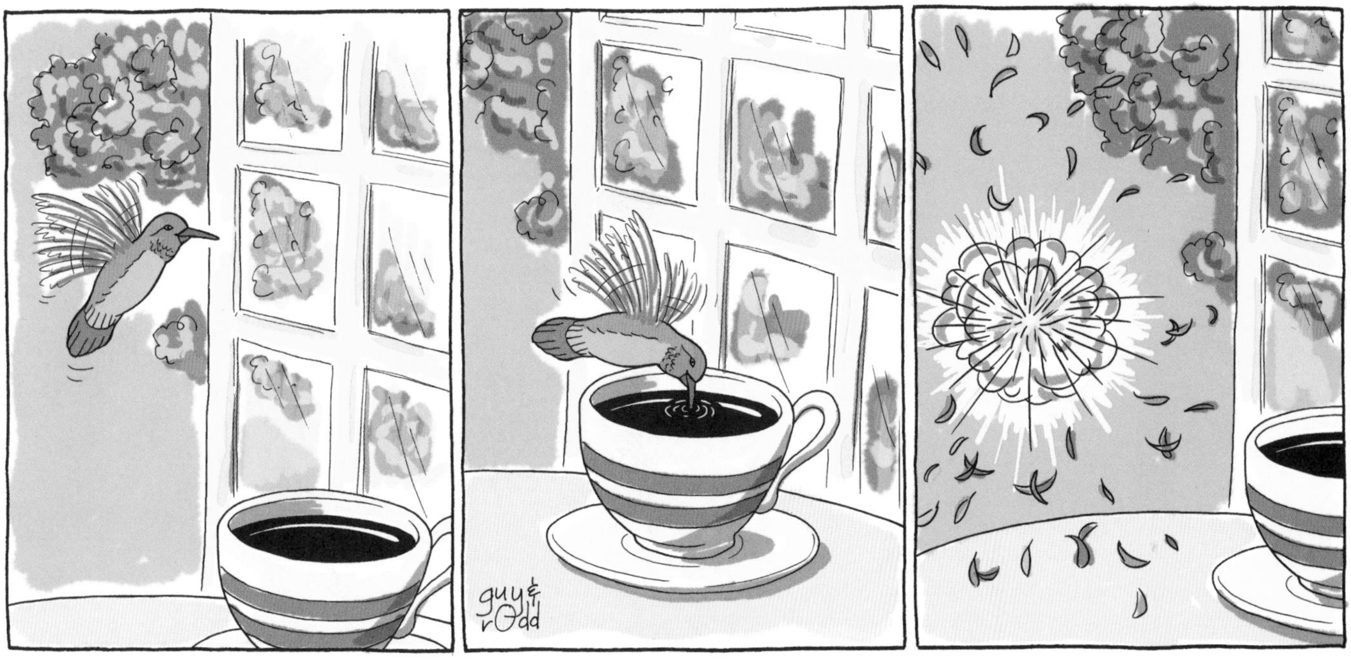
guy & rodd

YOU GUYS ARE THE BEST!
THIS TONGUE RULES!
WE'RE ALL FRIENDS!
TASTE BUDS
guy & rOdd

ICE CREAM
IDIOT.
guy & rOdd

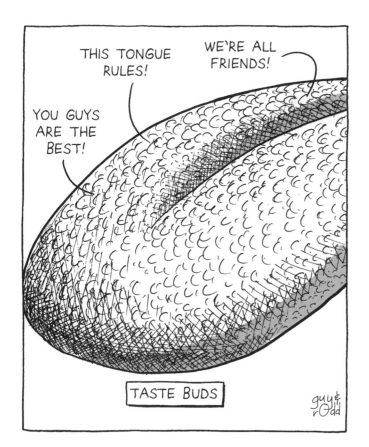

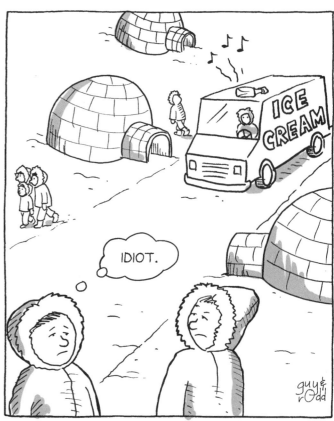

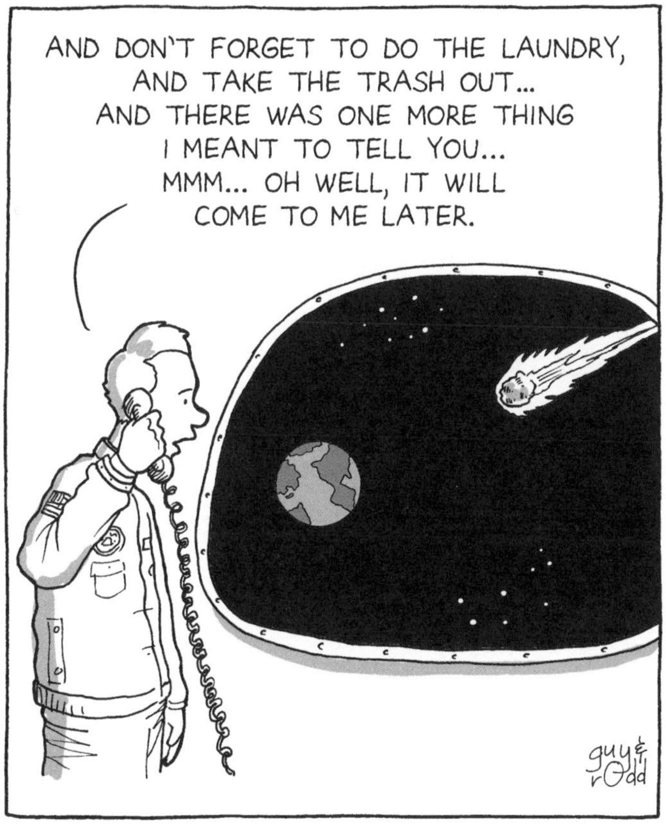
AND DON'T FORGET TO DO THE LAUNDRY, AND TAKE THE TRASH OUT... AND THERE WAS ONE MORE THING I MEANT TO TELL YOU... MMM... OH WELL, IT WILL COME TO ME LATER.
guy & rOdd

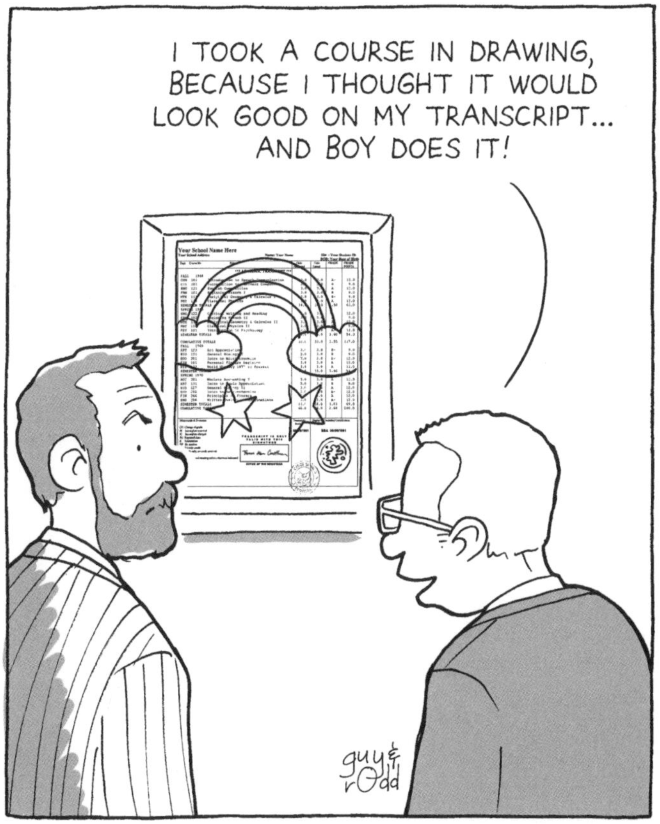
I TOOK A COURSE IN DRAWING, BECAUSE I THOUGHT IT WOULD LOOK GOOD ON MY TRANSCRIPT... AND BOY DOES IT!
guy & rOdd

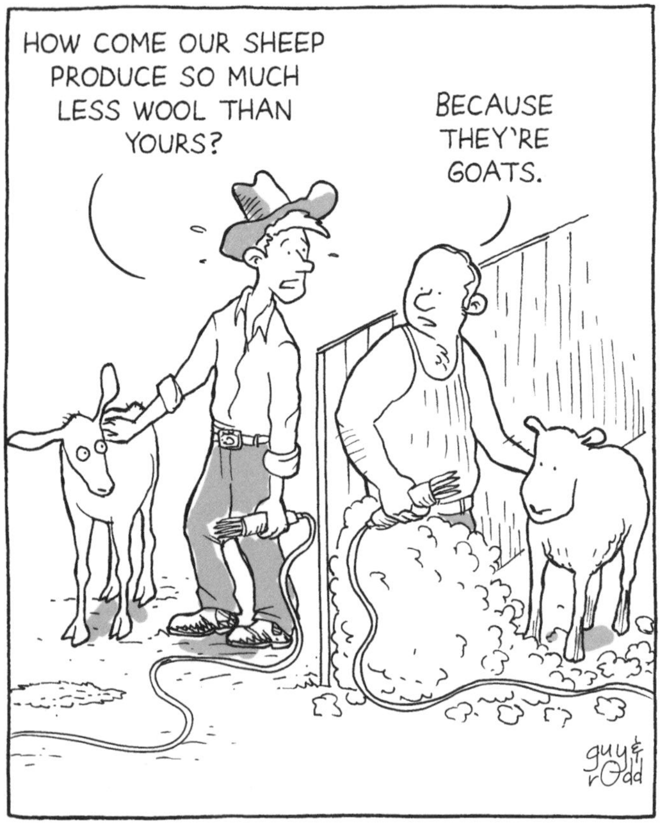
HOW COME OUR SHEEP PRODUCE SO MUCH LESS WOOL THAN YOURS?
BECAUSE THEY'RE GOATS.
guy & rOdd

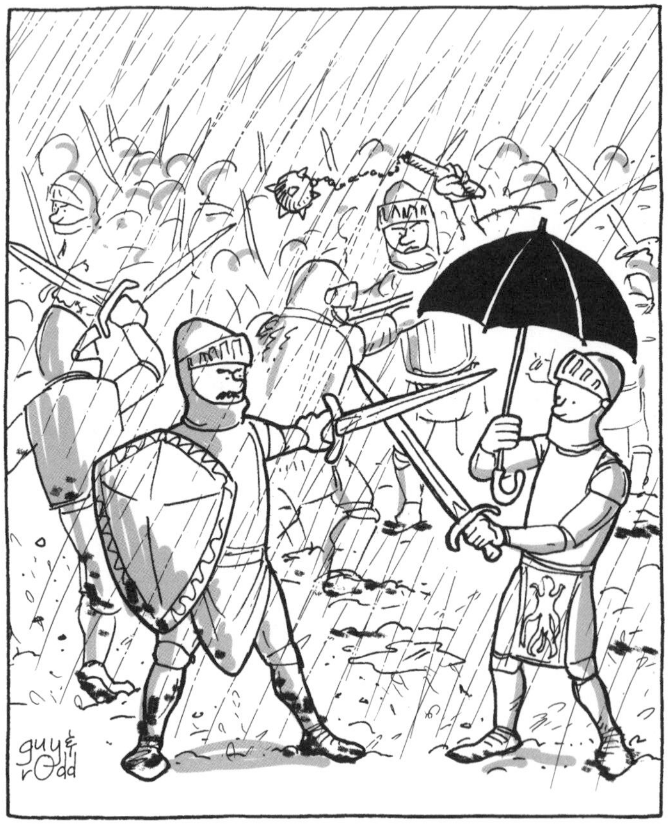
guy & rOdd

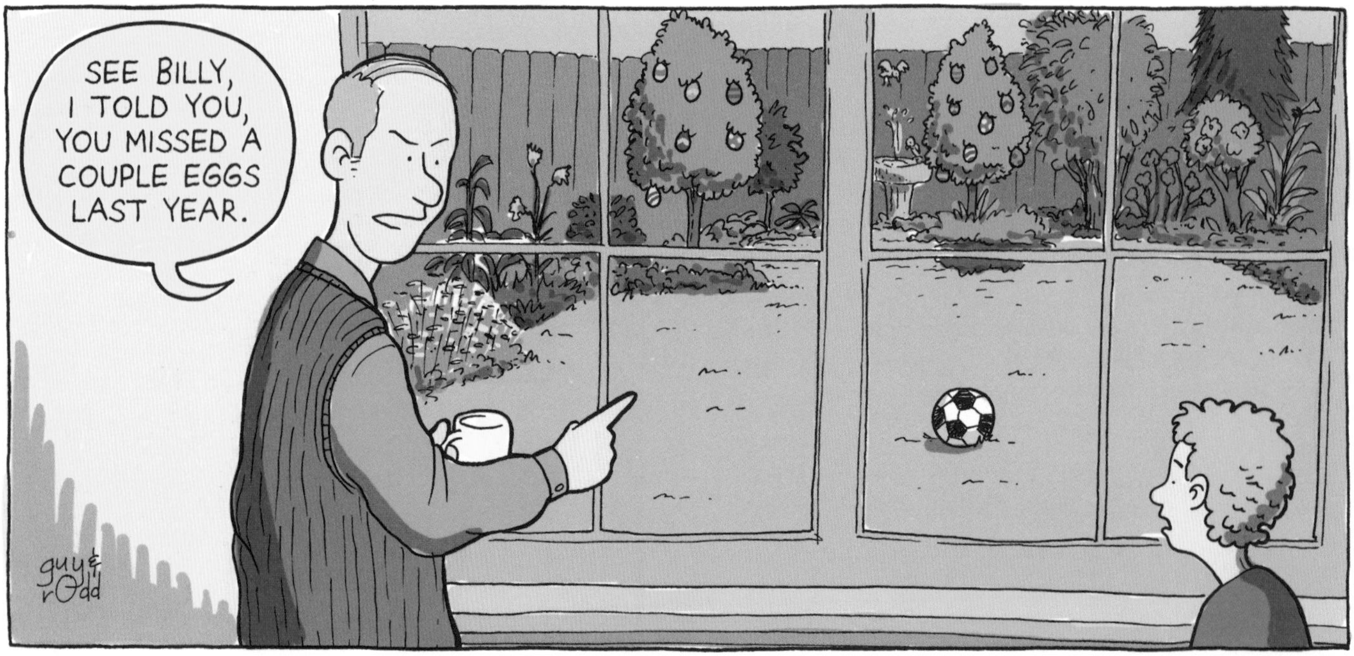
SEE BILLY, I TOLD YOU, YOU MISSED A COUPLE EGGS LAST YEAR.
guy & rOdd

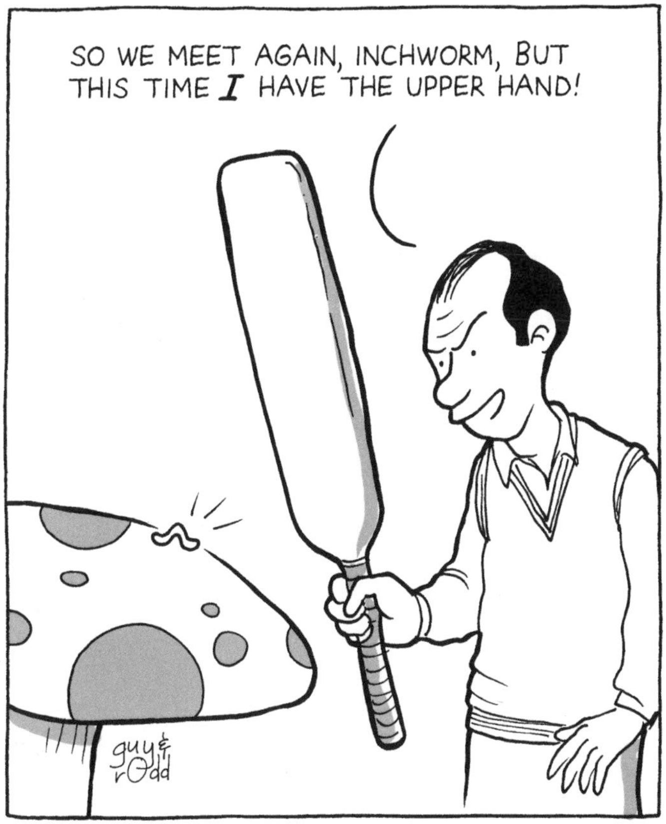
SO WE MEET AGAIN, INCHWORM, BUT THIS TIME *I* HAVE THE UPPER HAND!
guy & rodd

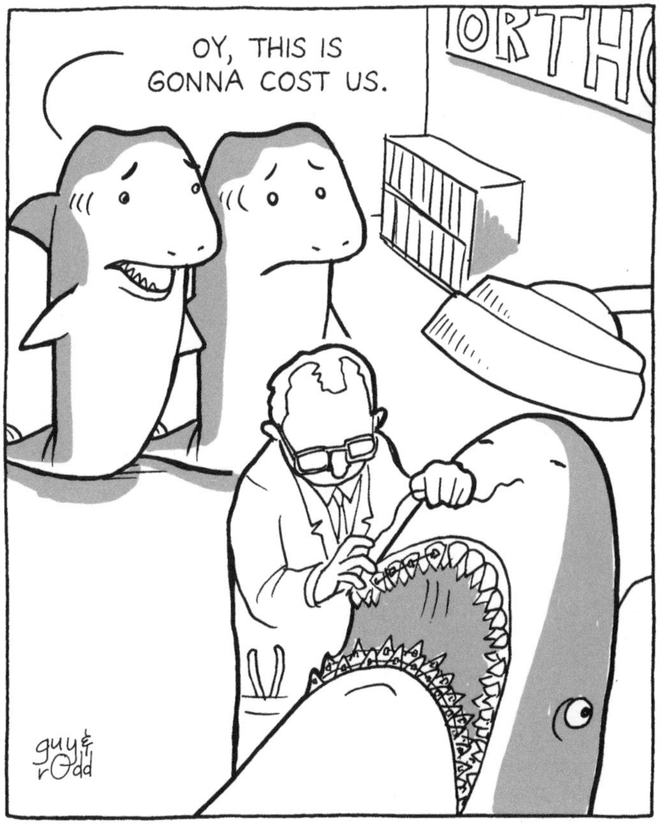
OY, THIS IS GONNA COST US.
ORTHO
guy & rodd

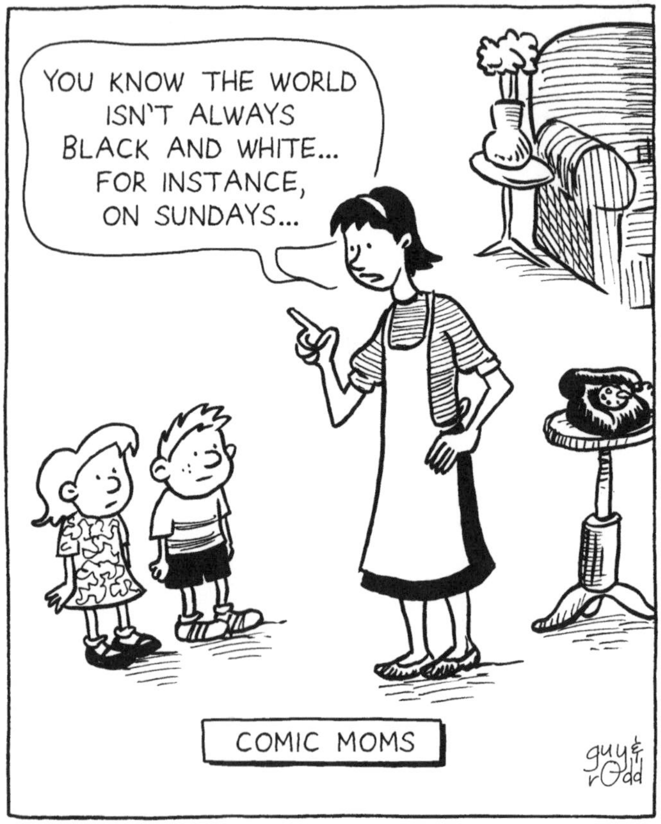
YOU KNOW THE WORLD ISN'T ALWAYS BLACK AND WHITE... FOR INSTANCE, ON SUNDAYS...
COMIC MOMS
guy & rOdd

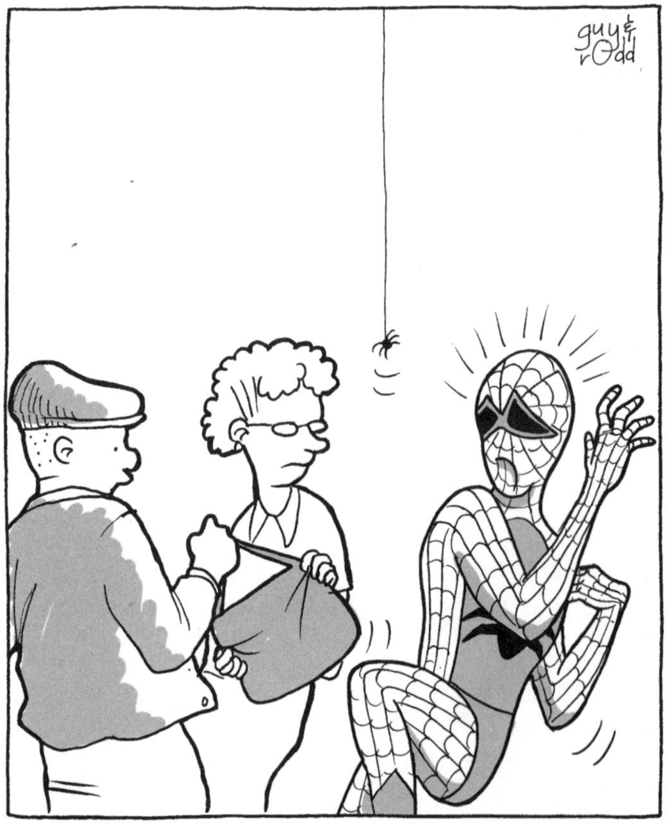
guy & rOdd

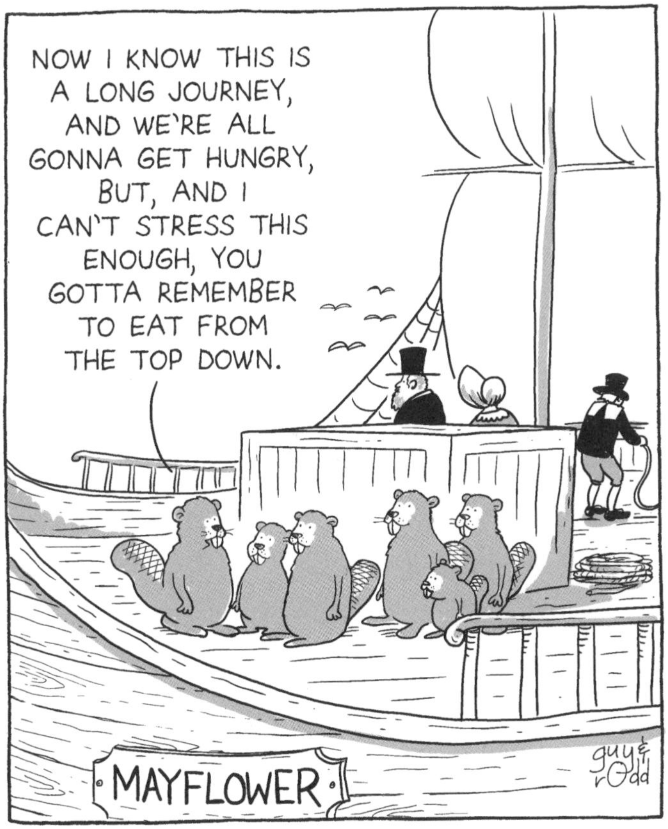
NOW I KNOW THIS IS A LONG JOURNEY, AND WE'RE ALL GONNA GET HUNGRY, BUT, AND I CAN'T STRESS THIS ENOUGH, YOU GOTTA REMEMBER TO EAT FROM THE TOP DOWN.
MAYFLOWER
guy & rOdd

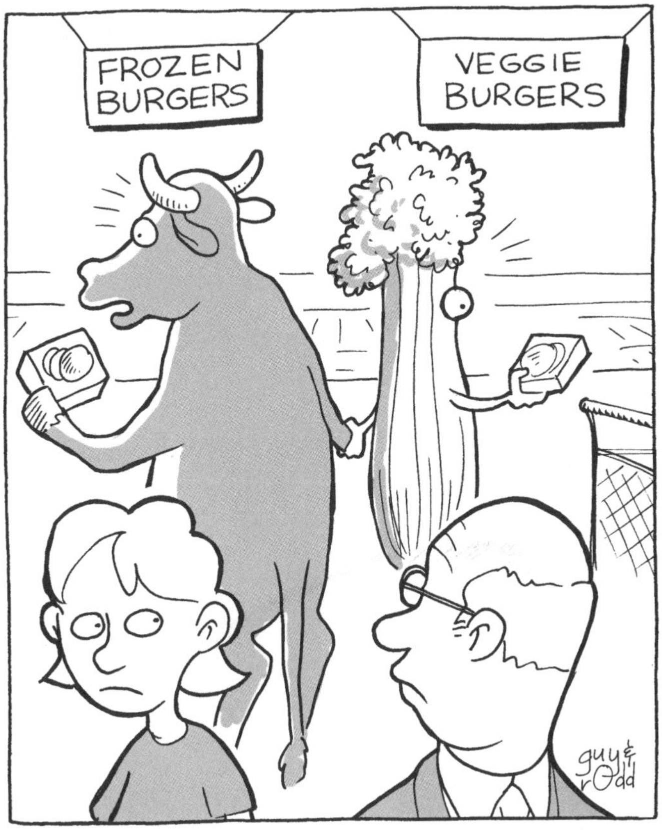
FROZEN BURGERS
VEGGIE BURGERS
guy & rOdd

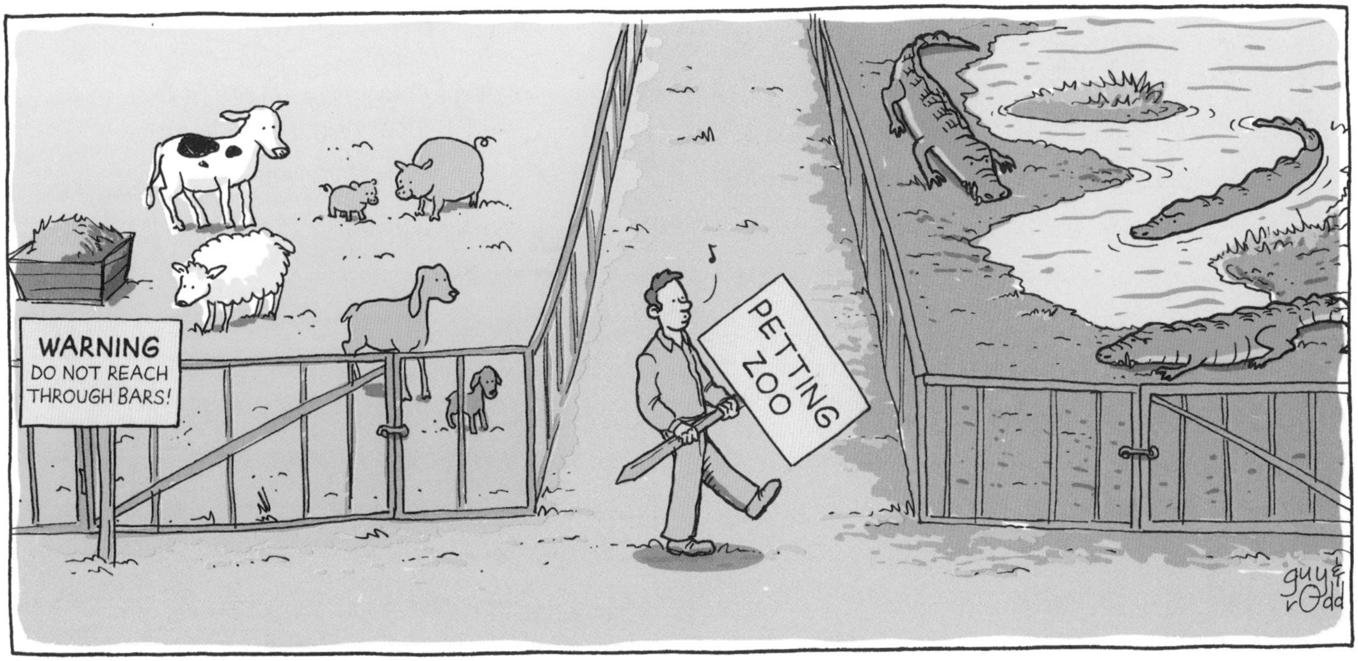
WARNING
DO NOT REACH THROUGH BARS!
PETTING ZOO
guy & rOdd

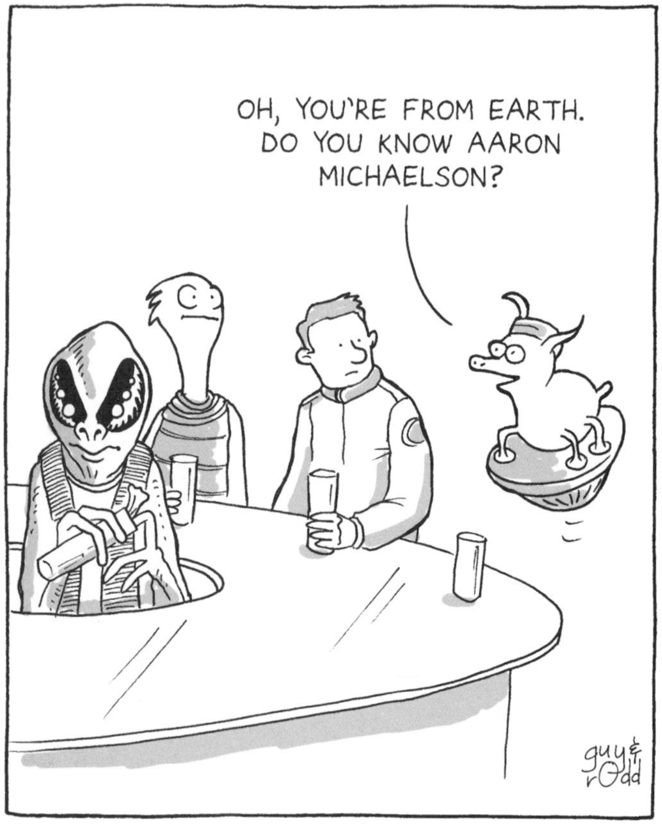
OH, YOU'RE FROM EARTH. DO YOU KNOW AARON MICHAELSON?
guy & rOdd

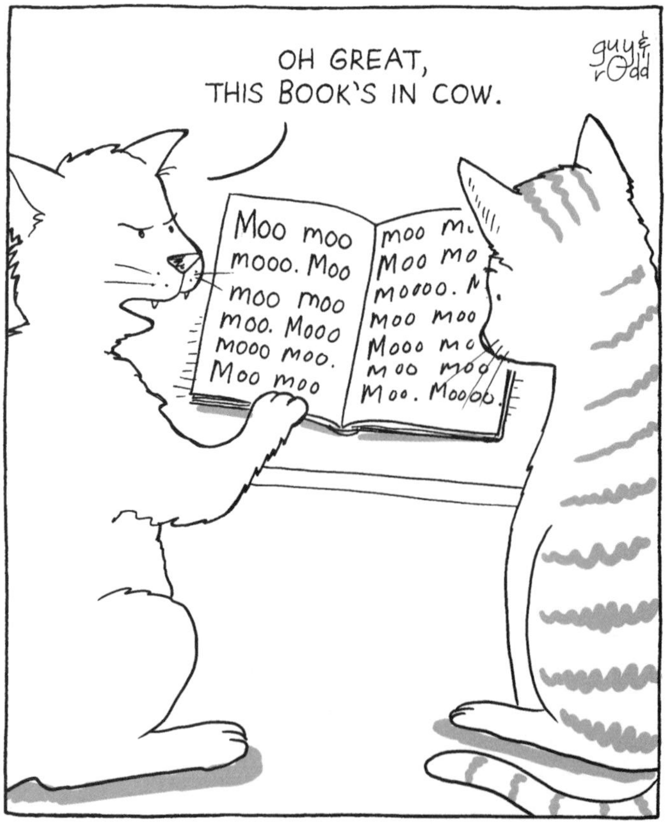
OH GREAT, THIS BOOK'S IN COW.
Moo moo mooo. Moo moo moo moo. Mooo mooo moo. Moo moo
guy & rOdd

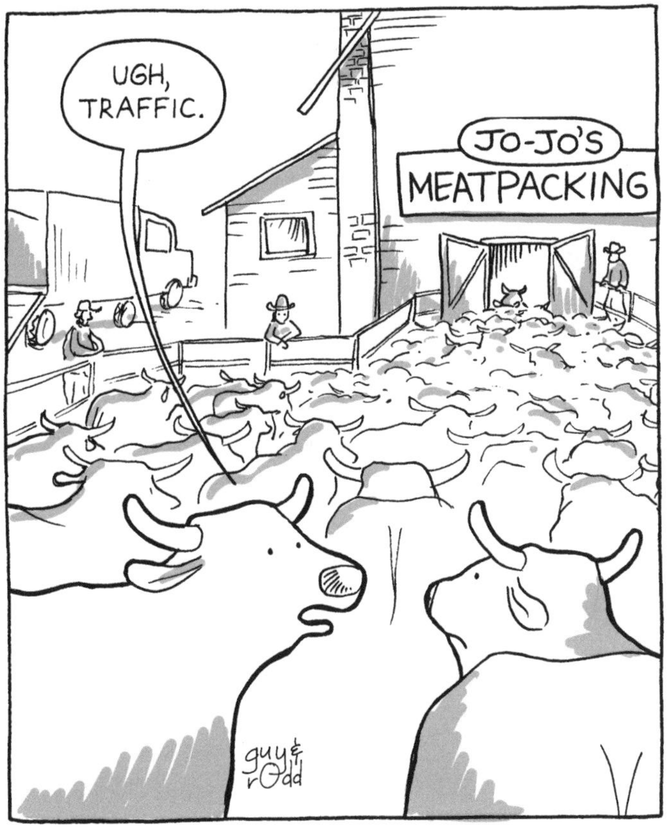
UGH, TRAFFIC.
JO-JO'S MEATPACKING
guy & rOdd

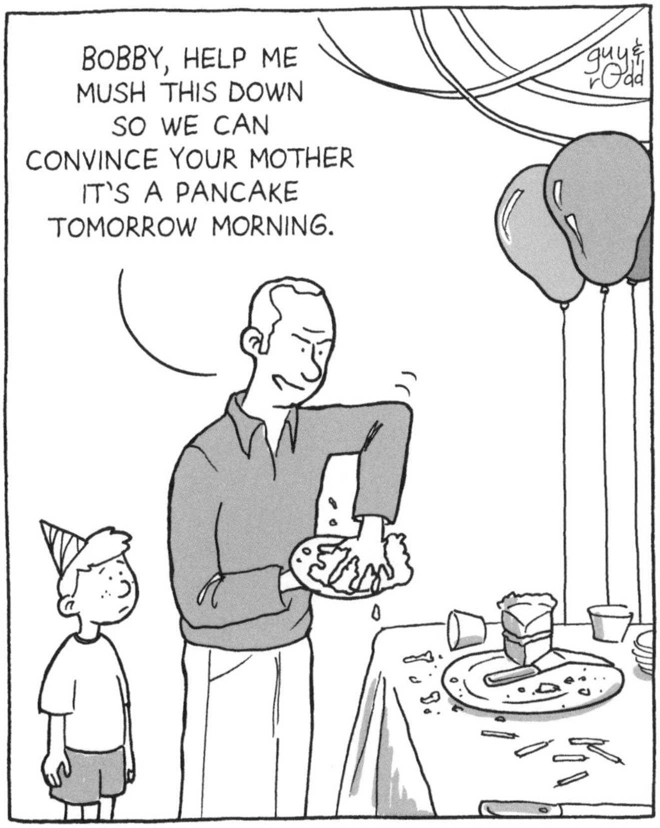
guy & rOdd
BOBBY, HELP ME MUSH THIS DOWN SO WE CAN CONVINCE YOUR MOTHER IT'S A PANCAKE TOMORROW MORNING.

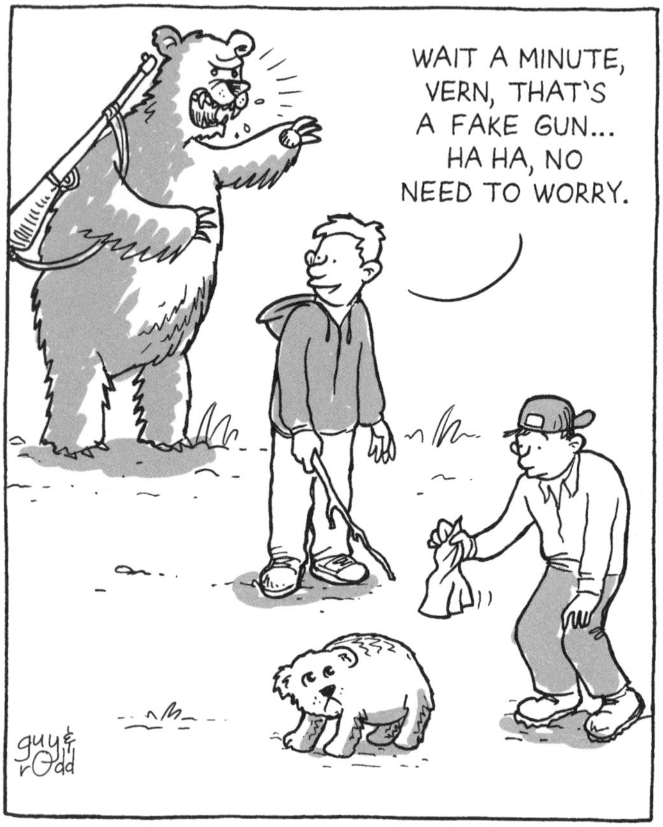
WAIT A MINUTE, VERN, THAT'S A FAKE GUN... HA HA, NO NEED TO WORRY.

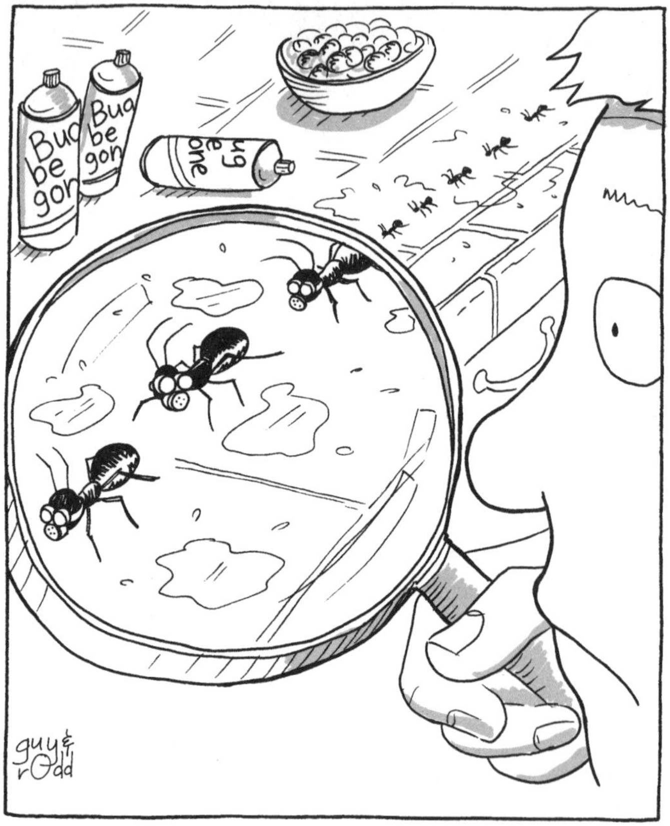

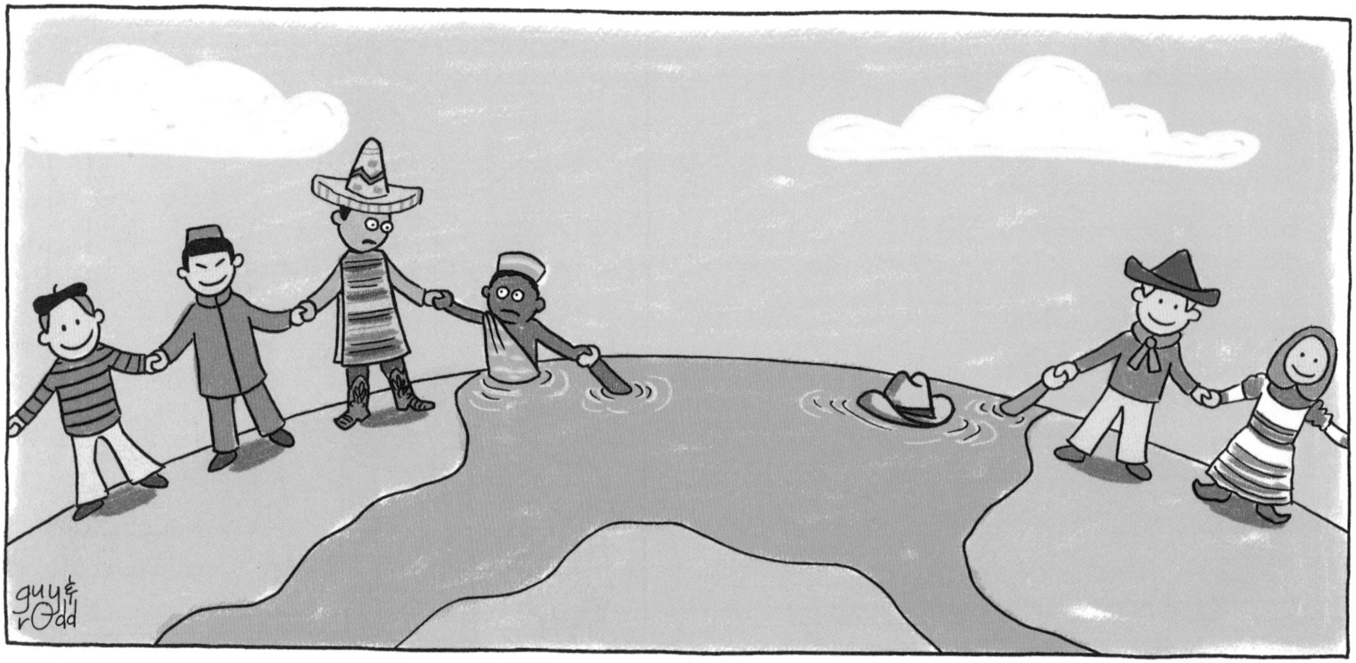

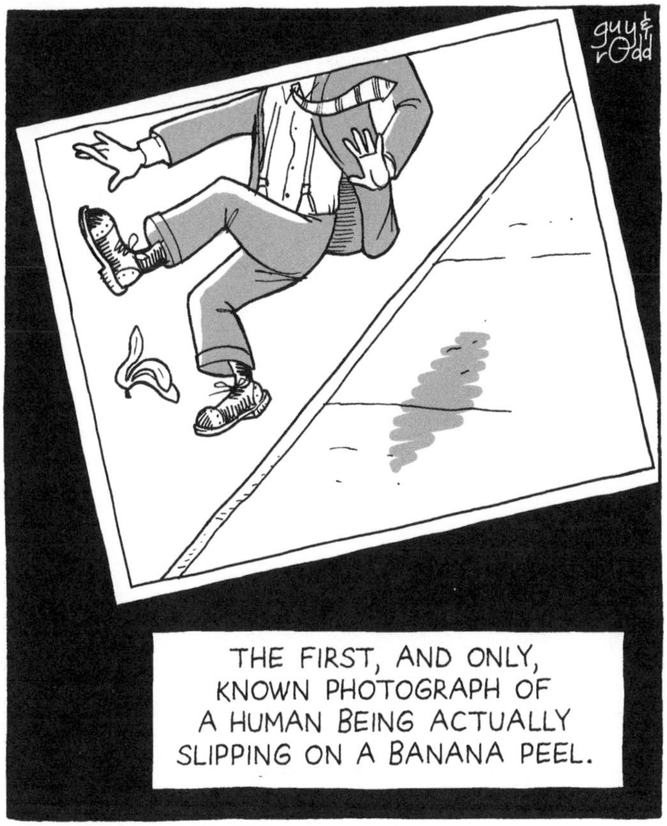
guy & rOdd
THE FIRST, AND ONLY, KNOWN PHOTOGRAPH OF A HUMAN BEING ACTUALLY SLIPPING ON A BANANA PEEL.

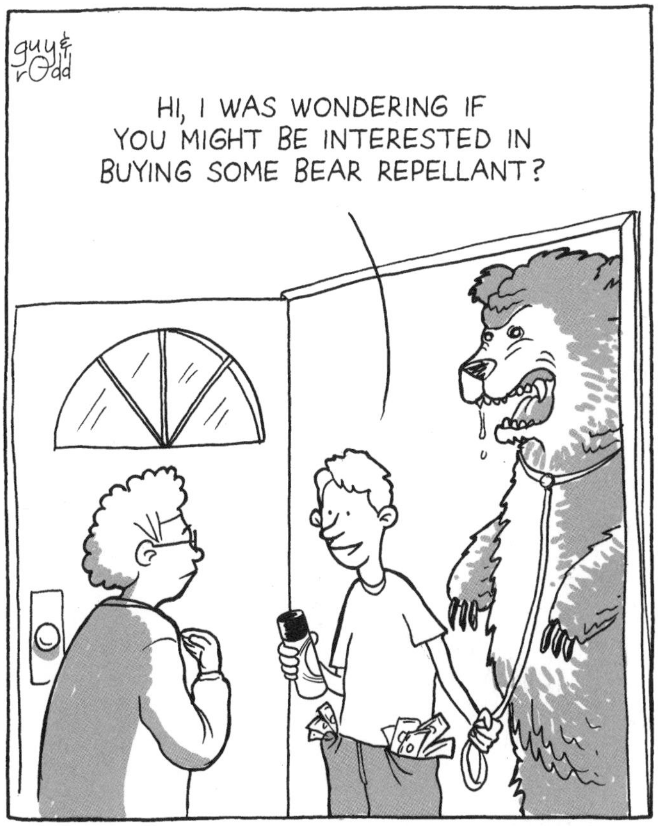
guy & rOdd
HI, I WAS WONDERING IF YOU MIGHT BE INTERESTED IN BUYING SOME BEAR REPELLANT?

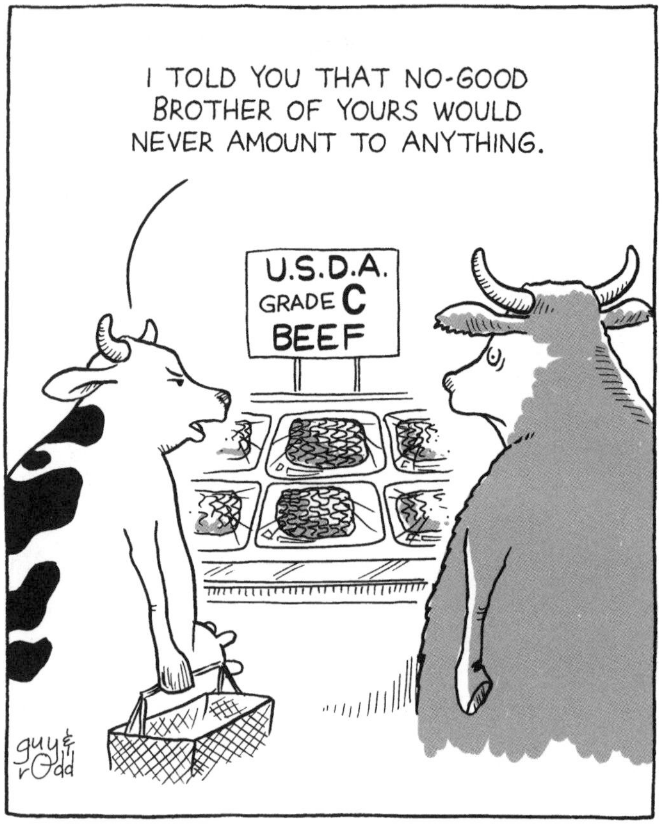
I TOLD YOU THAT NO-GOOD BROTHER OF YOURS WOULD NEVER AMOUNT TO ANYTHING.
U.S.D.A. GRADE C BEEF
guy & rOdd

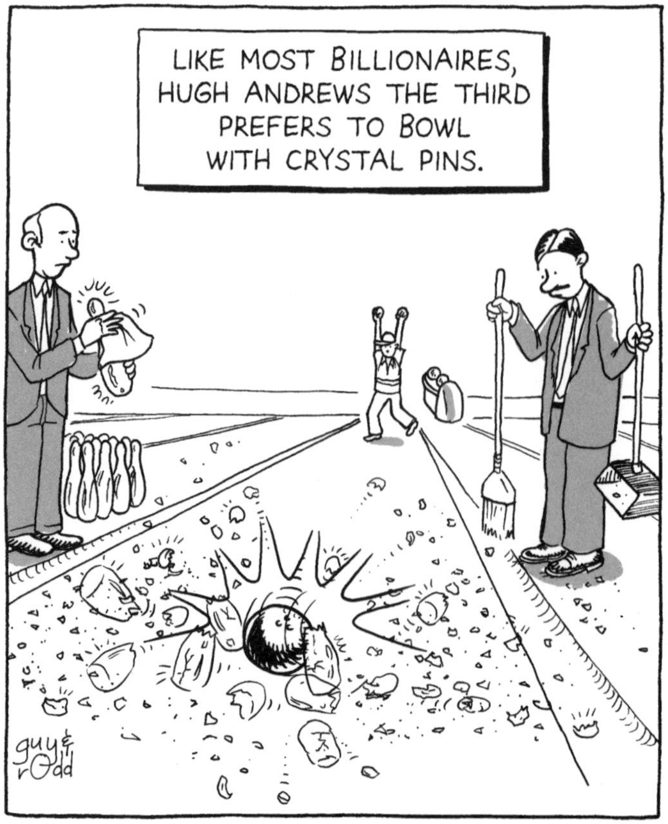
LIKE MOST BILLIONAIRES, HUGH ANDREWS THE THIRD PREFERS TO BOWL WITH CRYSTAL PINS.
guy & rOdd

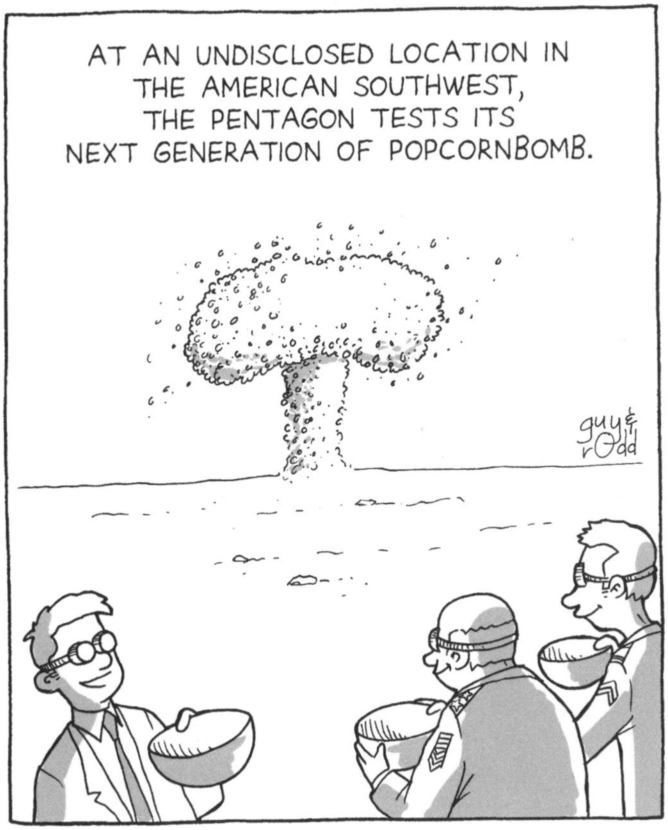
AT AN UNDISCLOSED LOCATION IN THE AMERICAN SOUTHWEST, THE PENTAGON TESTS ITS NEXT GENERATION OF POPCORNBOMB.

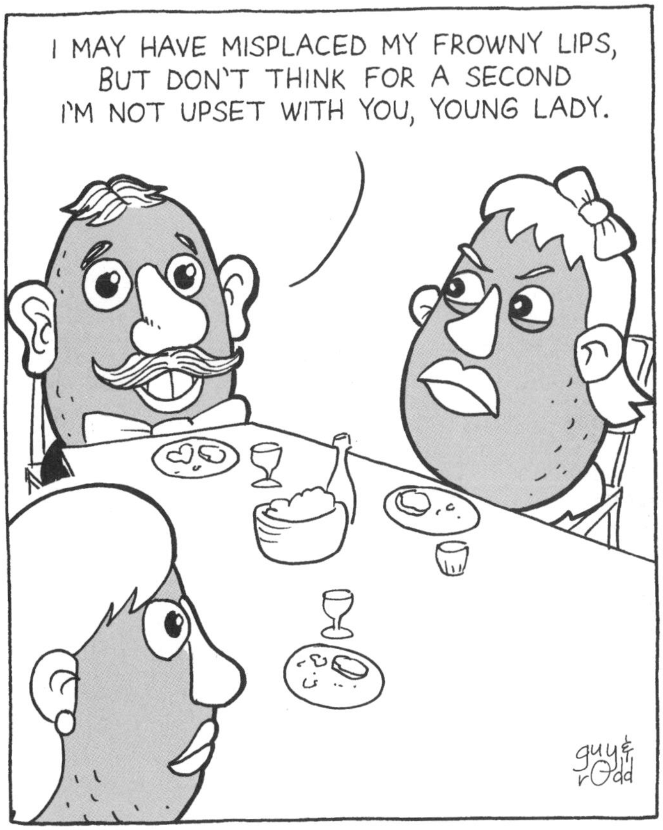
I MAY HAVE MISPLACED MY FROWNY LIPS, BUT DON'T THINK FOR A SECOND I'M NOT UPSET WITH YOU, YOUNG LADY.

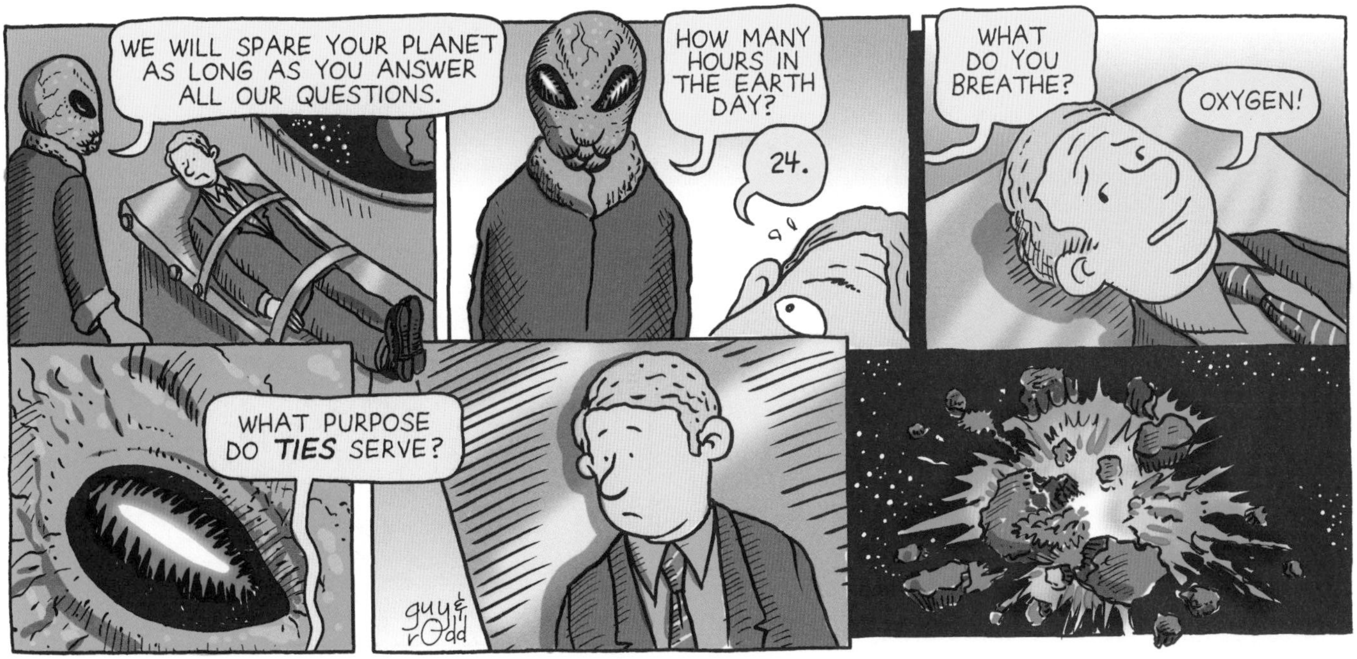
WE WILL SPARE YOUR PLANET AS LONG AS YOU ANSWER ALL OUR QUESTIONS.
HOW MANY HOURS IN THE EARTH DAY?
24.
WHAT DO YOU BREATHE?
OXYGEN!
WHAT PURPOSE DO **TIES** SERVE?

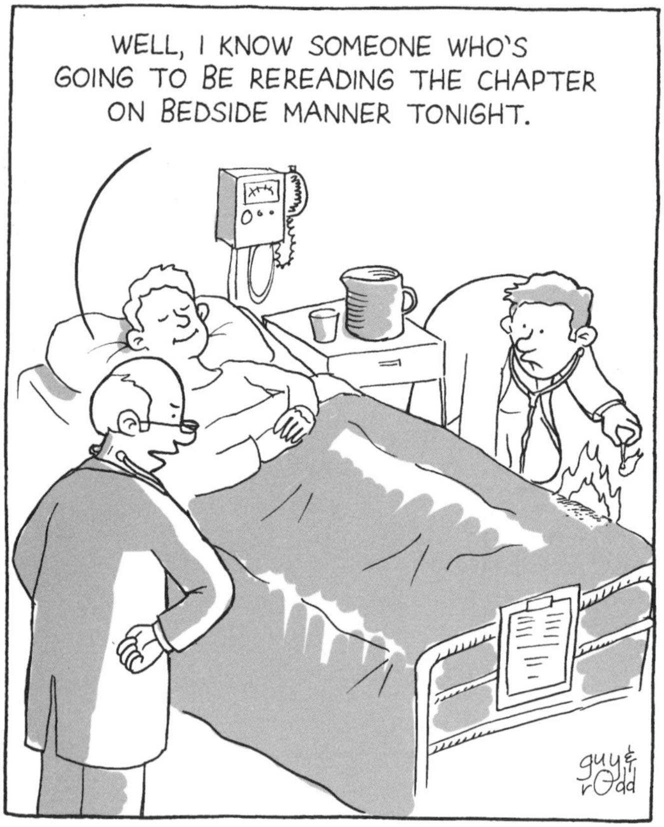
WELL, I KNOW SOMEONE WHO'S GOING TO BE REREADING THE CHAPTER ON BEDSIDE MANNER TONIGHT.
guy & rOdd

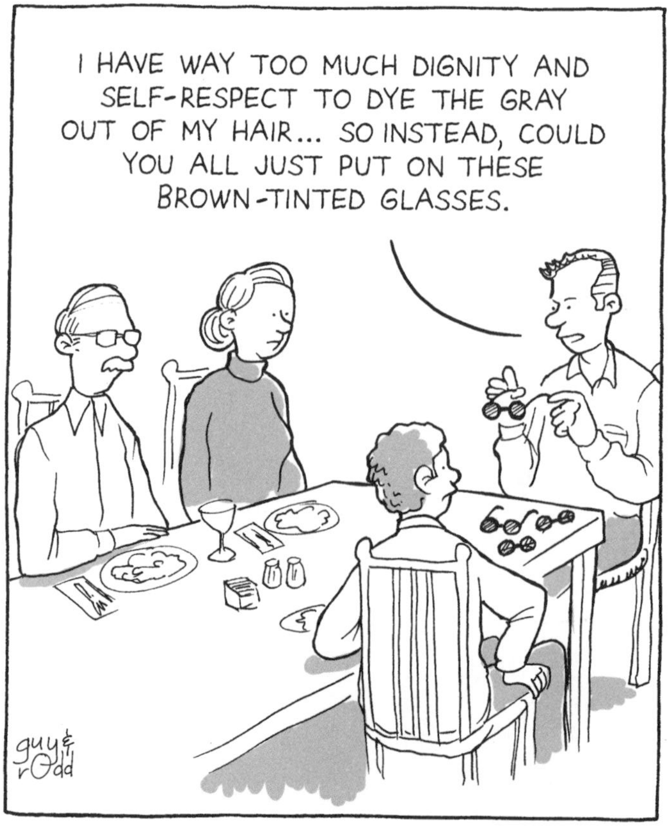
I HAVE WAY TOO MUCH DIGNITY AND SELF-RESPECT TO DYE THE GRAY OUT OF MY HAIR... SO INSTEAD, COULD YOU ALL JUST PUT ON THESE BROWN-TINTED GLASSES.
guy & rOdd

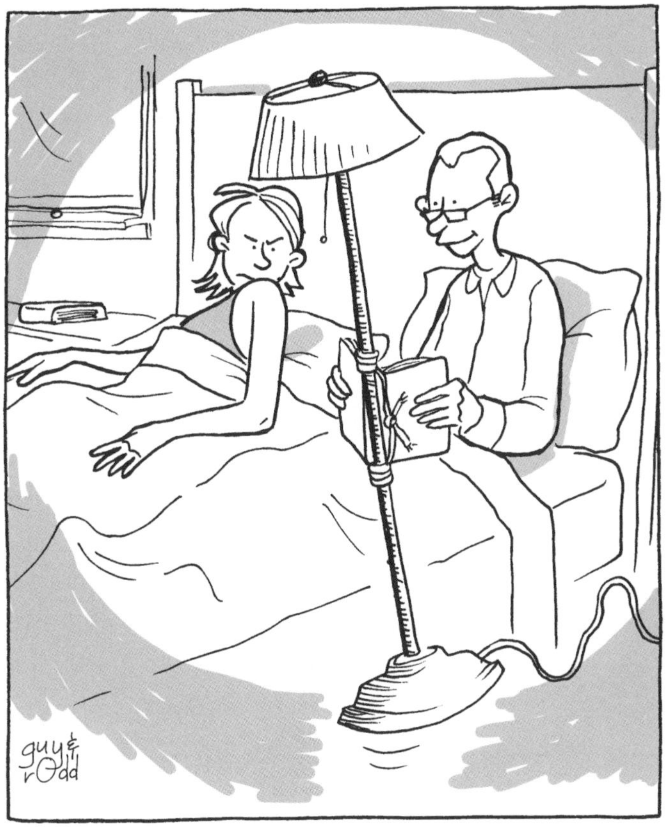
guy & rOdd

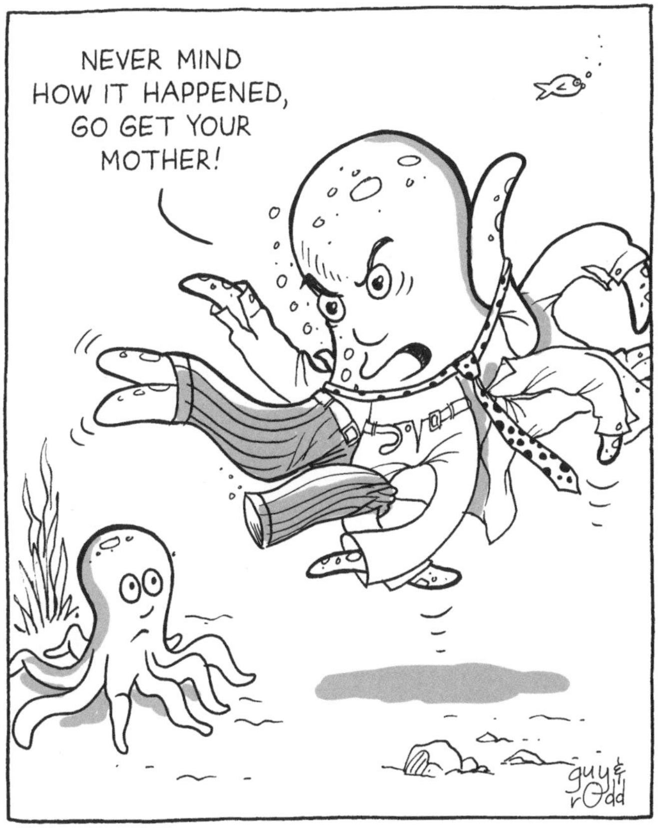
NEVER MIND HOW IT HAPPENED, GO GET YOUR MOTHER!
guy & rOdd

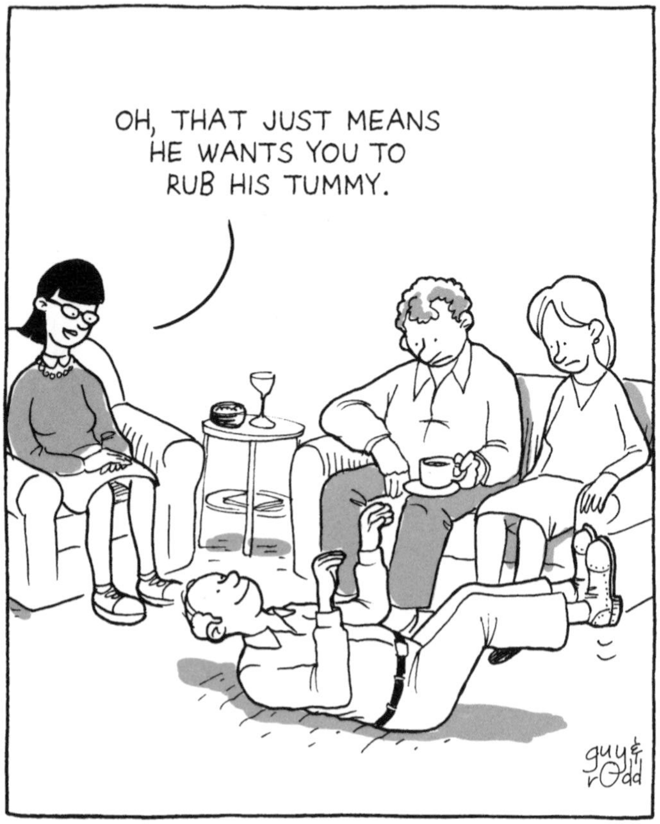
OH, THAT JUST MEANS HE WANTS YOU TO RUB HIS TUMMY.
guy & rOdd

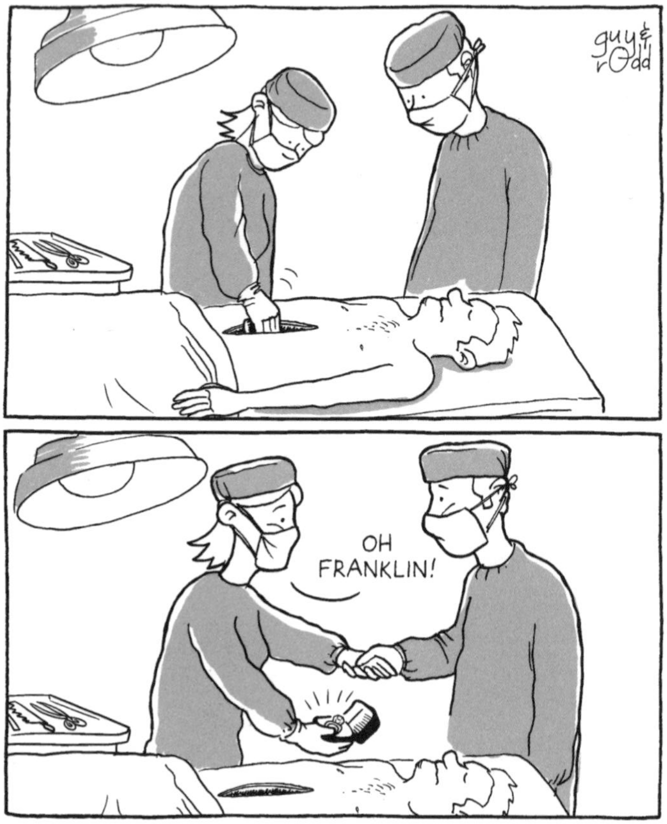
guy & rOdd
OH FRANKLIN!

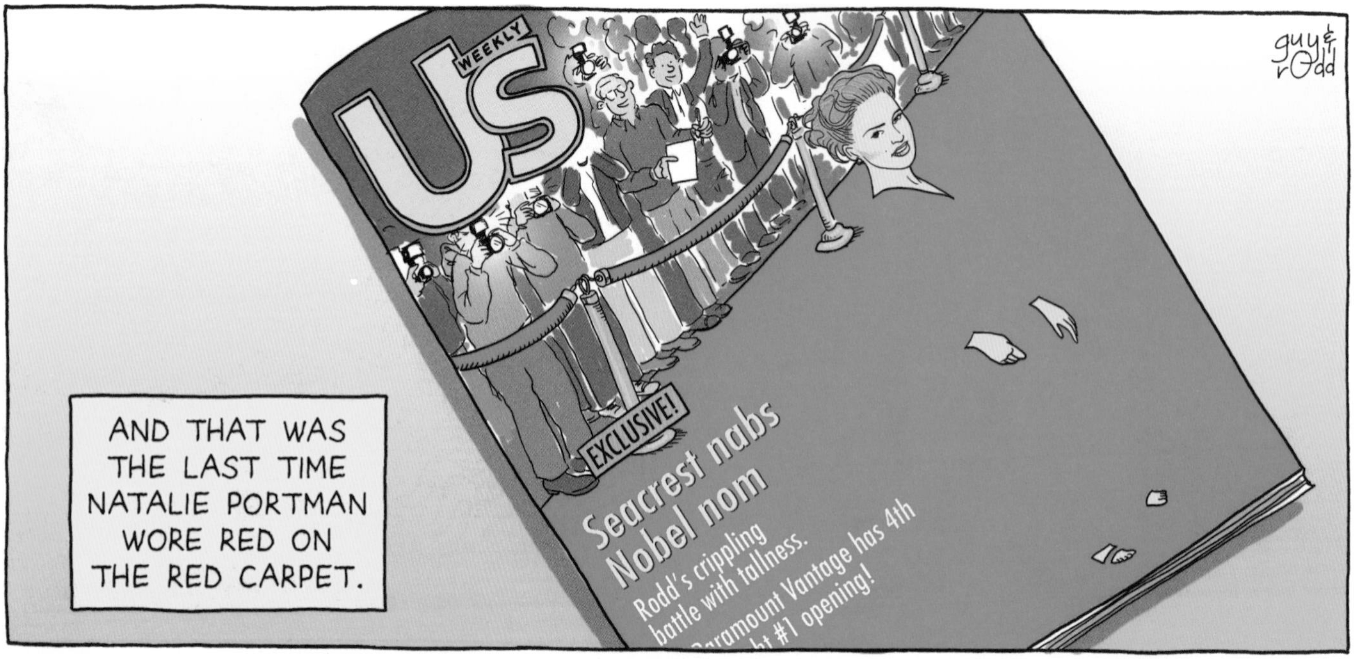
guy & rOdd
US
WEEKLY
EXCLUSIVE!
Seacrest nabs Nobel nom
Rodd's crippling battle with tallness.
aramount Vantage has 4th
#1 opening!
AND THAT WAS THE LAST TIME NATALIE PORTMAN WORE RED ON THE RED CARPET.

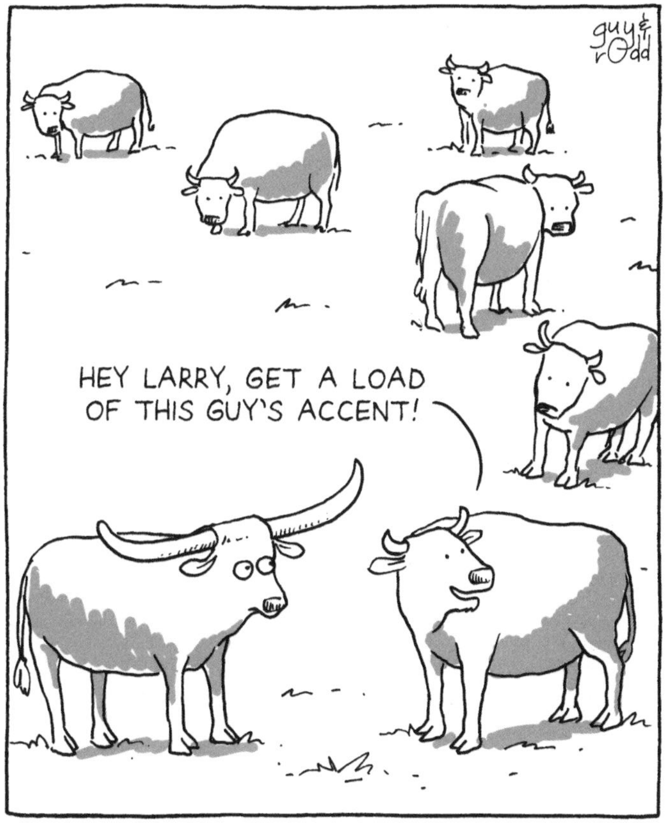
guy & rOdd
HEY LARRY, GET A LOAD OF THIS GUY'S ACCENT!

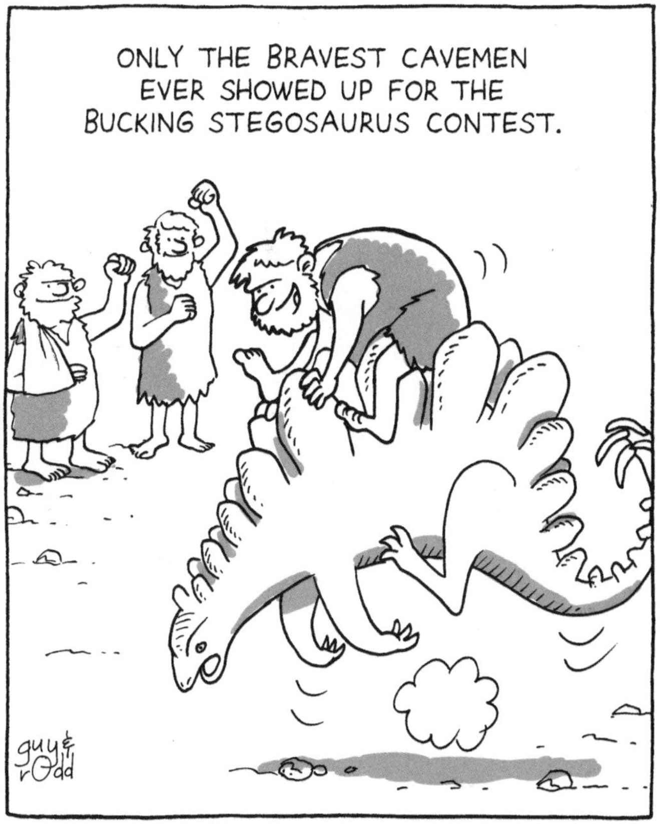
ONLY THE BRAVEST CAVEMEN EVER SHOWED UP FOR THE BUCKING STEGOSAURUS CONTEST.
guy & rOdd

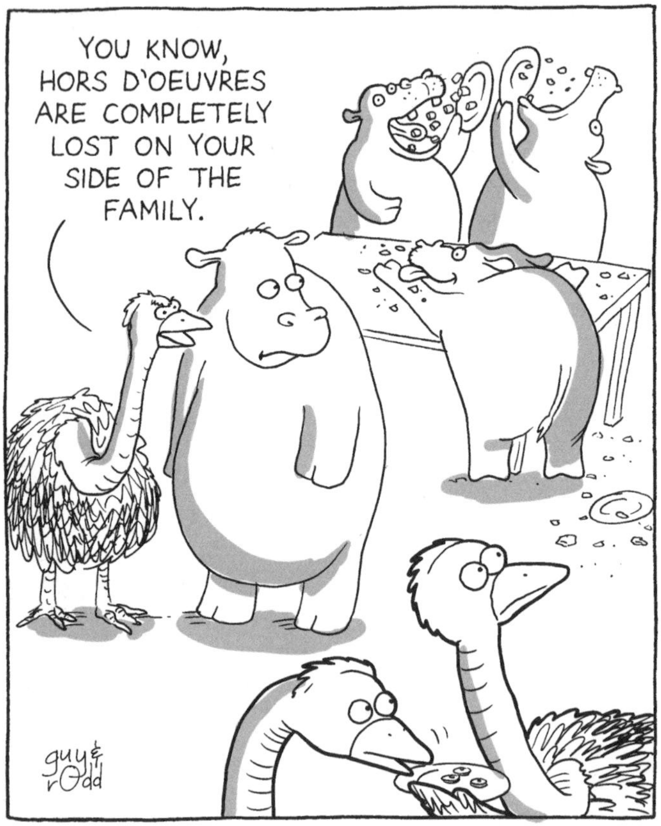
YOU KNOW, HORS D'OEUVRES ARE COMPLETELY LOST ON YOUR SIDE OF THE FAMILY.
guy & rodd

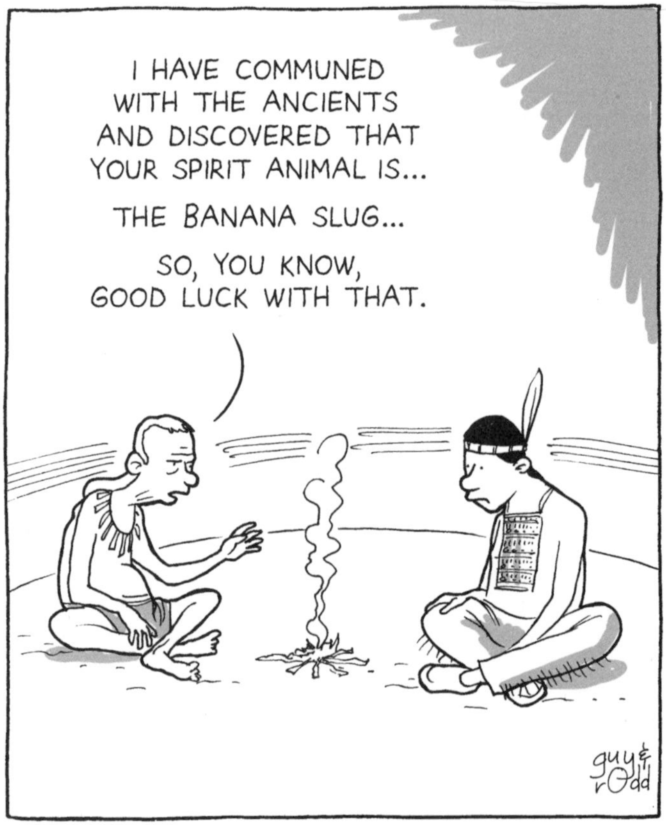
I HAVE COMMUNED WITH THE ANCIENTS AND DISCOVERED THAT YOUR SPIRIT ANIMAL IS...
THE BANANA SLUG...
SO, YOU KNOW, GOOD LUCK WITH THAT.
guy & rodd

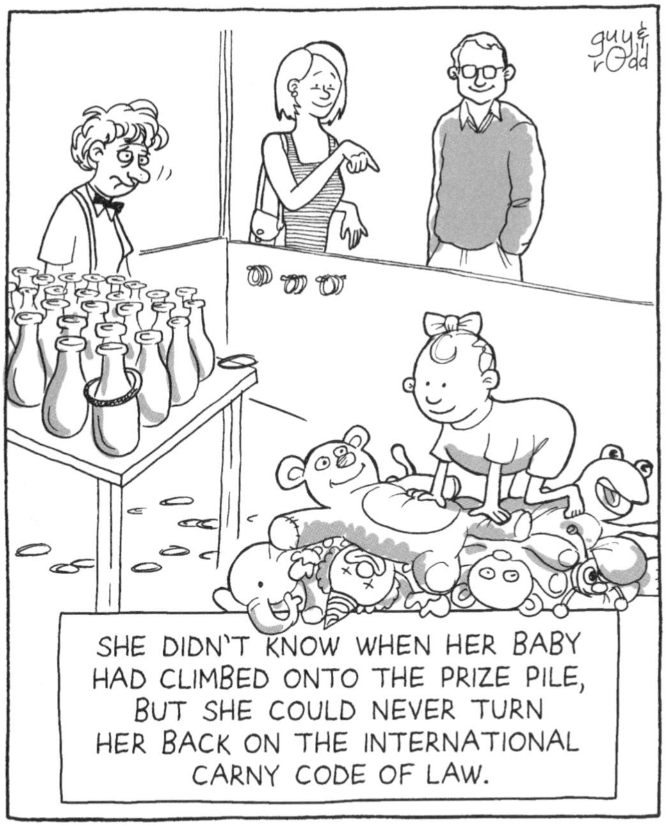
guy & rodd
SHE DIDN'T KNOW WHEN HER BABY HAD CLIMBED ONTO THE PRIZE PILE, BUT SHE COULD NEVER TURN HER BACK ON THE INTERNATIONAL CARNY CODE OF LAW.

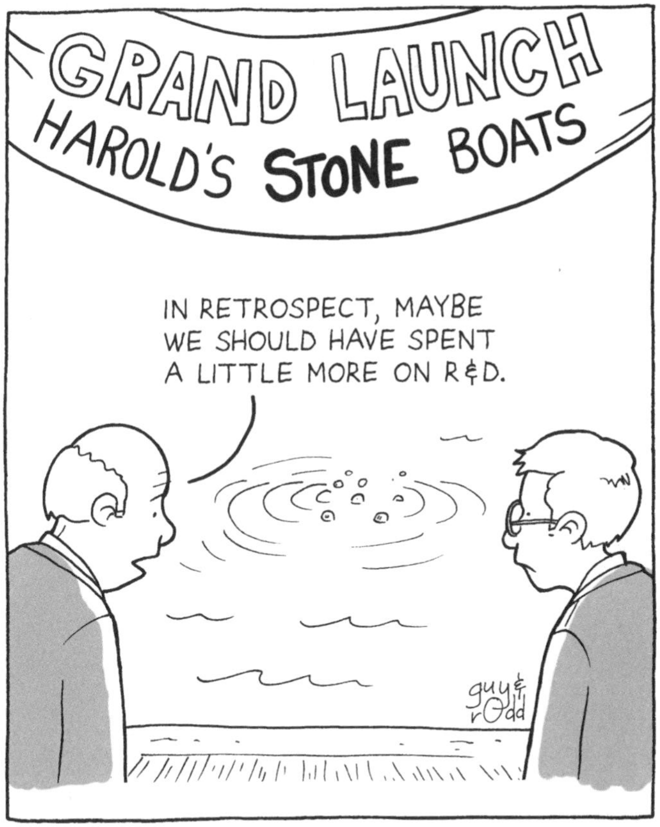
GRAND LAUNCH
HAROLD'S STONE BOATS
IN RETROSPECT, MAYBE WE SHOULD HAVE SPENT A LITTLE MORE ON R&D.
guy & rodd

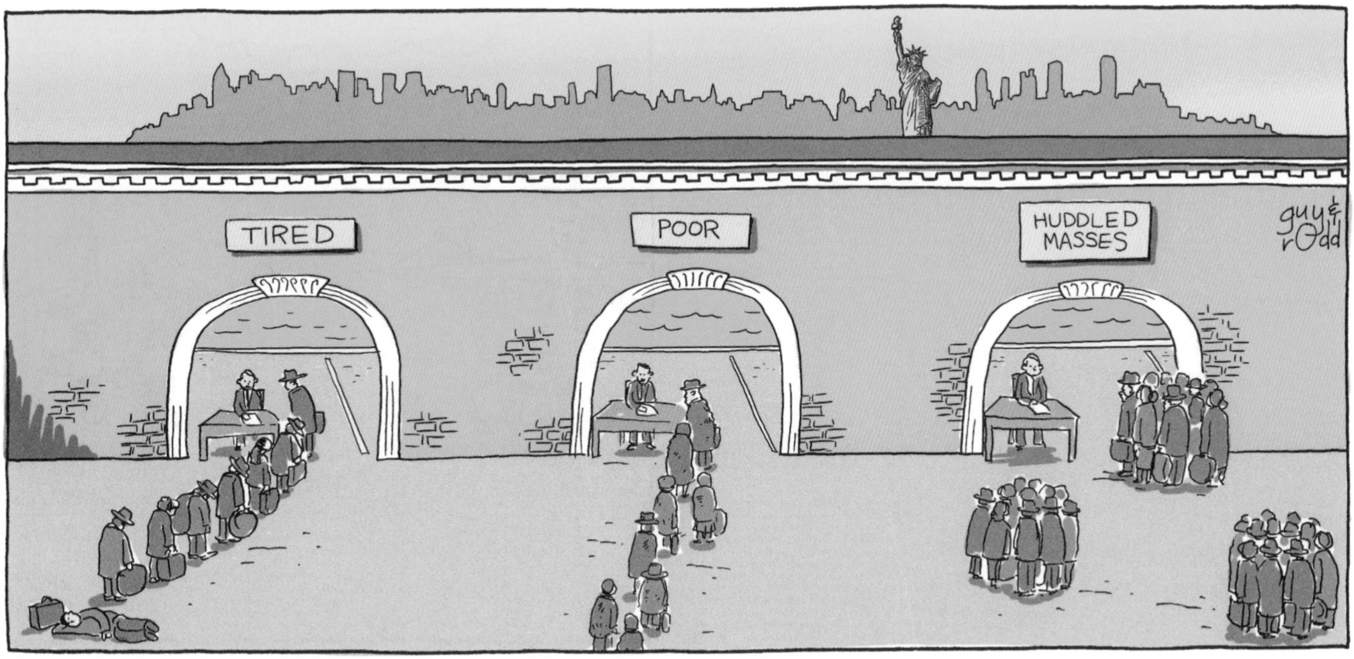
TIRED
POOR
HUDDLED MASSES
guy & rodd

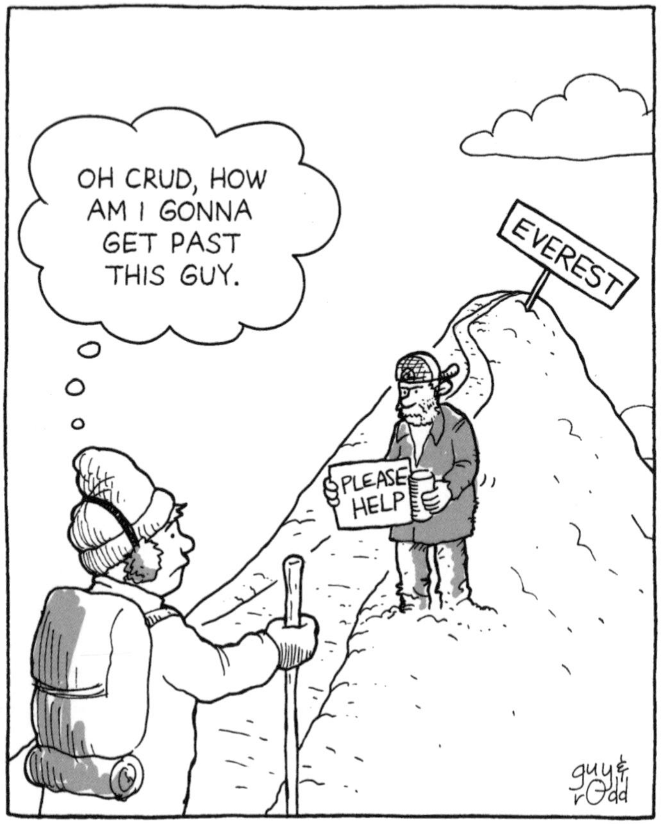
OH CRUD, HOW AM I GONNA GET PAST THIS GUY.
EVEREST
PLEASE HELP
guy & rOdd

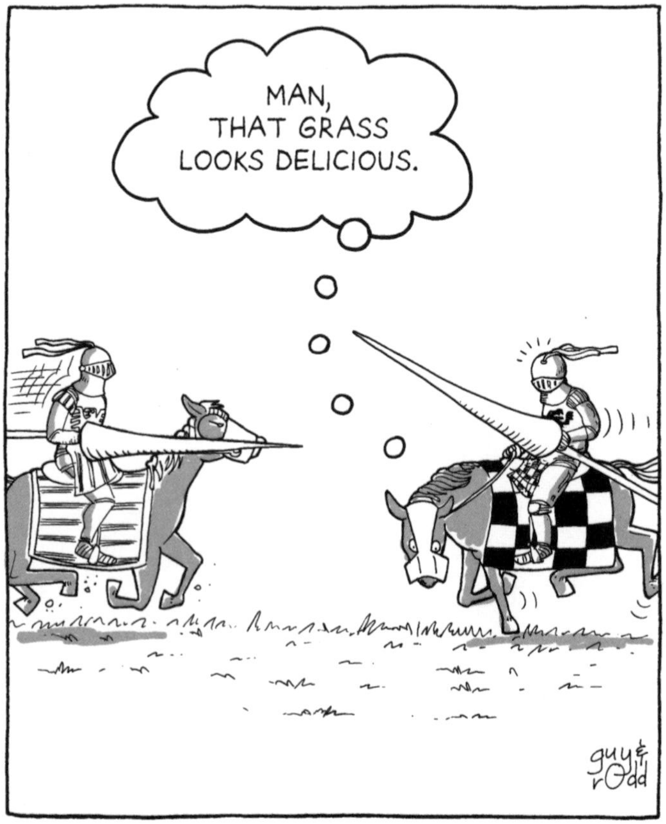
MAN, THAT GRASS LOOKS DELICIOUS.
guy & rOdd

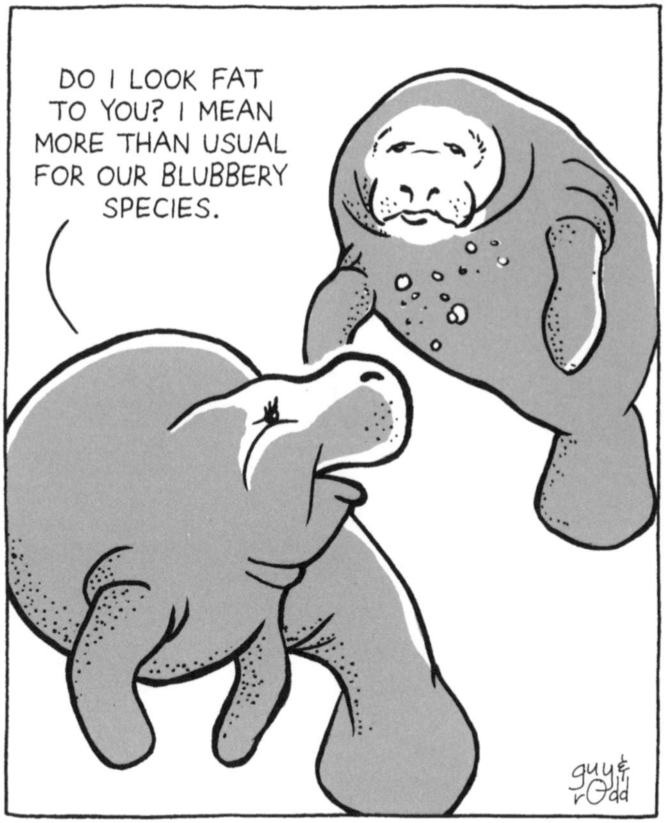
DO I LOOK FAT TO YOU? I MEAN MORE THAN USUAL FOR OUR BLUBBERY SPECIES.
guy & rOdd

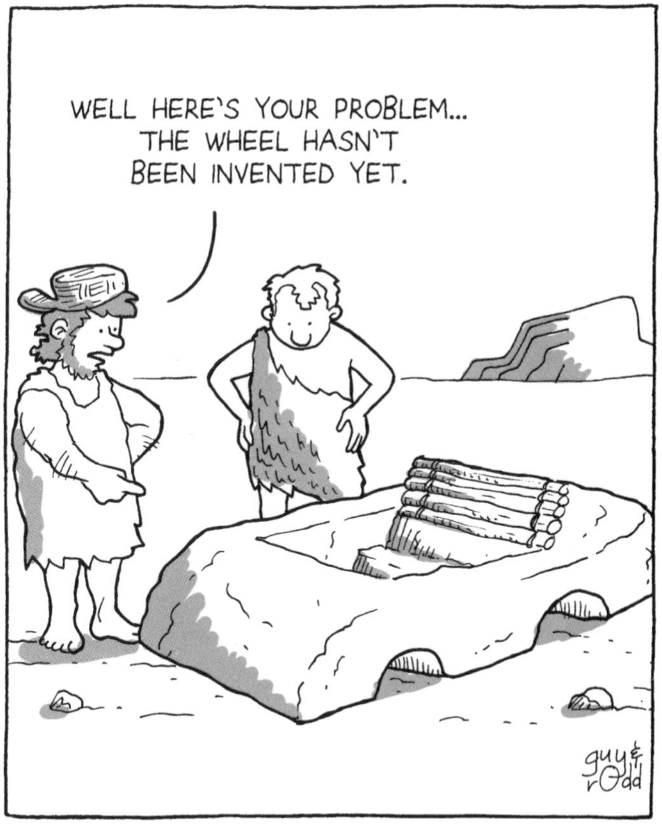
WELL HERE'S YOUR PROBLEM... THE WHEEL HASN'T BEEN INVENTED YET.
guy & rOdd

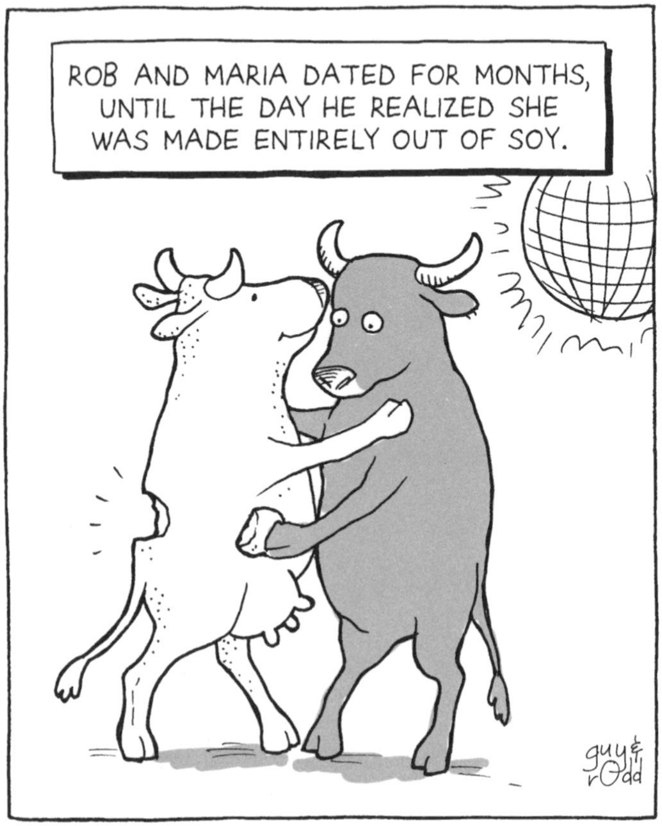
ROB AND MARIA DATED FOR MONTHS, UNTIL THE DAY HE REALIZED SHE WAS MADE ENTIRELY OUT OF SOY.
guy & rodd

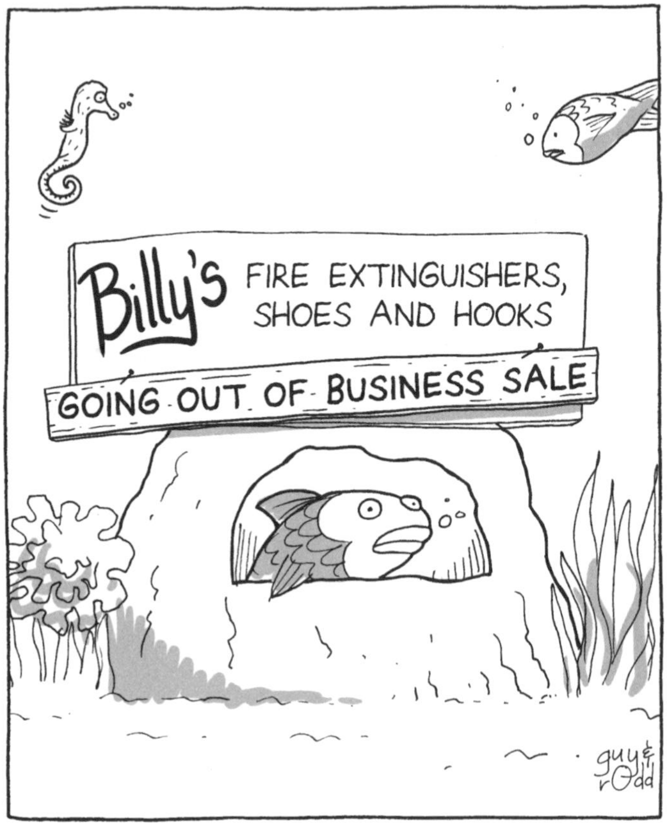
Billy's FIRE EXTINGUISHERS, SHOES AND HOOKS
GOING OUT OF BUSINESS SALE
guy & rodd

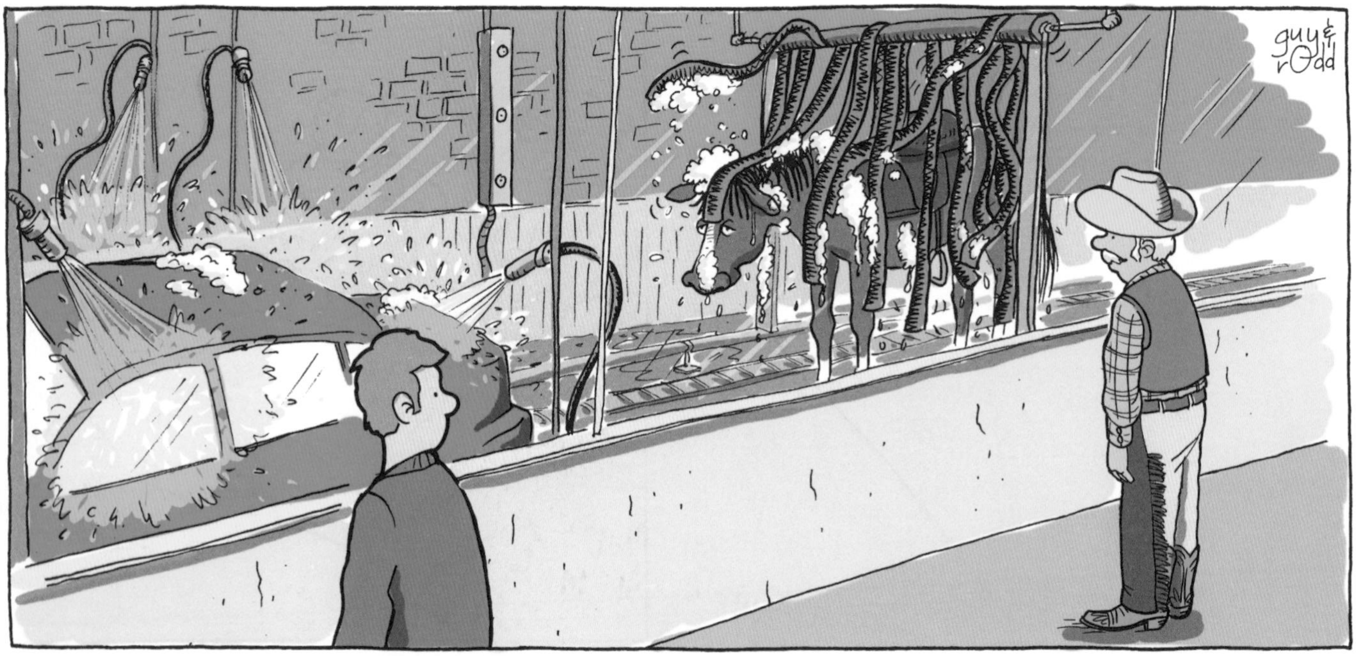
guy & rodd

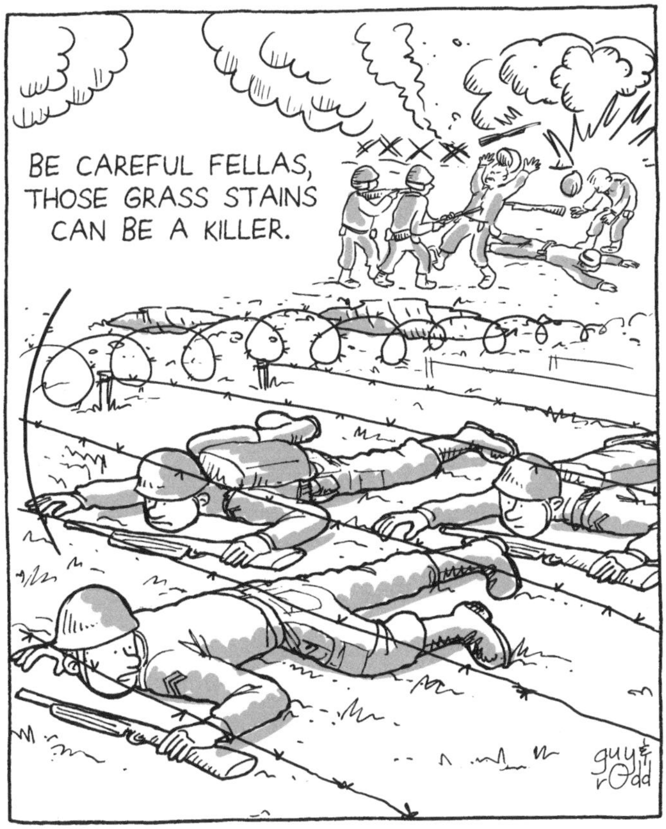
BE CAREFUL FELLAS, THOSE GRASS STAINS CAN BE A KILLER.
guy & rOdd

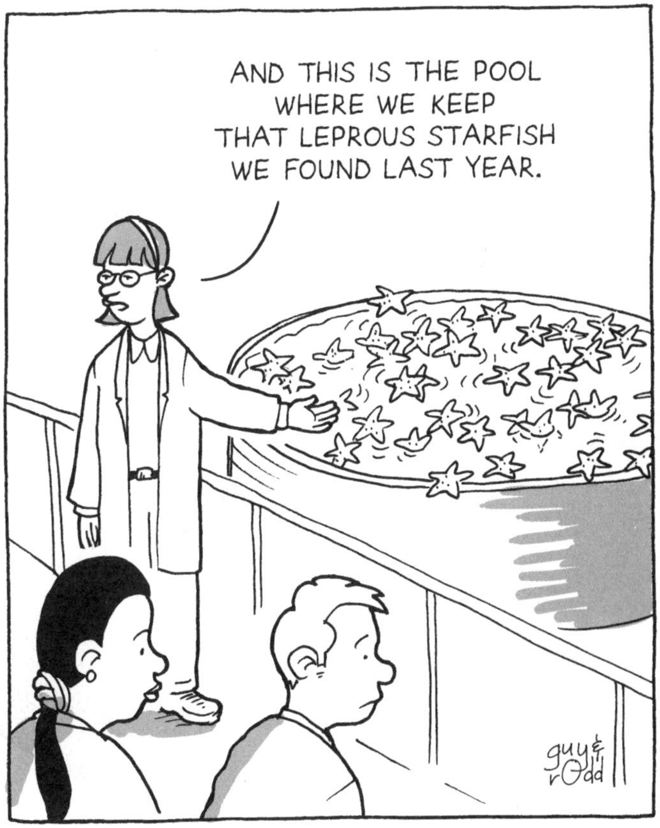
AND THIS IS THE POOL WHERE WE KEEP THAT LEPROUS STARFISH WE FOUND LAST YEAR.
guy & rOdd

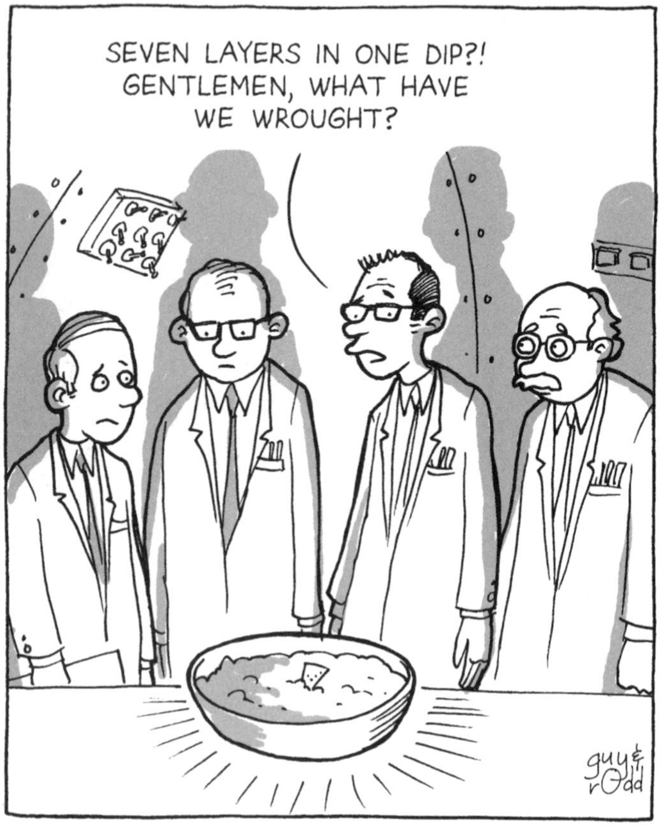
SEVEN LAYERS IN ONE DIP?! GENTLEMEN, WHAT HAVE WE WROUGHT?
guy & rOdd

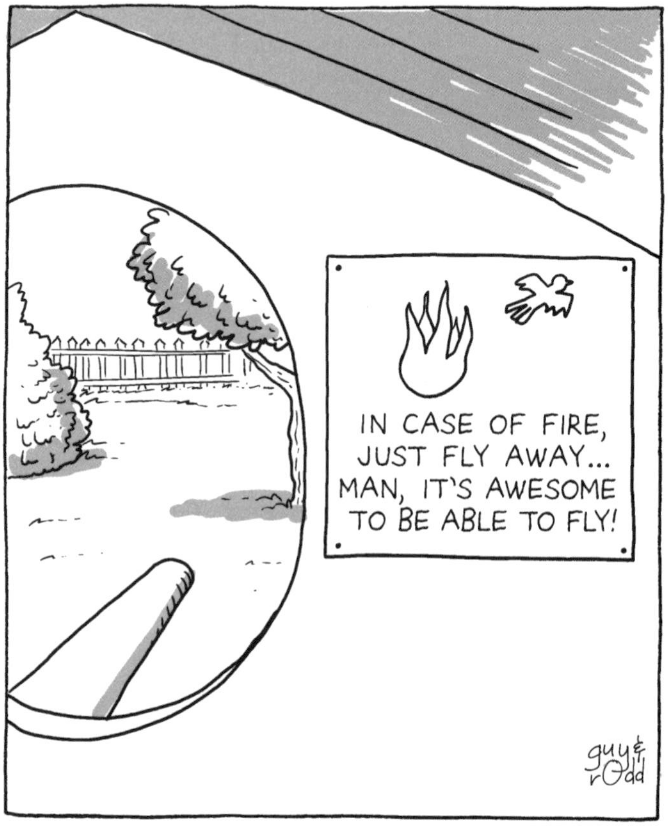
IN CASE OF FIRE, JUST FLY AWAY... MAN, IT'S AWESOME TO BE ABLE TO FLY!
guy & rOdd

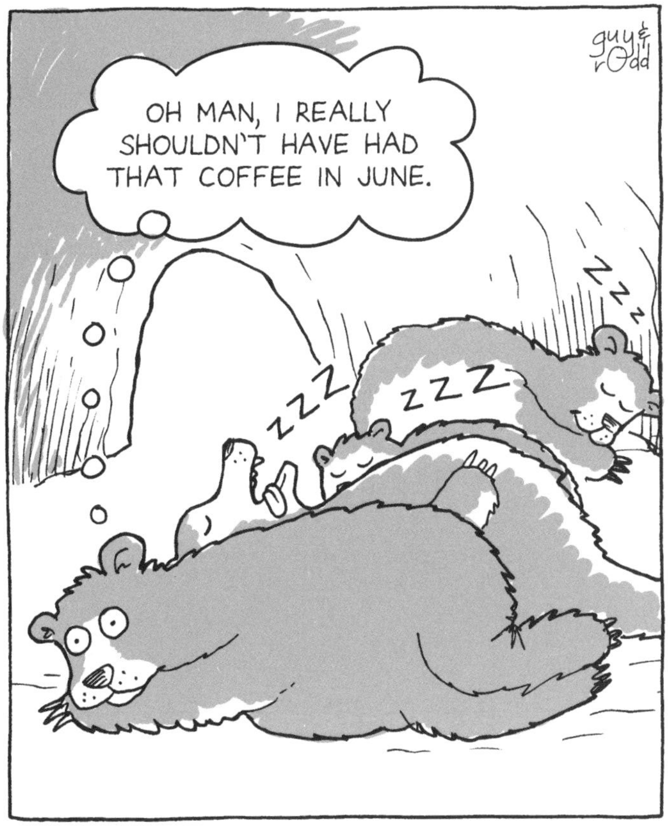
OH MAN, I REALLY SHOULDN'T HAVE HAD THAT COFFEE IN JUNE.
ZZZ
ZZZ
ZZZ

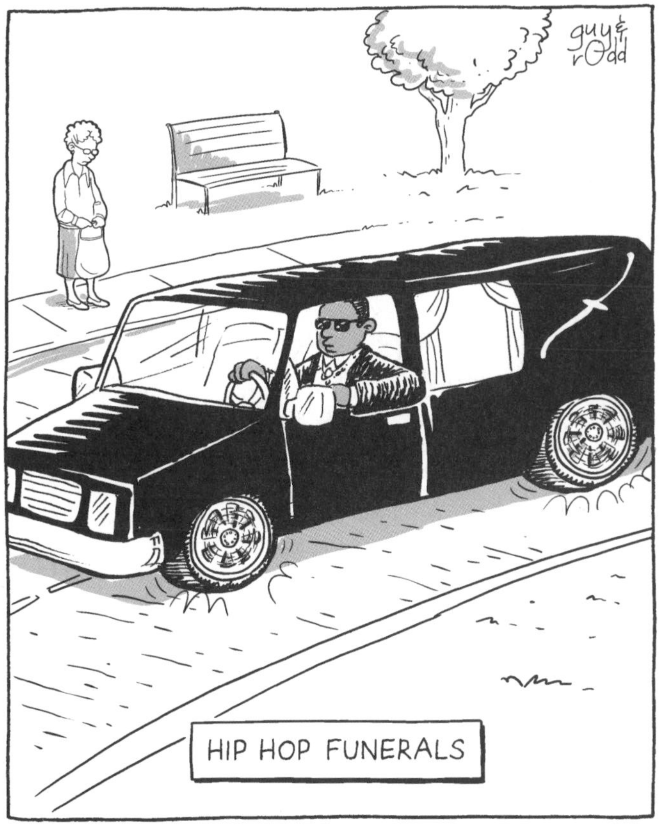
HIP HOP FUNERALS

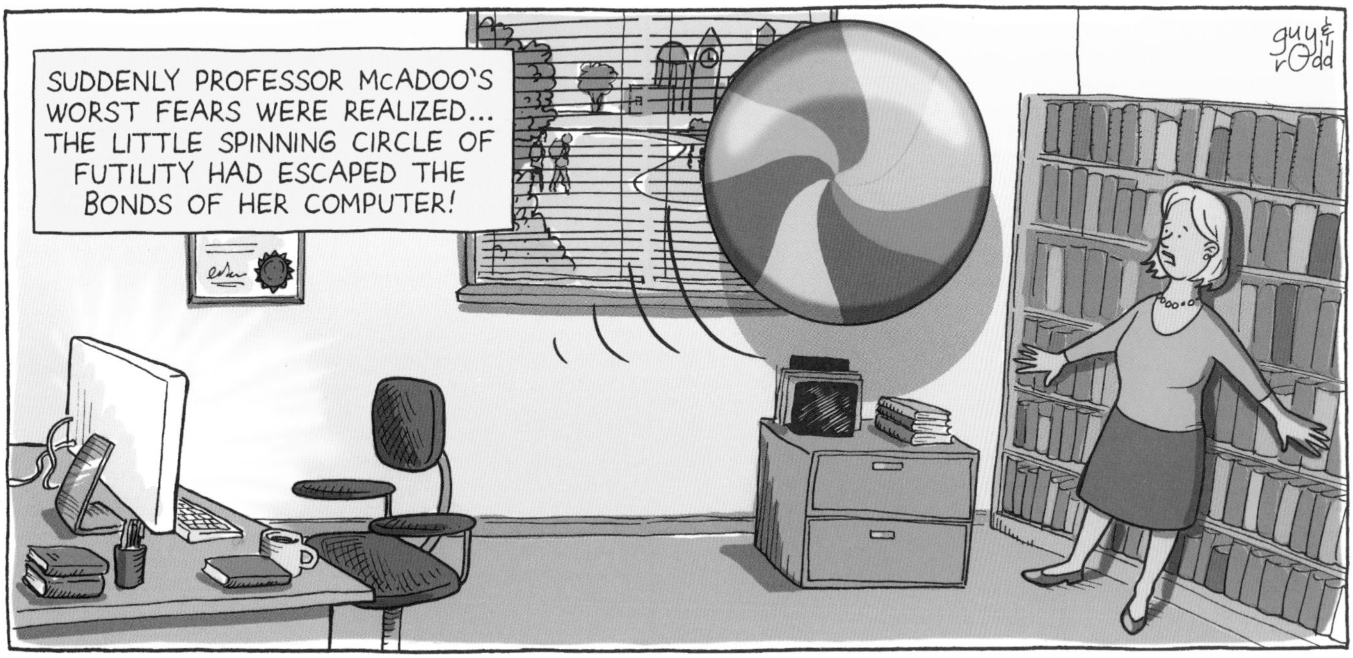
SUDDENLY PROFESSOR McADOO'S WORST FEARS WERE REALIZED... THE LITTLE SPINNING CIRCLE OF FUTILITY HAD ESCAPED THE BONDS OF HER COMPUTER!

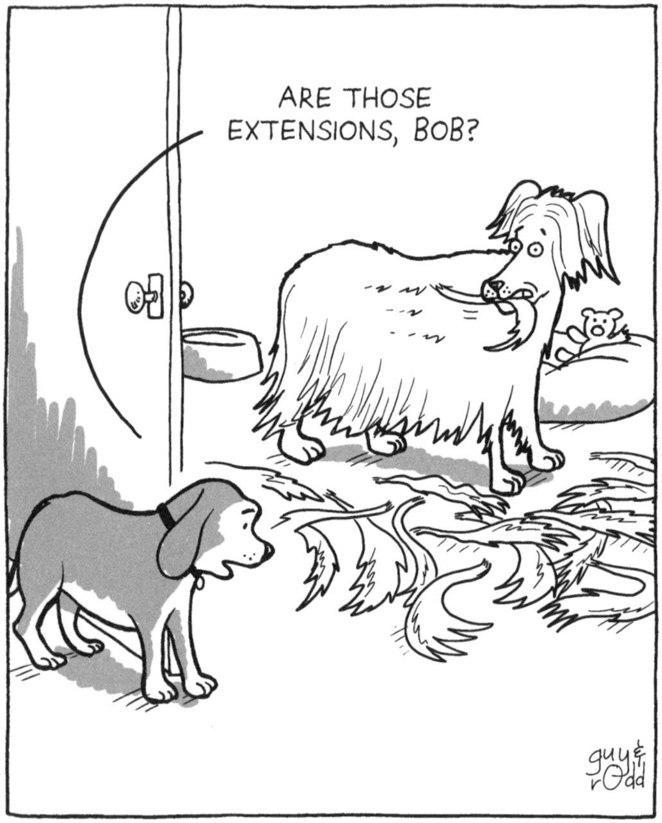
ARE THOSE EXTENSIONS, BOB?
guy & rodd

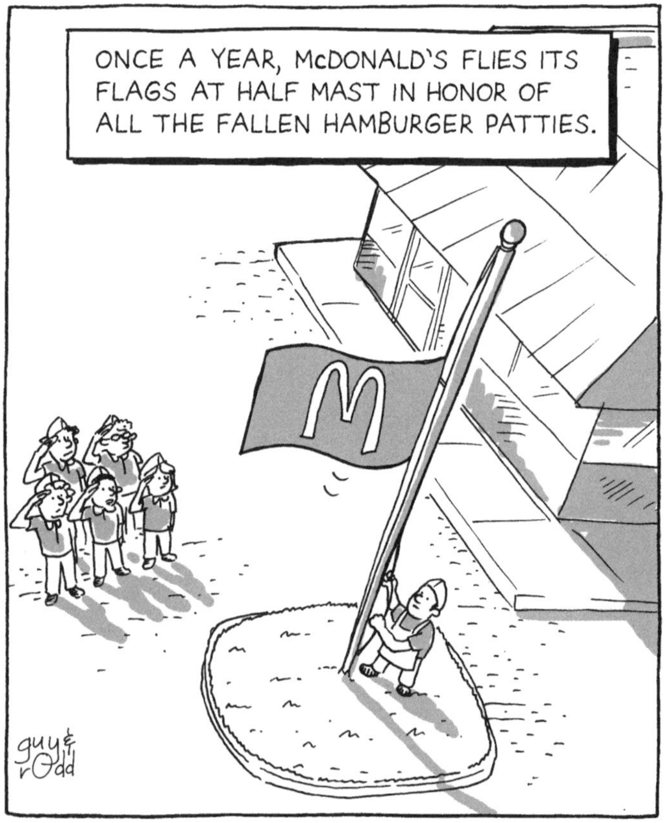
ONCE A YEAR, McDONALD'S FLIES ITS FLAGS AT HALF MAST IN HONOR OF ALL THE FALLEN HAMBURGER PATTIES.
M
guy & rodd

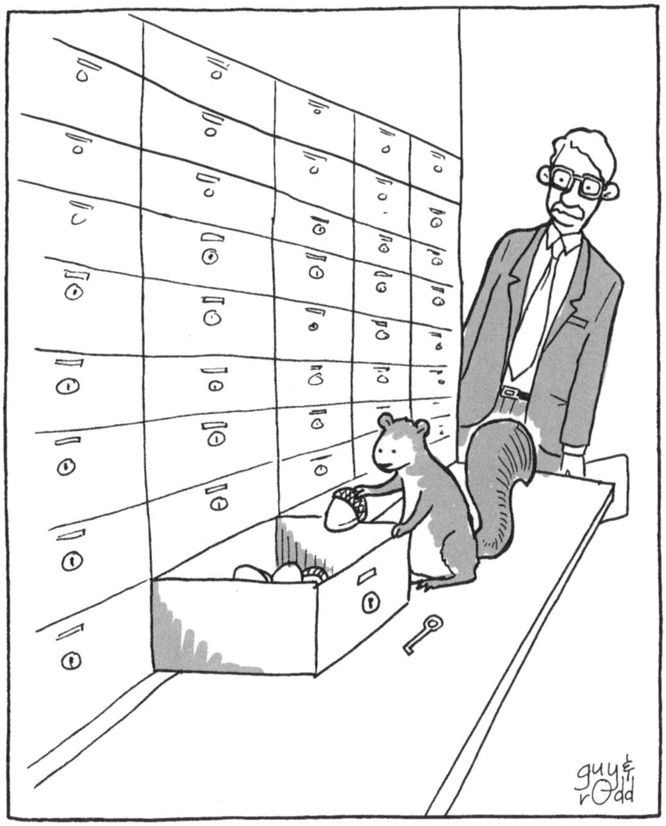
guy & rOdd

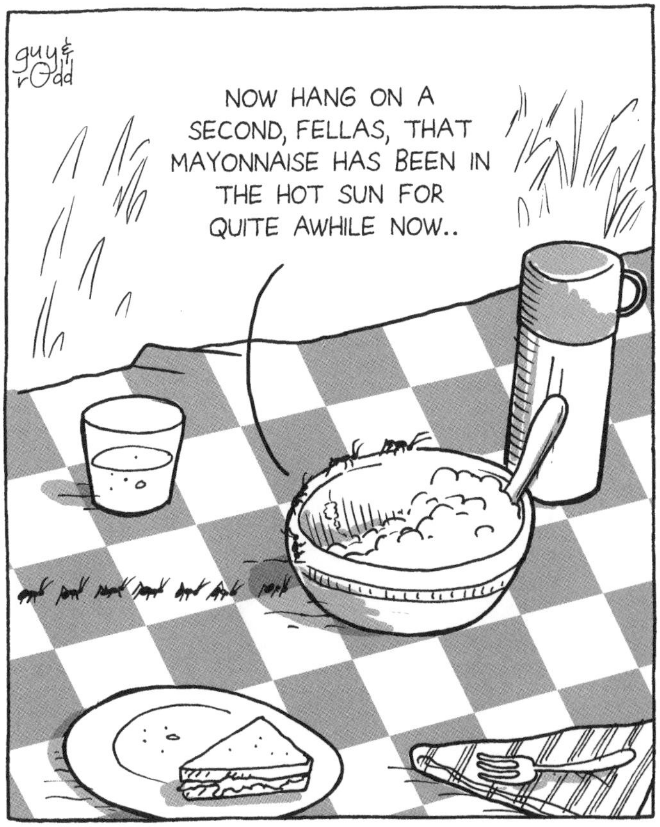
guy & rOdd
NOW HANG ON A SECOND, FELLAS, THAT MAYONNAISE HAS BEEN IN THE HOT SUN FOR QUITE AWHILE NOW..

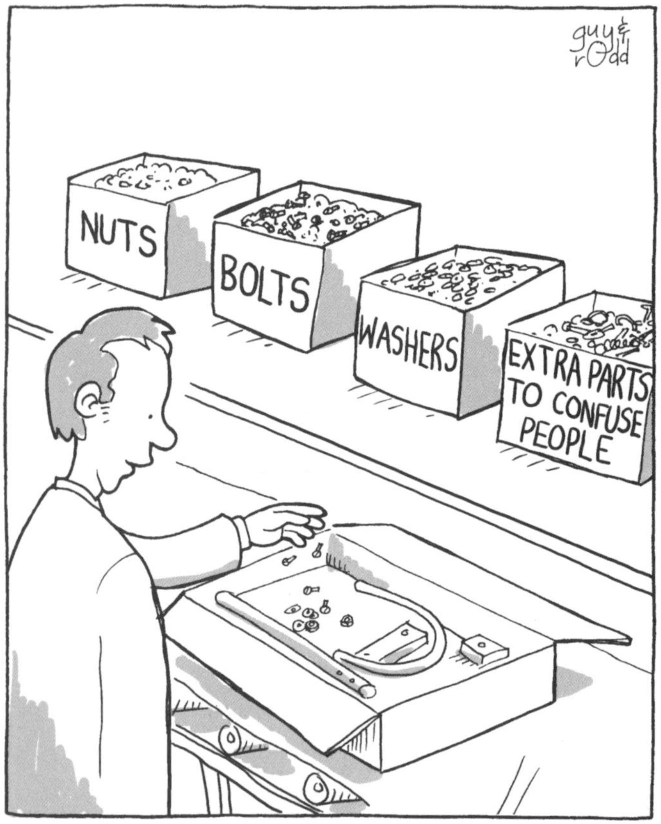
NUTS
BOLTS
WASHERS
EXTRA PARTS TO CONFUSE PEOPLE
guy & rodd

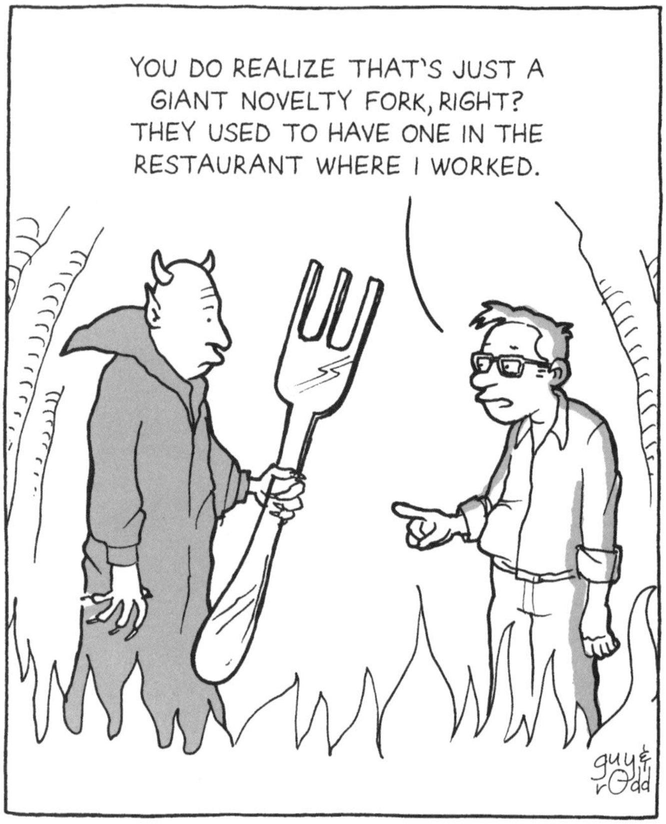
YOU DO REALIZE THAT'S JUST A GIANT NOVELTY FORK, RIGHT? THEY USED TO HAVE ONE IN THE RESTAURANT WHERE I WORKED.
guy & rodd

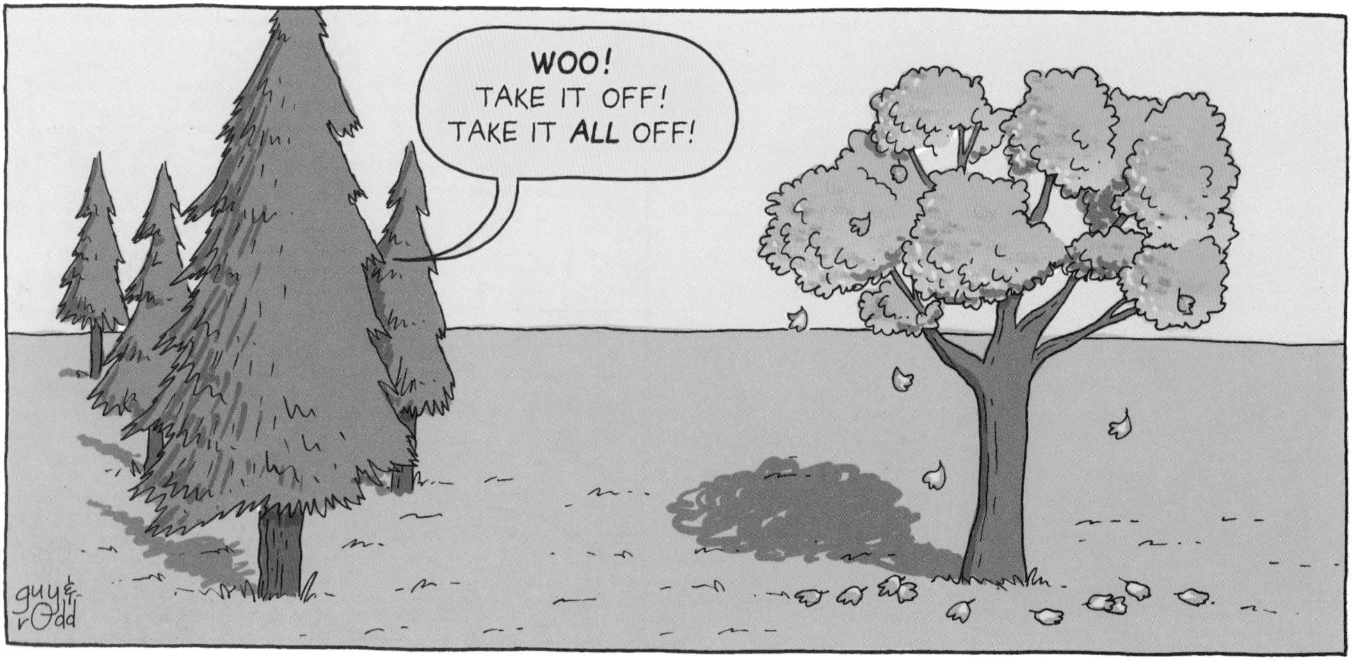
WOO! TAKE IT OFF! TAKE IT ALL OFF!
guy & rodd

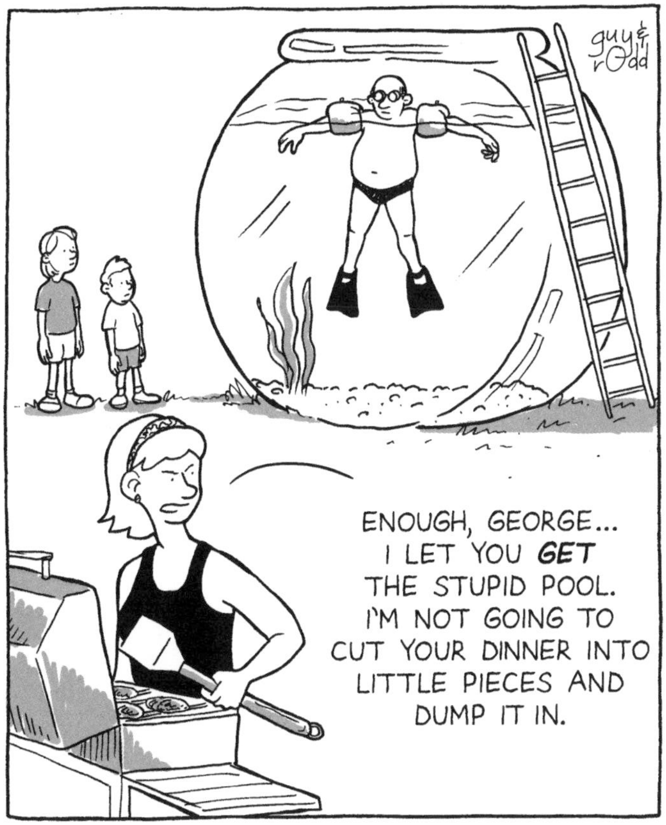
guy & rOdd
ENOUGH, GEORGE... I LET YOU **GET** THE STUPID POOL. I'M NOT GOING TO CUT YOUR DINNER INTO LITTLE PIECES AND DUMP IT IN.

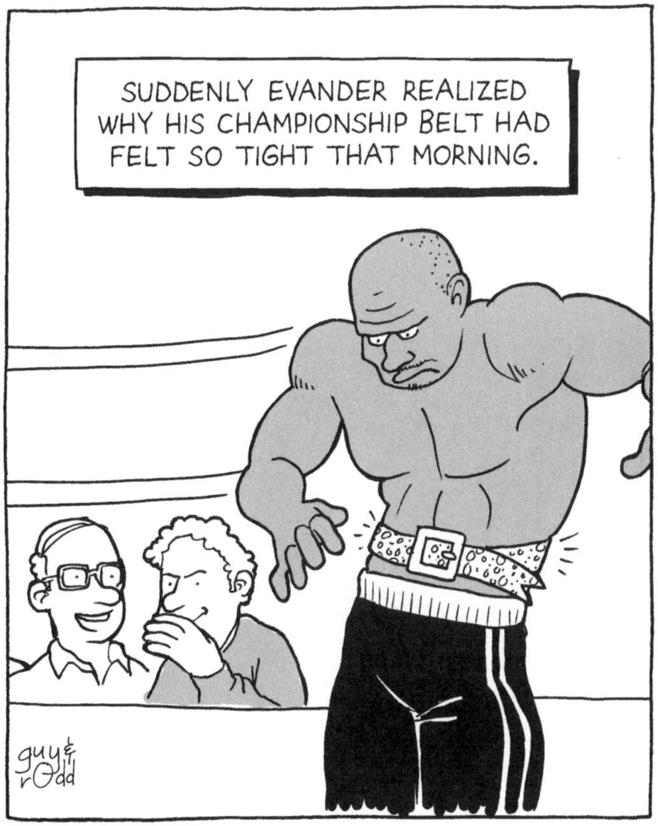
SUDDENLY EVANDER REALIZED WHY HIS CHAMPIONSHIP BELT HAD FELT SO TIGHT THAT MORNING.
guy & rOdd

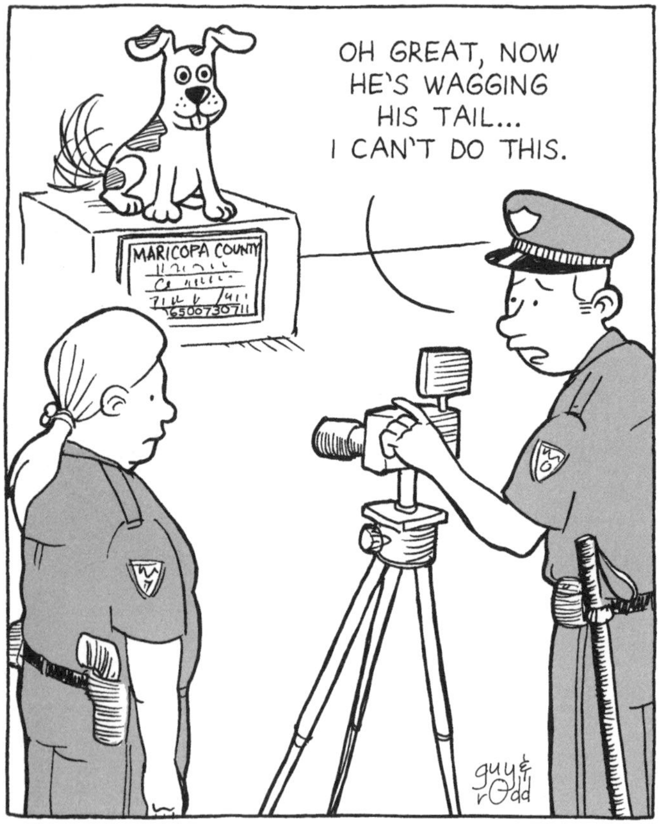
OH GREAT, NOW HE'S WAGGING HIS TAIL... I CAN'T DO THIS.
MARICOPA COUNTY
guy & rOdd

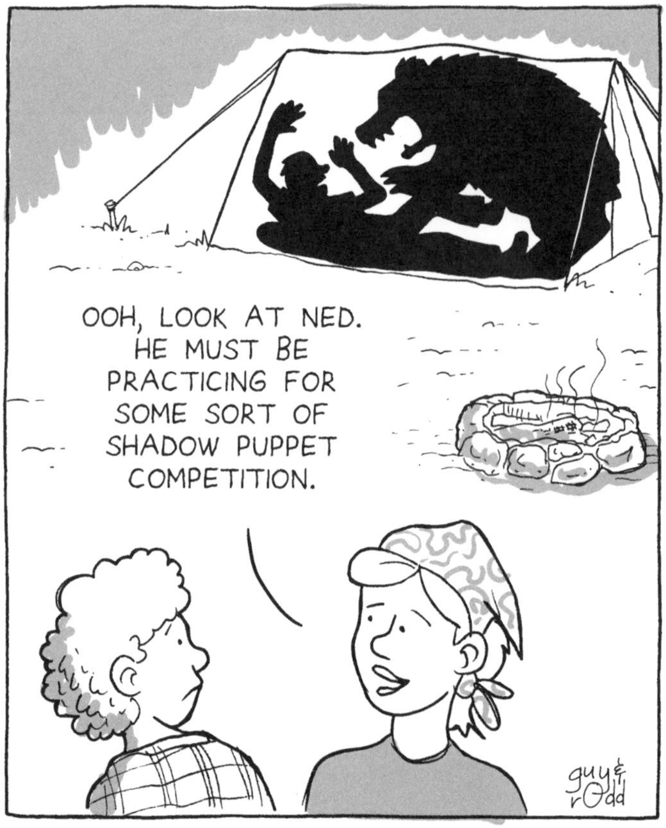
OOH, LOOK AT NED. HE MUST BE PRACTICING FOR SOME SORT OF SHADOW PUPPET COMPETITION.
guy & rOdd

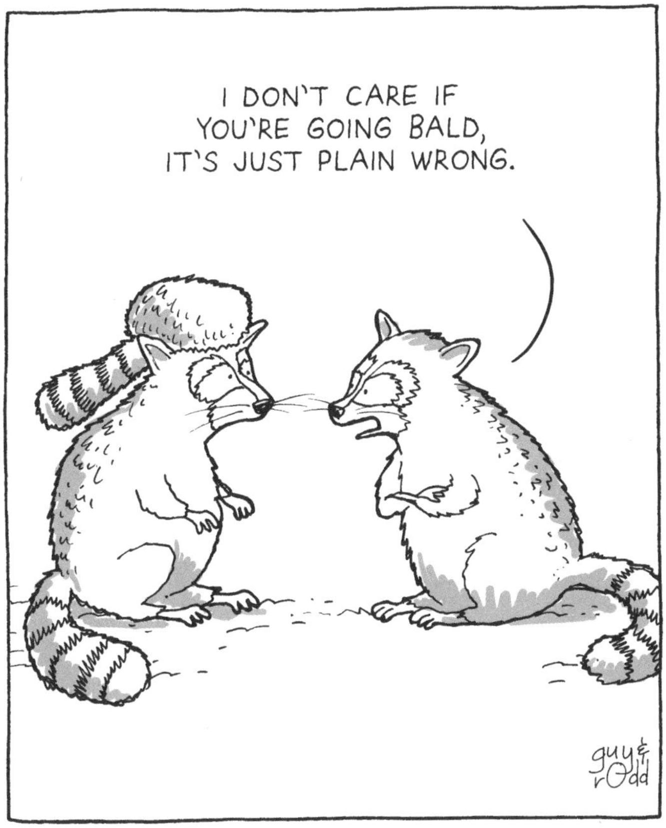
I DON'T CARE IF YOU'RE GOING BALD, IT'S JUST PLAIN WRONG.

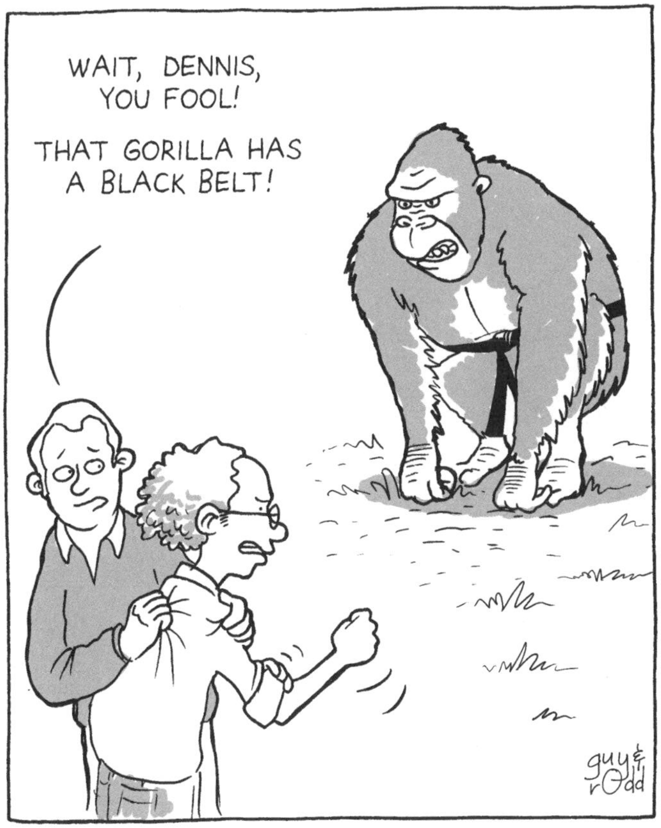
WAIT, DENNIS, YOU FOOL!
THAT GORILLA HAS A BLACK BELT!

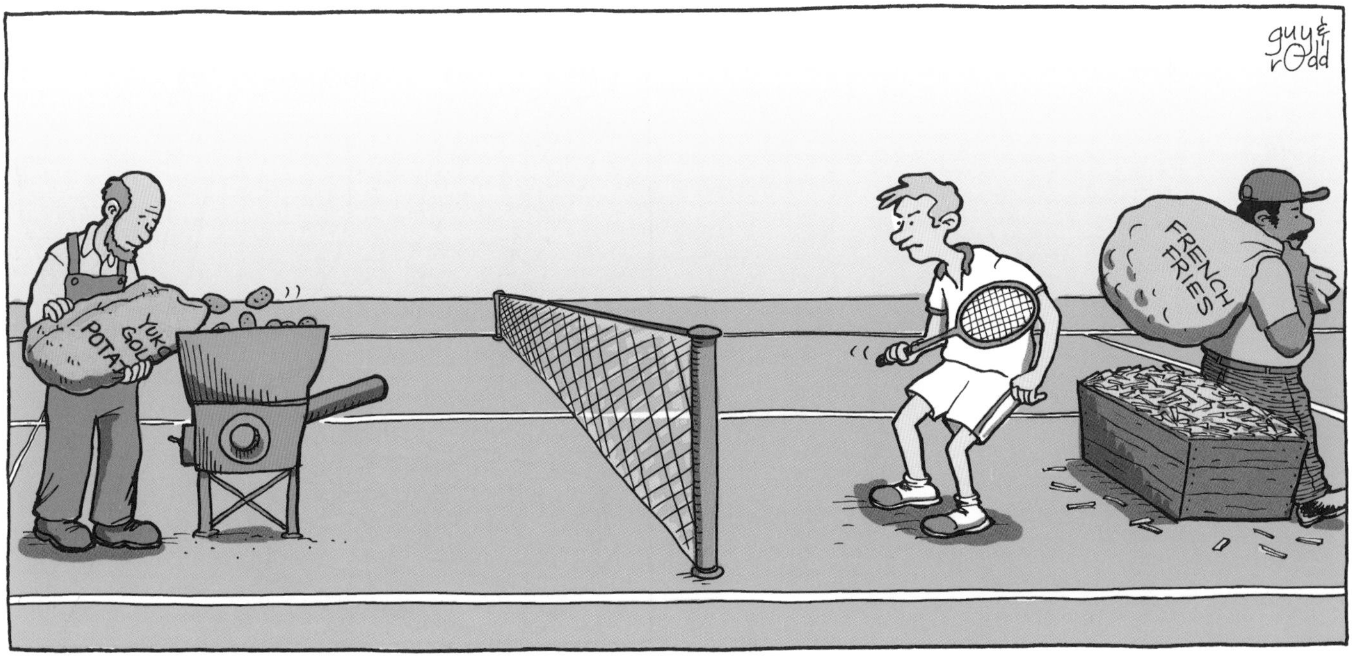
FRENCH FRIES

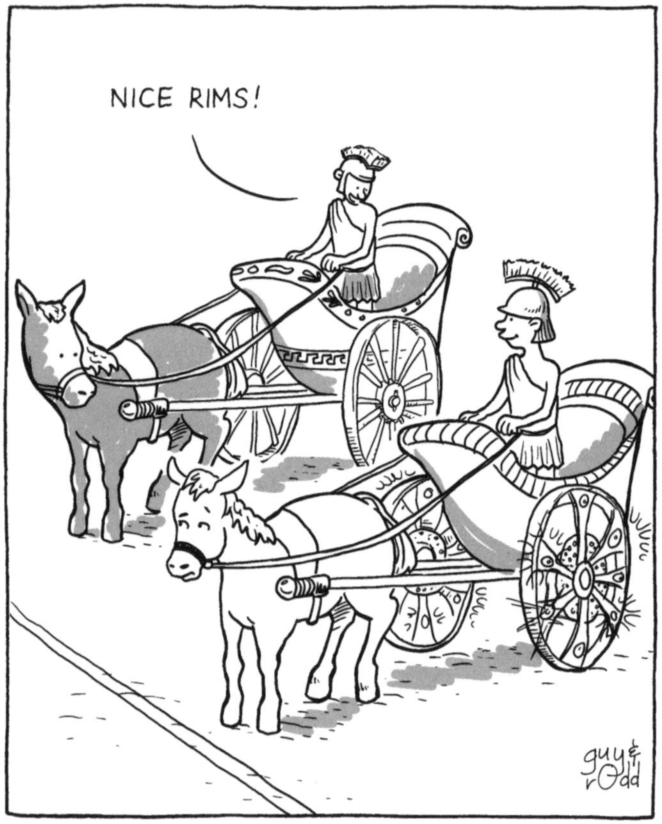
NICE RIMS!
guy & rOdd

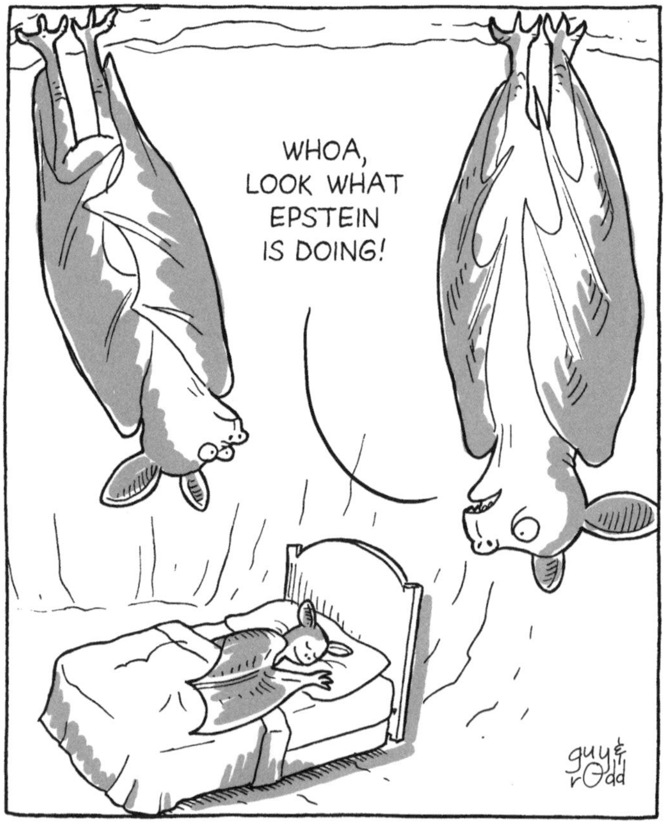
WHOA, LOOK WHAT EPSTEIN IS DOING!
guy & rOdd

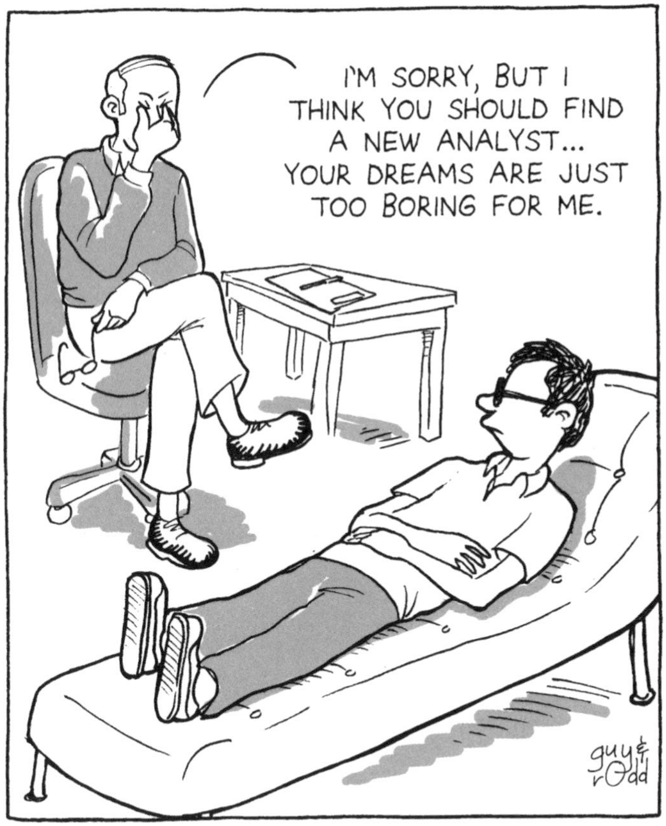
I'M SORRY, BUT I THINK YOU SHOULD FIND A NEW ANALYST... YOUR DREAMS ARE JUST TOO BORING FOR ME.
guy & rodd

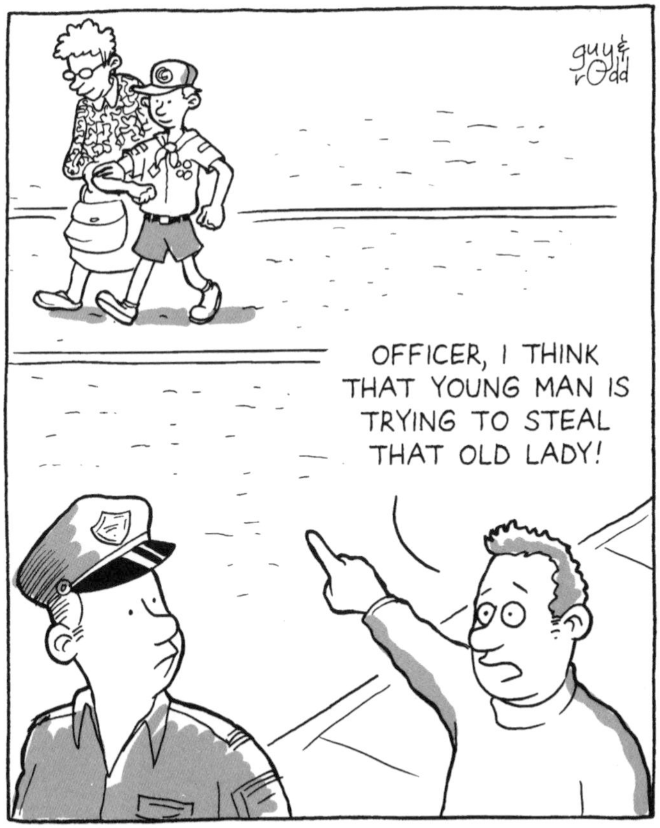
guy & rodd
OFFICER, I THINK THAT YOUNG MAN IS TRYING TO STEAL THAT OLD LADY!

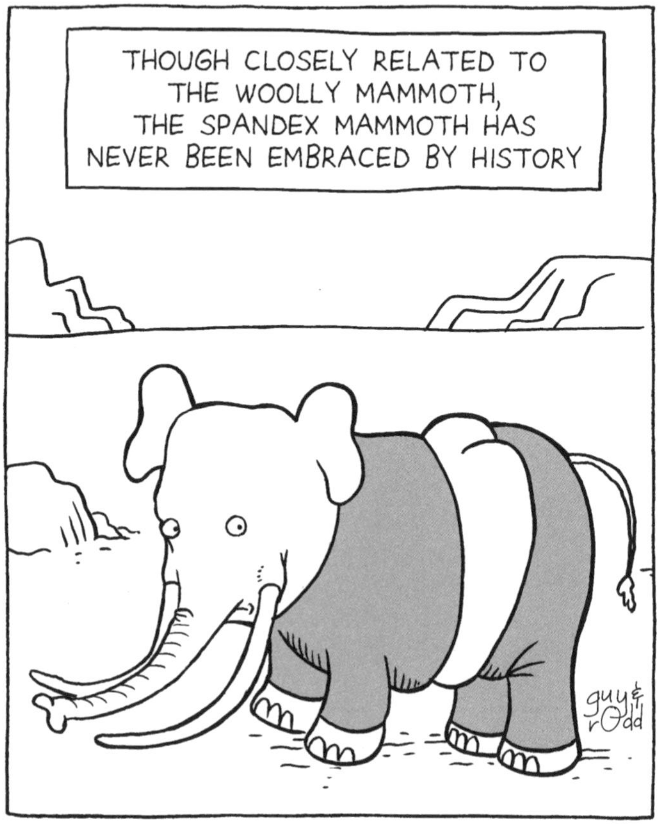
THOUGH CLOSELY RELATED TO THE WOOLLY MAMMOTH, THE SPANDEX MAMMOTH HAS NEVER BEEN EMBRACED BY HISTORY

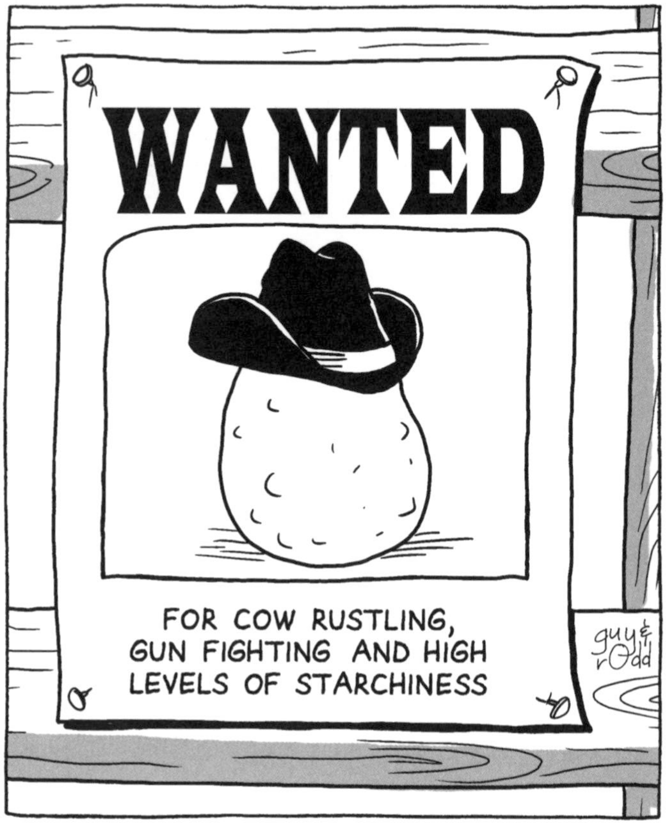
WANTED
FOR COW RUSTLING, GUN FIGHTING AND HIGH LEVELS OF STARCHINESS

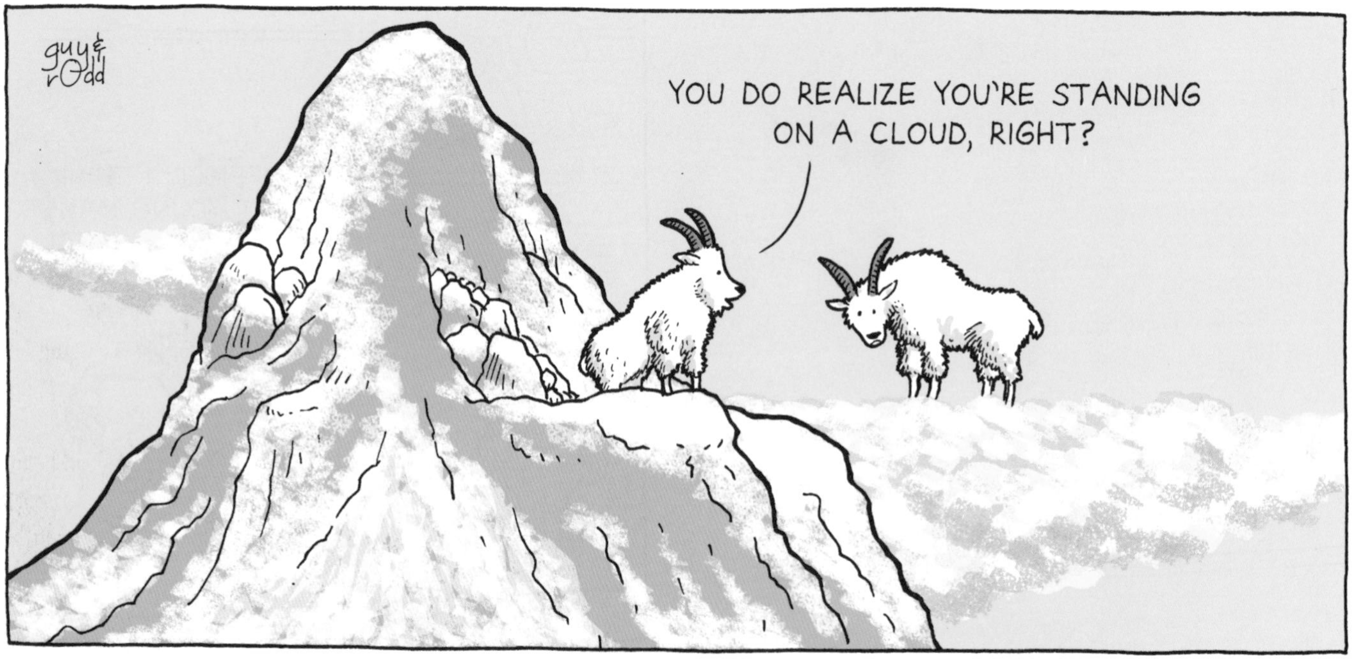
YOU DO REALIZE YOU'RE STANDING ON A CLOUD, RIGHT?

AND THOUGH HE DIED DURING THE HUNT, WE CAN ONLY ASSUME THAT SIR GEORGE L. JONES WOULD WANT THIS NEW SPECIES OF *BUTT-FACED CLOWN MONKEY* TO FOREVER BEAR HIS NAME.

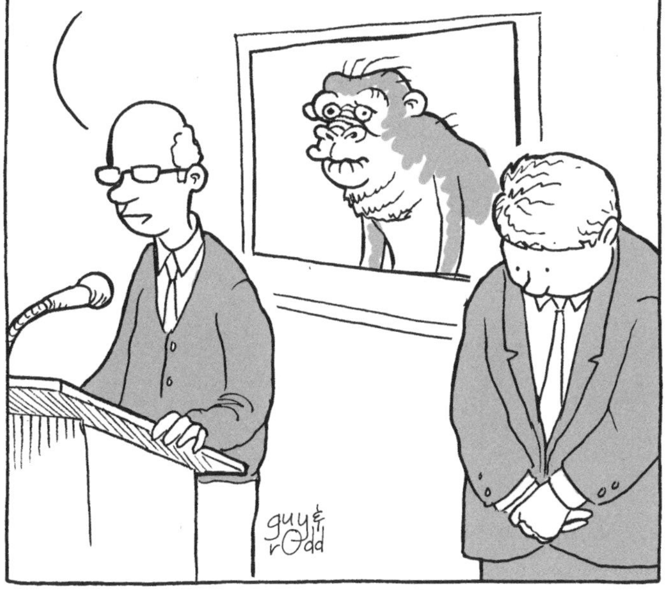
guy & rodd

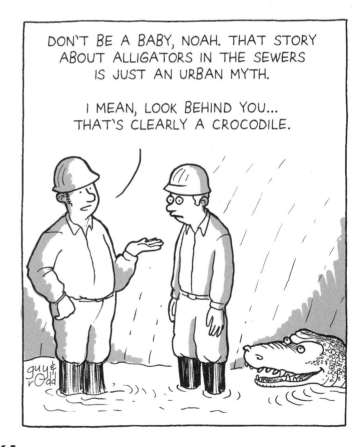

DON'T BE A BABY, NOAH. THAT STORY ABOUT ALLIGATORS IN THE SEWERS IS JUST AN URBAN MYTH.

I MEAN, LOOK BEHIND YOU... THAT'S CLEARLY A CROCODILE.

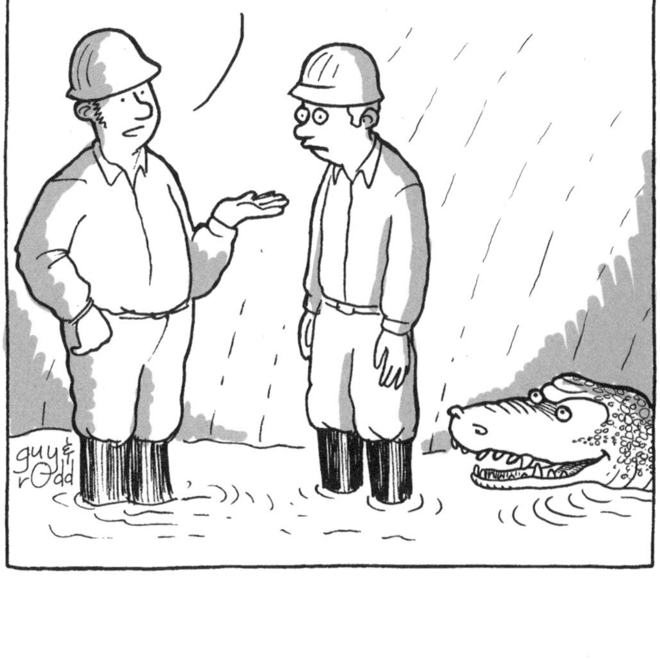
guy & rodd

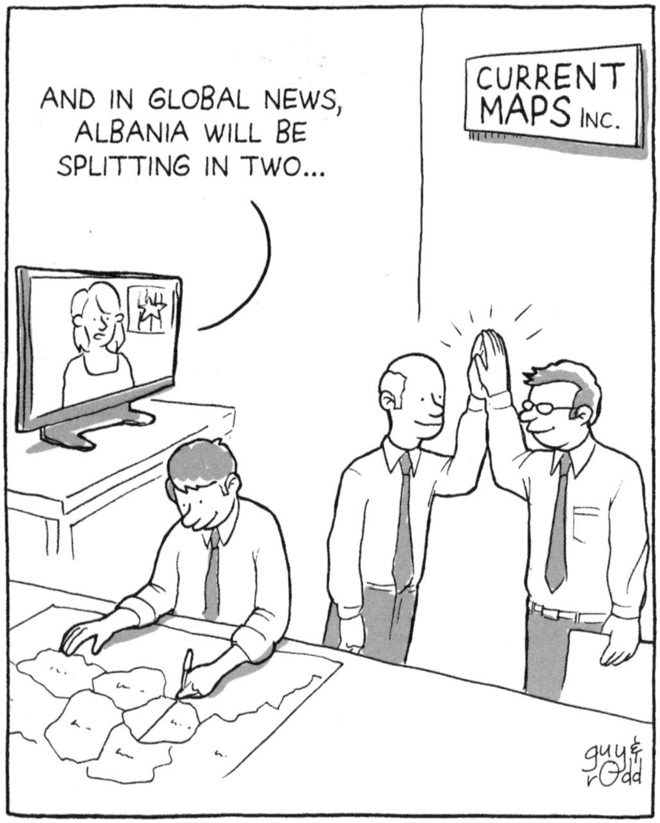
AND IN GLOBAL NEWS, ALBANIA WILL BE SPLITTING IN TWO...
CURRENT MAPS INC.
guy & rOdd

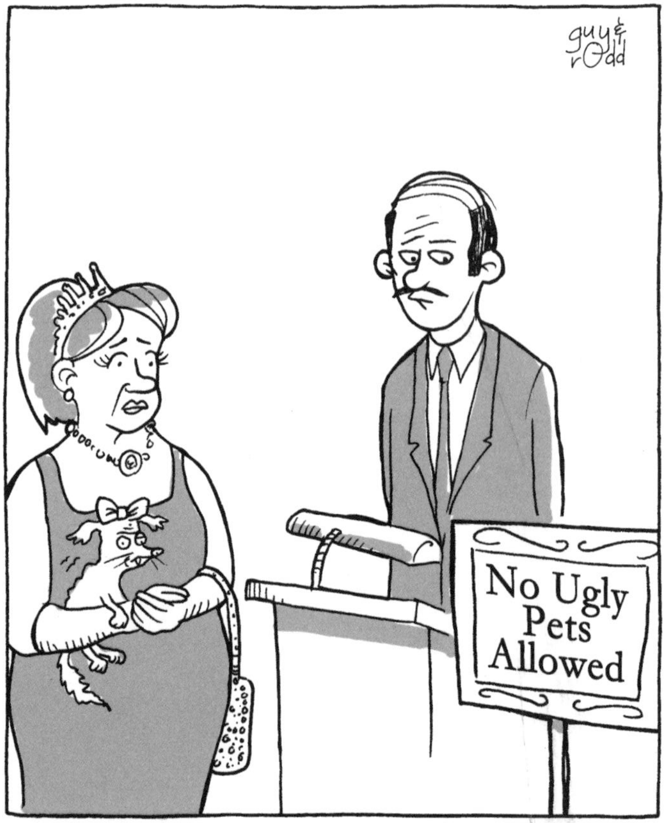
guy & rOdd
No Ugly Pets Allowed

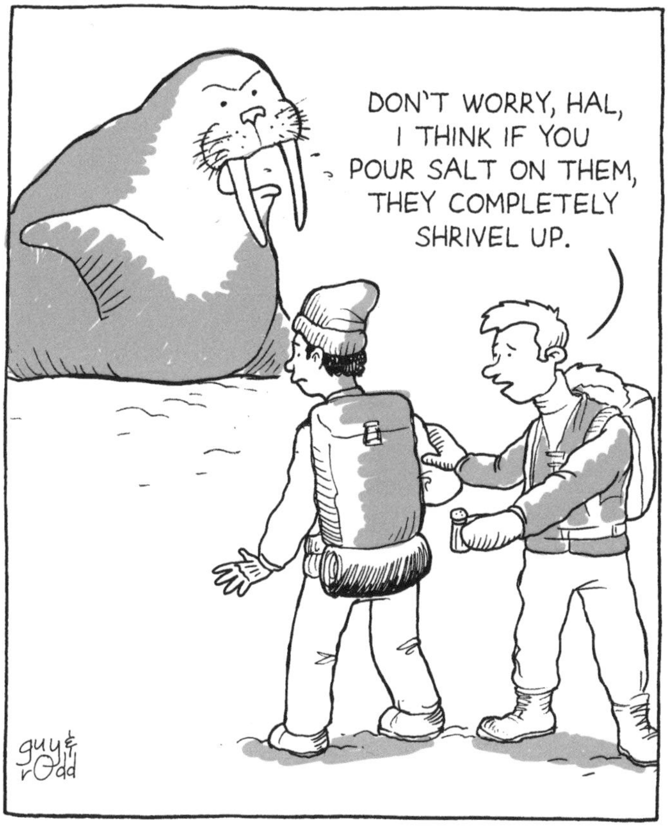
DON'T WORRY, HAL, I THINK IF YOU POUR SALT ON THEM, THEY COMPLETELY SHRIVEL UP.
guy & rOdd

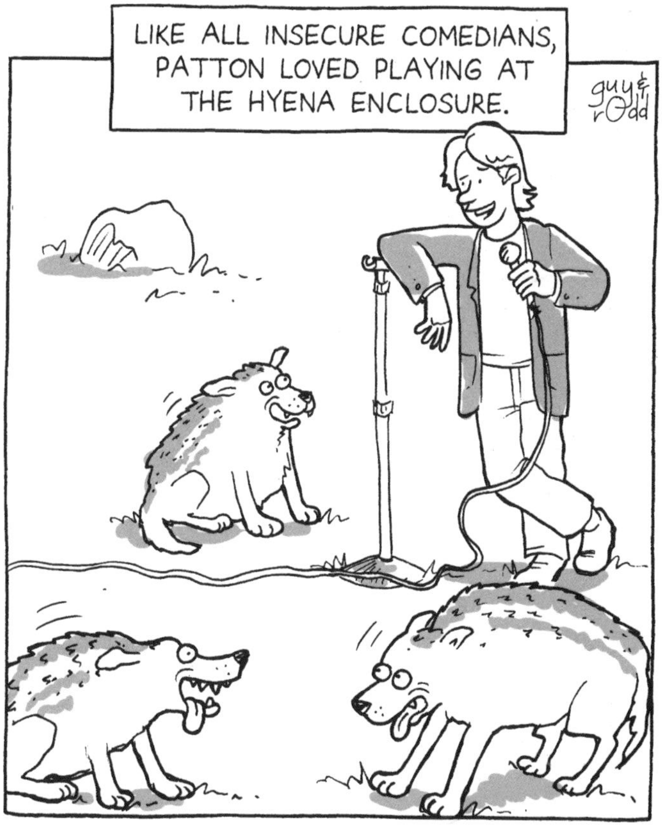
LIKE ALL INSECURE COMEDIANS, PATTON LOVED PLAYING AT THE HYENA ENCLOSURE.
guy & rOdd

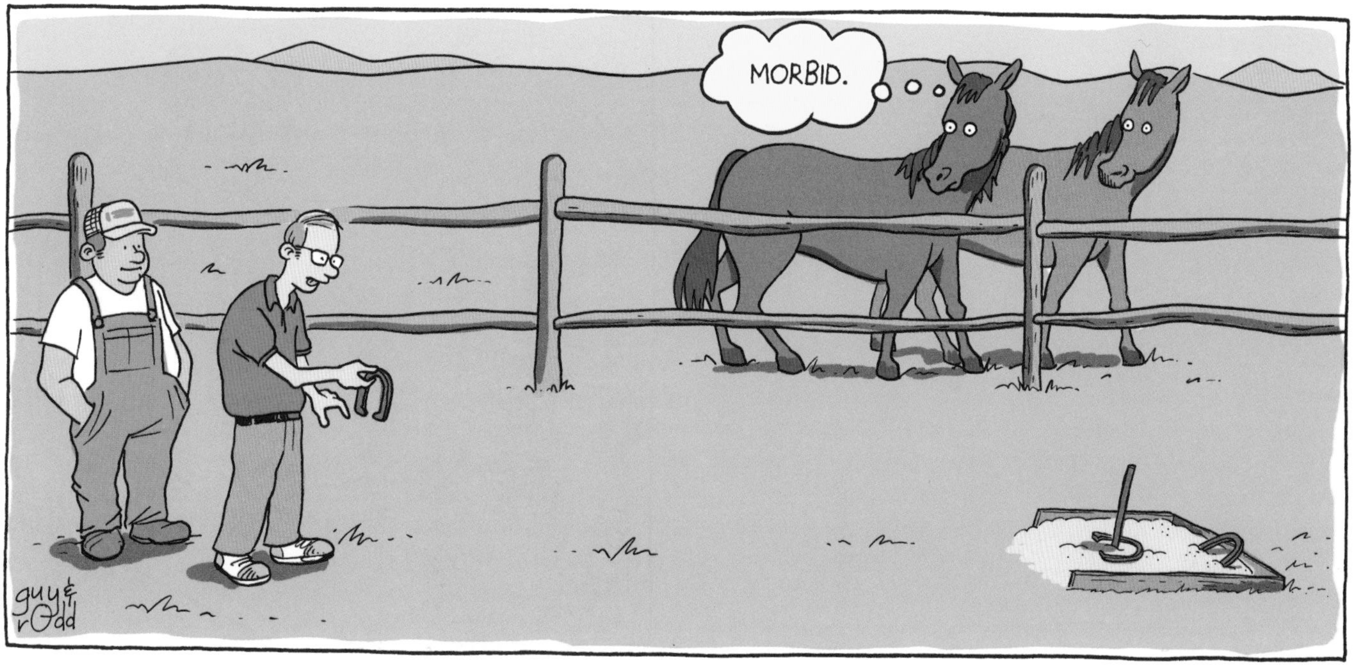
MORBID.
guy & rOdd

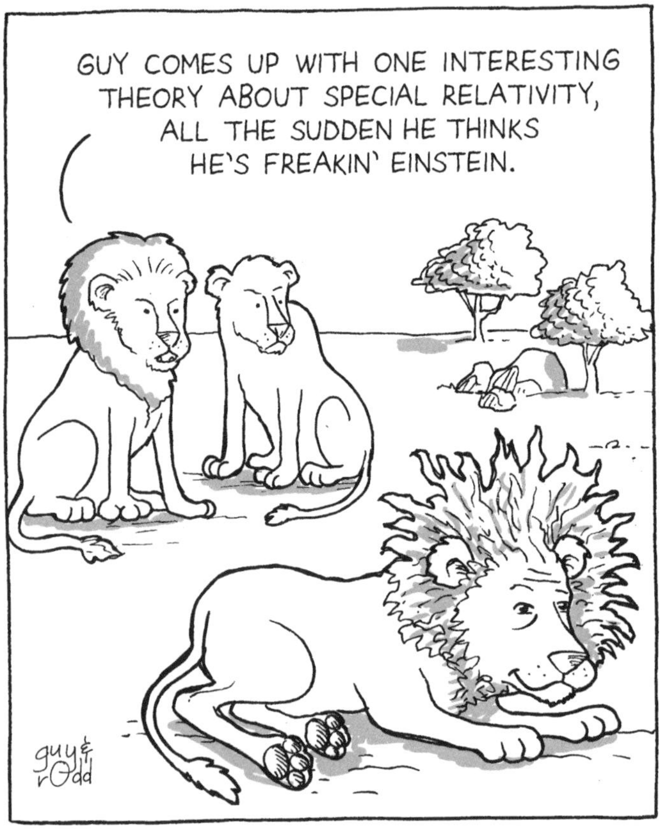
GUY COMES UP WITH ONE INTERESTING THEORY ABOUT SPECIAL RELATIVITY, ALL THE SUDDEN HE THINKS HE'S FREAKIN' EINSTEIN.
guy & rodd

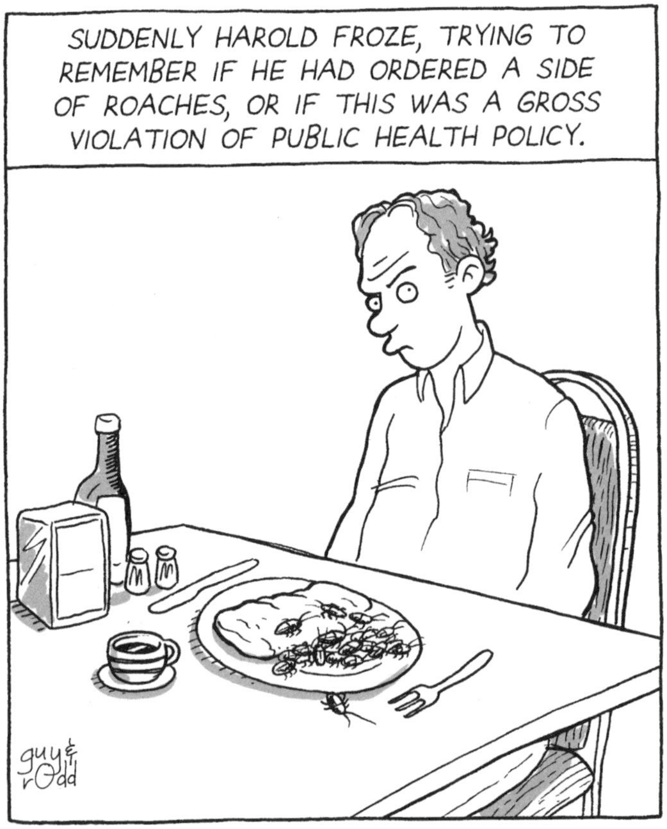
SUDDENLY HAROLD FROZE, TRYING TO REMEMBER IF HE HAD ORDERED A SIDE OF ROACHES, OR IF THIS WAS A GROSS VIOLATION OF PUBLIC HEALTH POLICY.
guy & rodd

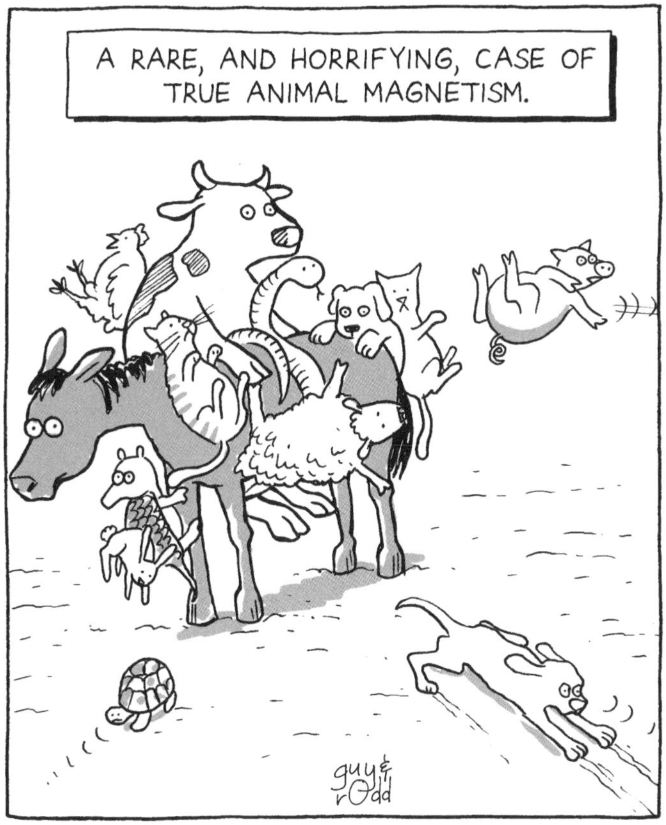
A RARE, AND HORRIFYING, CASE OF TRUE ANIMAL MAGNETISM.
guy & rodd

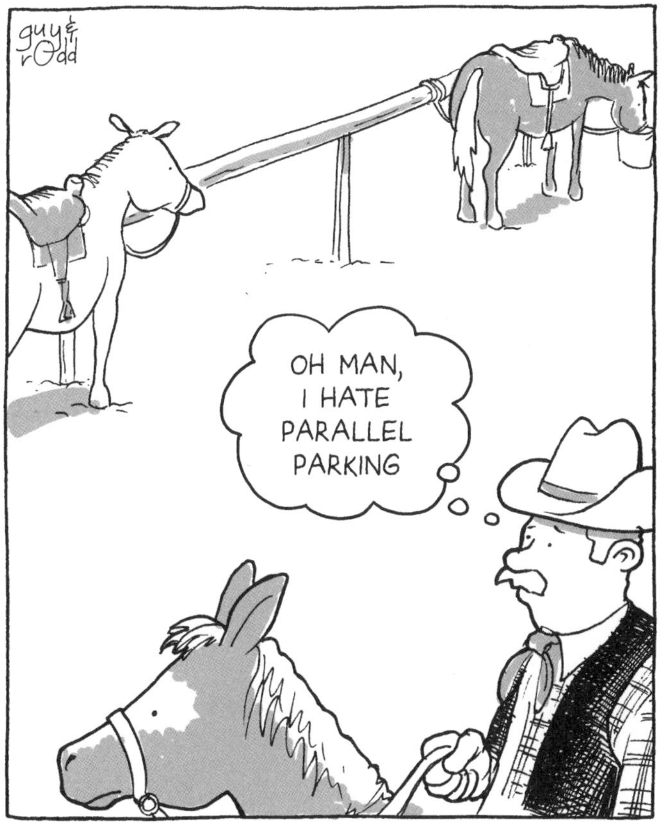
guy & rodd
OH MAN, I HATE PARALLEL PARKING

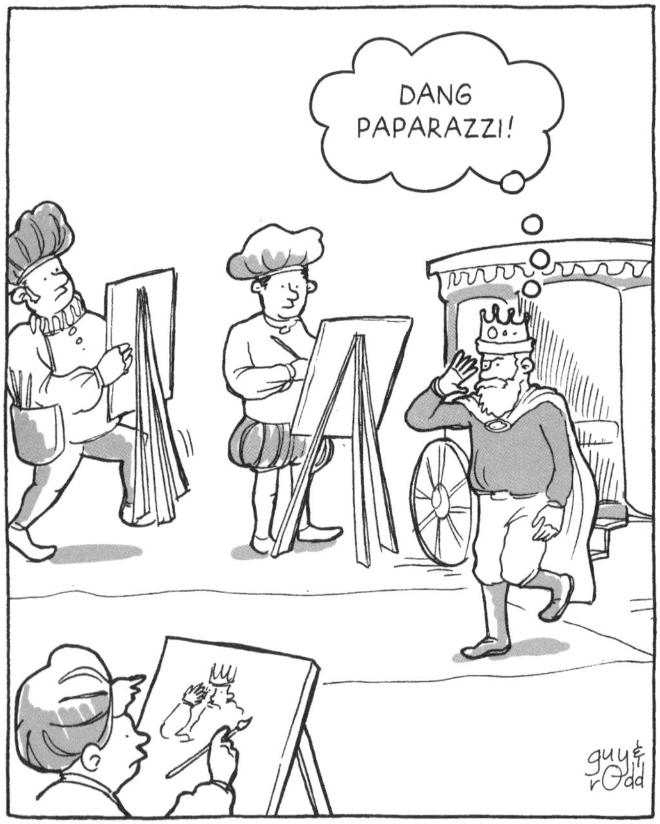
DANG PAPARAZZI!
guy & rOdd

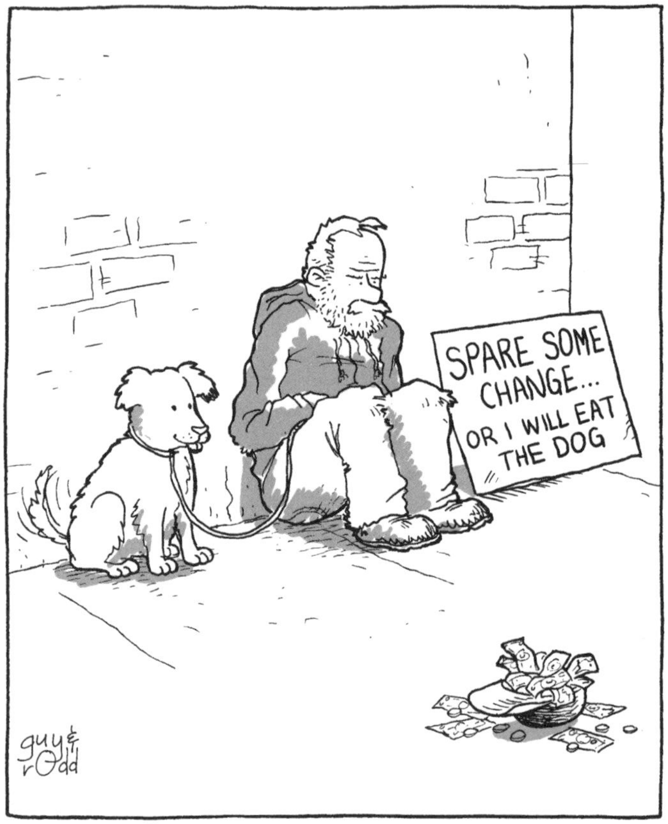
SPARE SOME CHANGE... OR I WILL EAT THE DOG
guy & rOdd

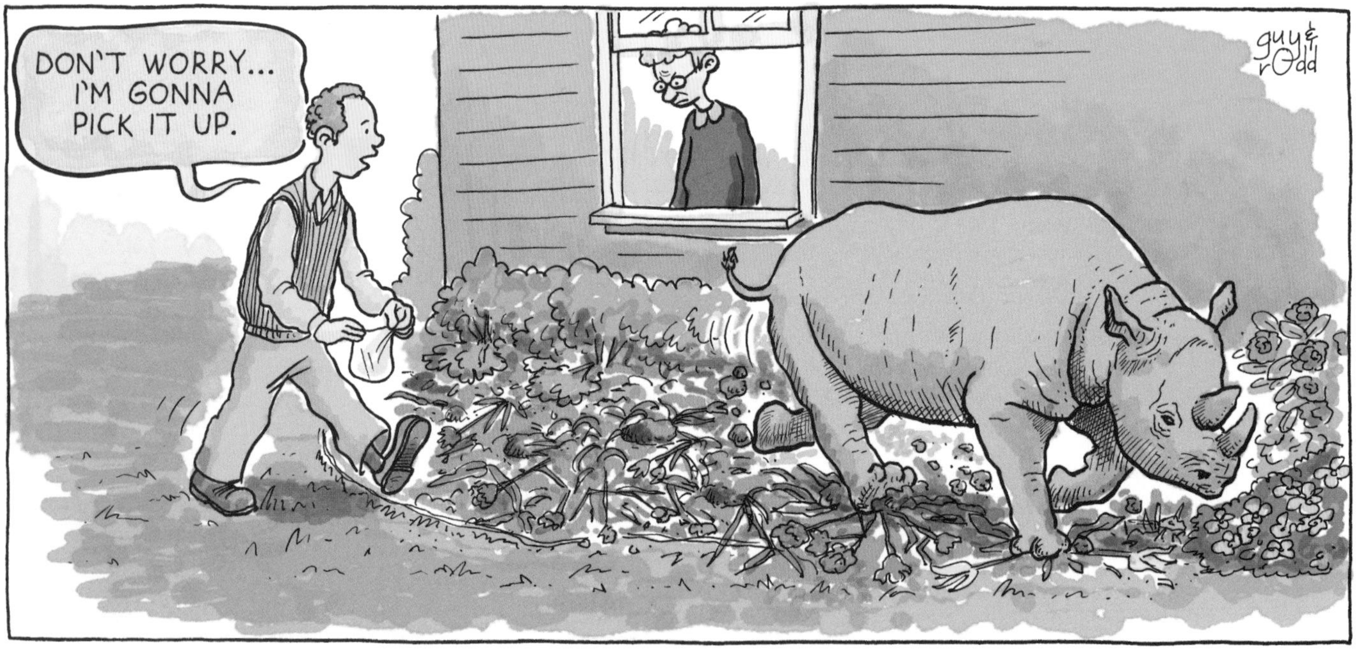
DON'T WORRY... I'M GONNA PICK IT UP.
guy & rOdd

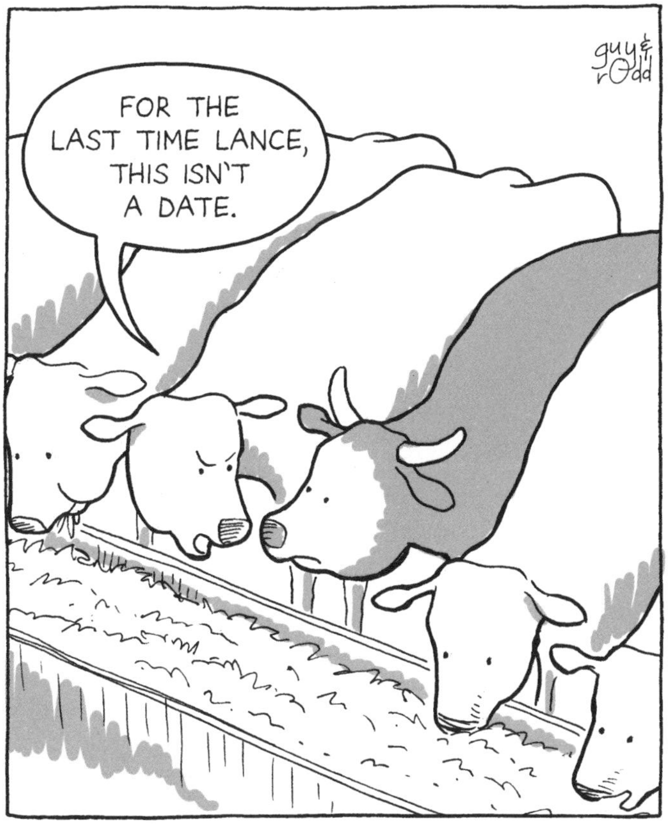
guy & rOdd
FOR THE LAST TIME LANCE, THIS ISN'T A DATE.

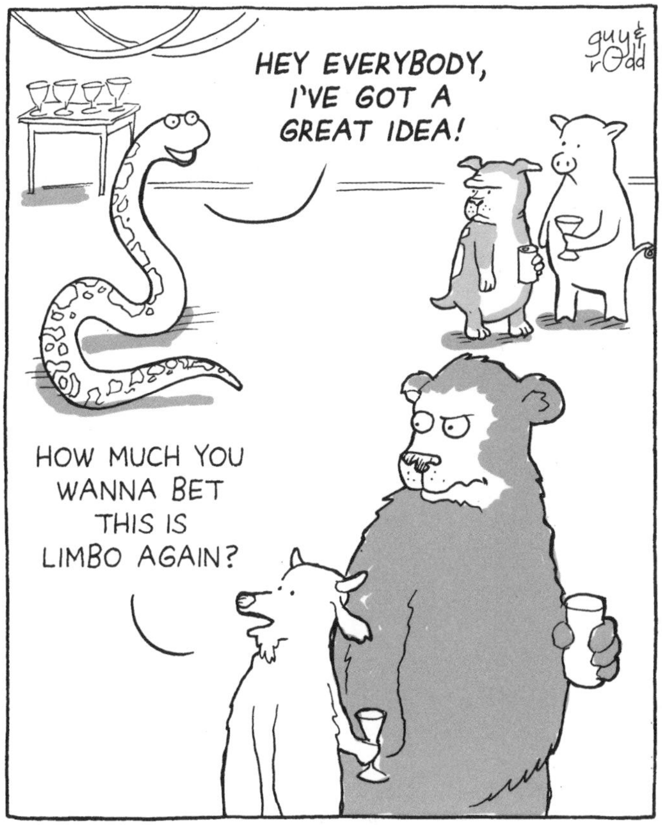
guy & rOdd
HEY EVERYBODY, I'VE GOT A GREAT IDEA!
HOW MUCH YOU WANNA BET THIS IS LIMBO AGAIN?

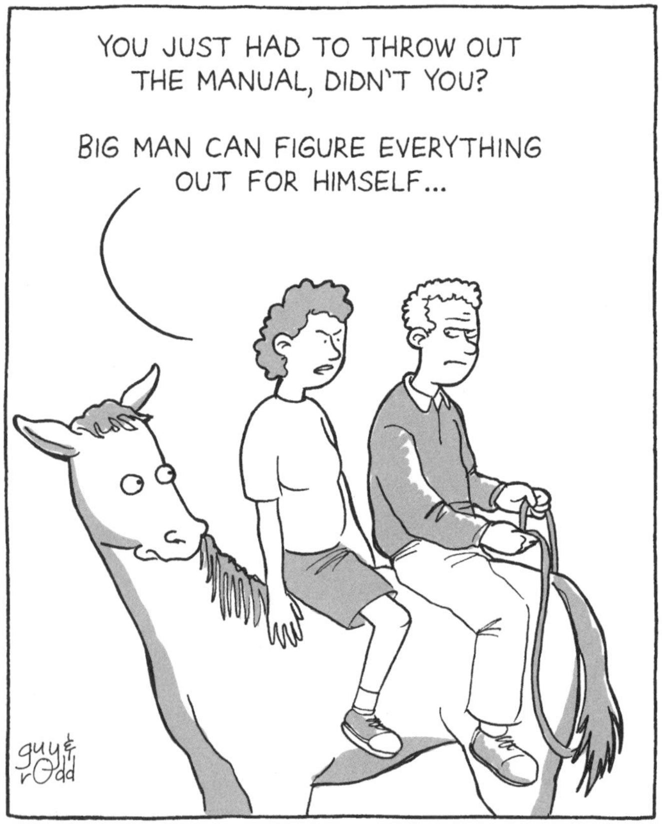
YOU JUST HAD TO THROW OUT THE MANUAL, DIDN'T YOU?
BIG MAN CAN FIGURE EVERYTHING OUT FOR HIMSELF...
guy & rOdd

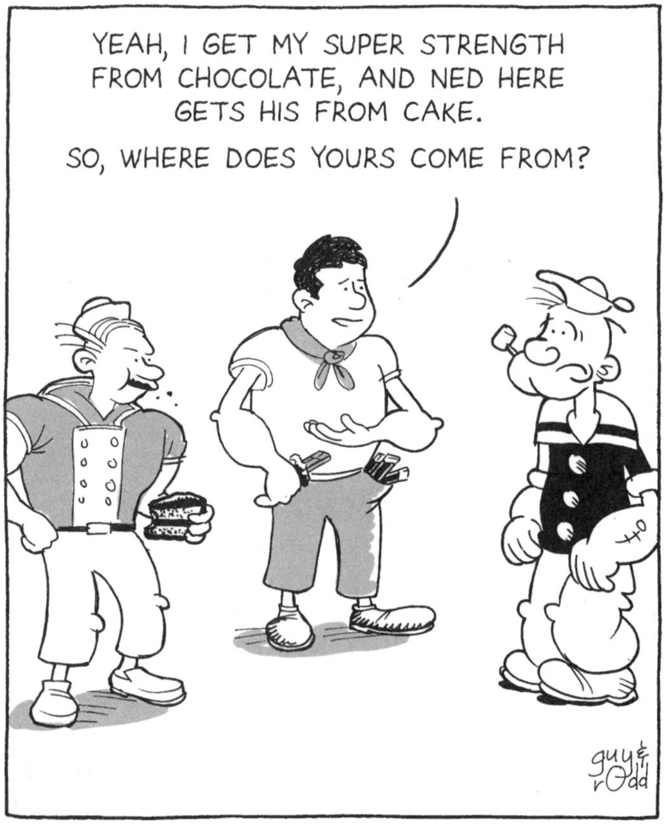
YEAH, I GET MY SUPER STRENGTH FROM CHOCOLATE, AND NED HERE GETS HIS FROM CAKE.
SO, WHERE DOES YOURS COME FROM?
guy & rOdd

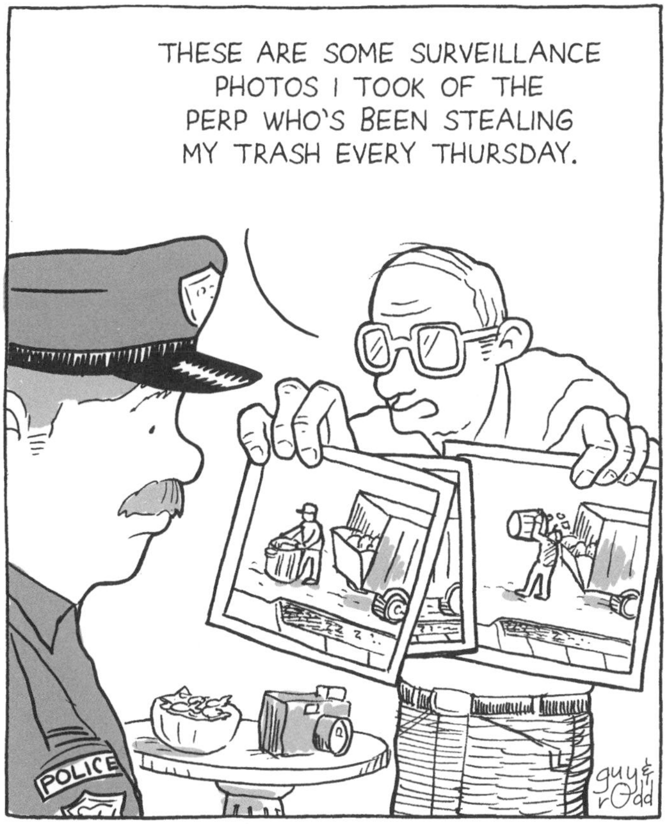
THESE ARE SOME SURVEILLANCE PHOTOS I TOOK OF THE PERP WHO'S BEEN STEALING MY TRASH EVERY THURSDAY.
POLICE
guy & rOdd

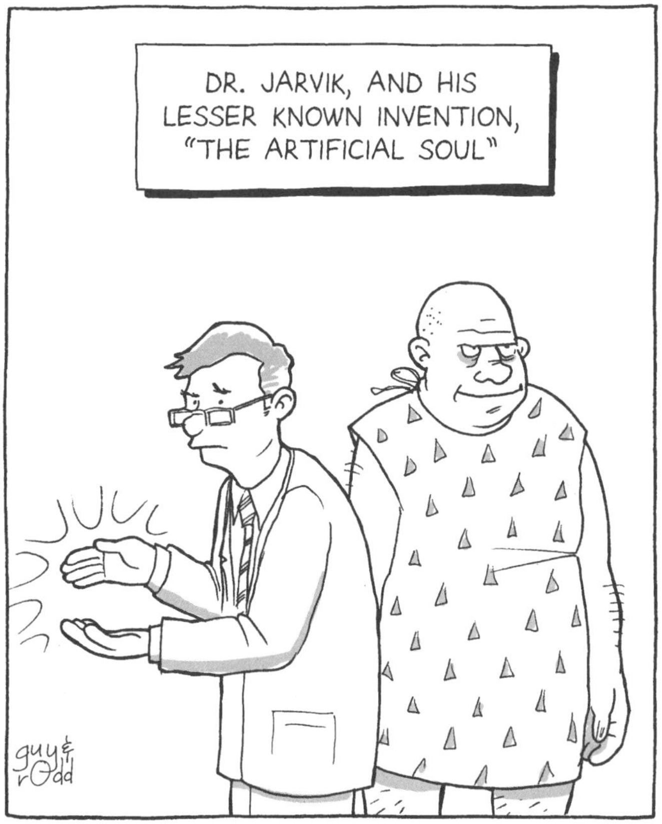
DR. JARVIK, AND HIS LESSER KNOWN INVENTION, "THE ARTIFICIAL SOUL"
guy & rOdd

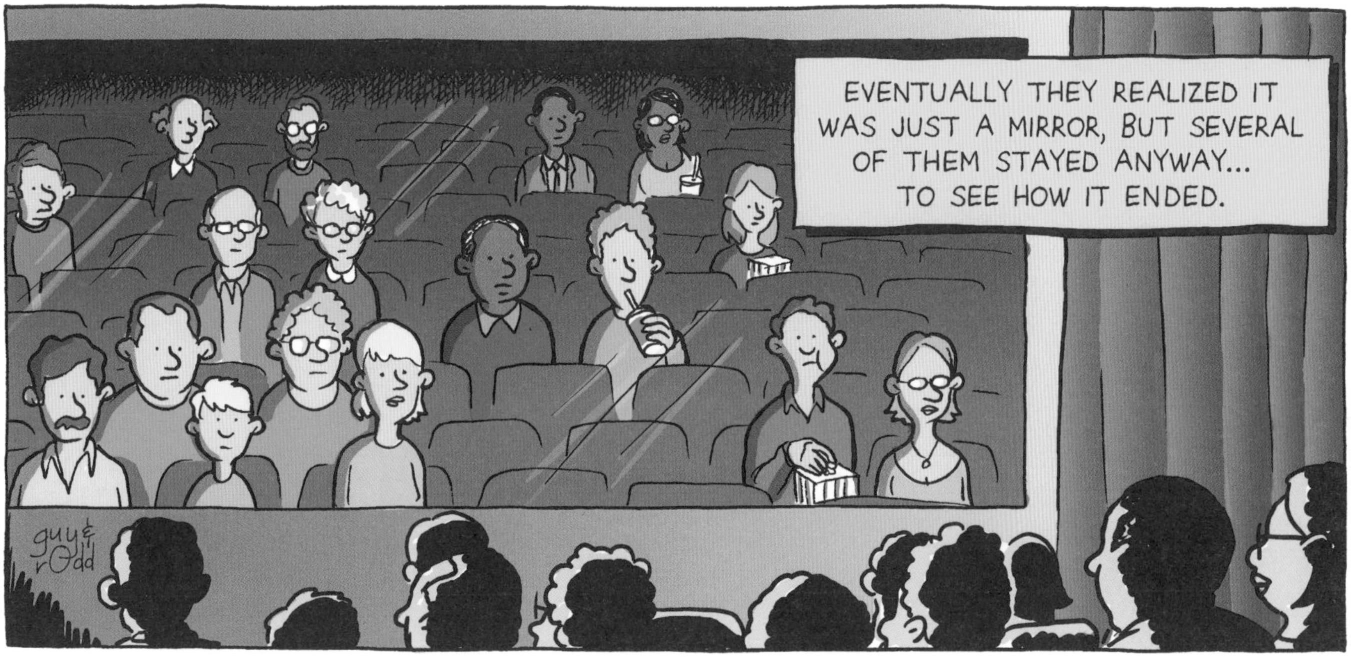
EVENTUALLY THEY REALIZED IT WAS JUST A MIRROR, BUT SEVERAL OF THEM STAYED ANYWAY... TO SEE HOW IT ENDED.
guy & rOdd

NOTHING, JUST TAKING A JACUZ'... HOW 'BOUT YOU?
guy & rOdd

SORRY FRIEND, YOU MUST HAVE TAKEN A WRONG TURN, THIS IS ACTUALLY THE MILD WEST... BUT WE'RE HAVING PILATES AFTER BRUNCH, IF YOU WANNA STAY.
guy & rOdd

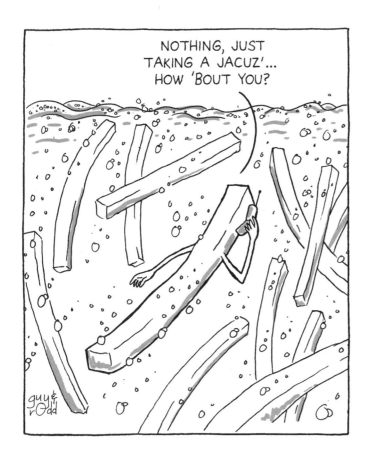

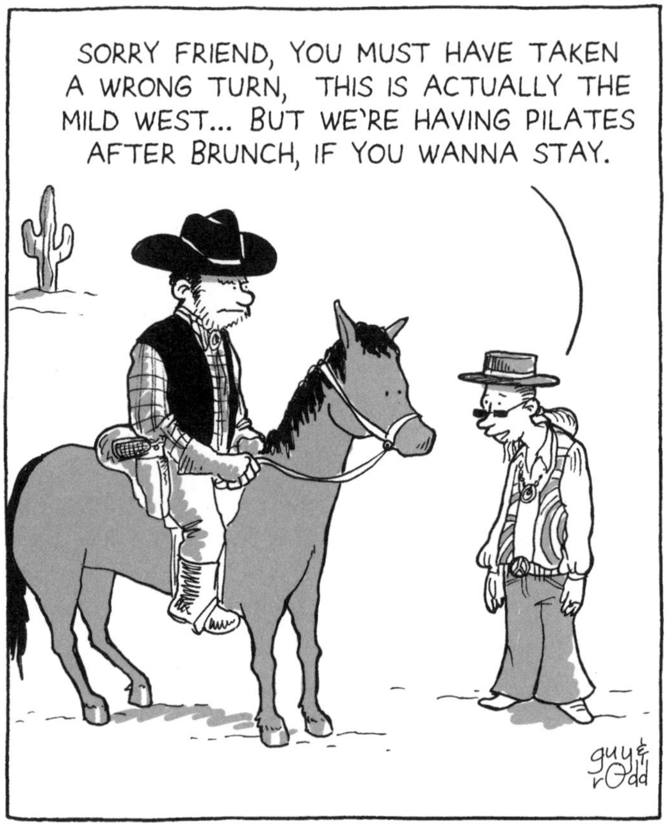

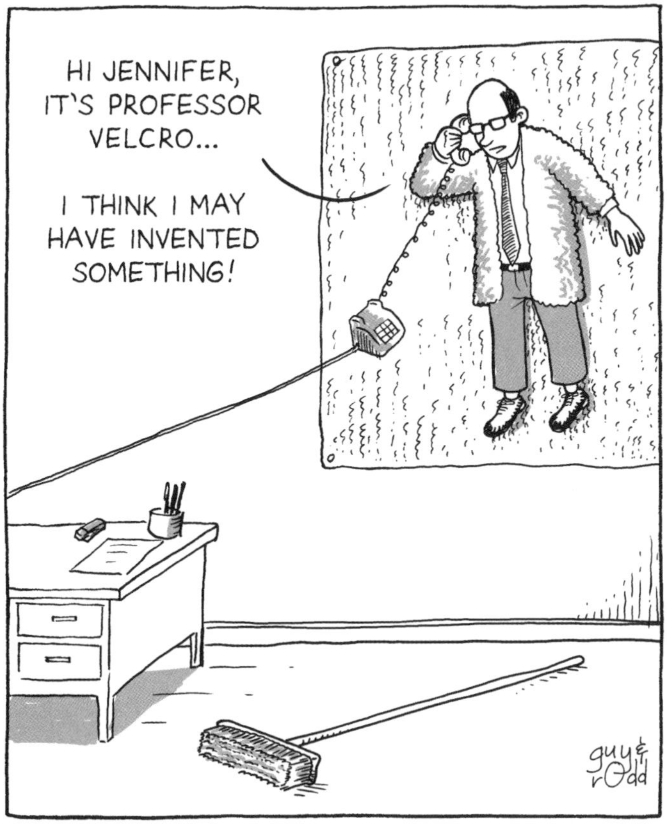
HI JENNIFER, IT'S PROFESSOR VELCRO...
I THINK I MAY HAVE INVENTED SOMETHING!
guy & rOdd

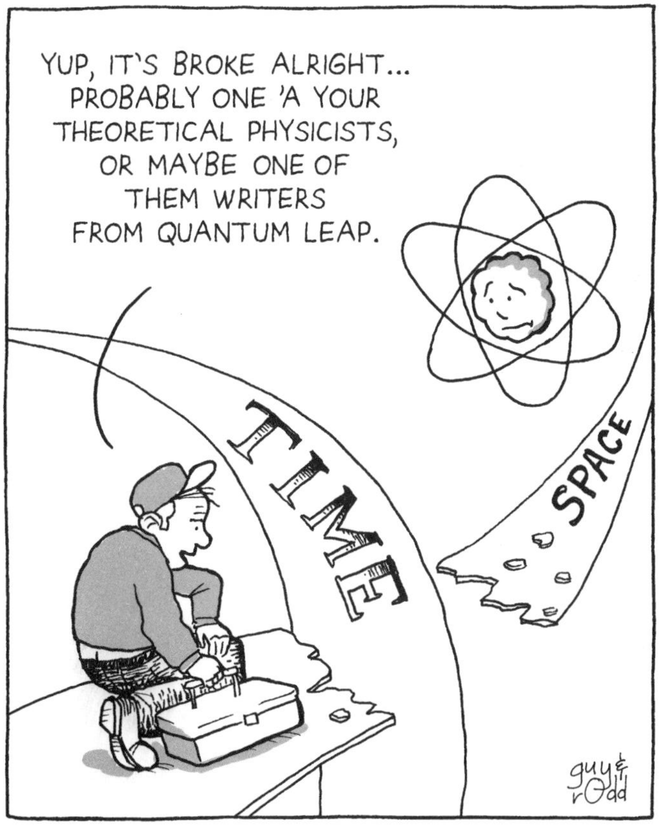
YUP, IT'S BROKE ALRIGHT... PROBABLY ONE 'A YOUR THEORETICAL PHYSICISTS, OR MAYBE ONE OF THEM WRITERS FROM QUANTUM LEAP.
TIME
SPACE
guy & rOdd

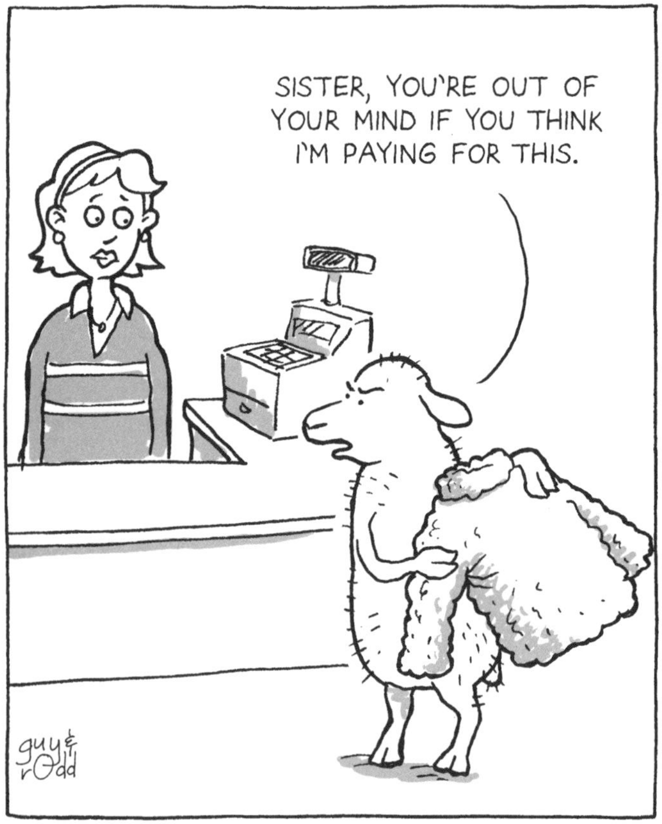
SISTER, YOU'RE OUT OF YOUR MIND IF YOU THINK I'M PAYING FOR THIS.
guy & rodd

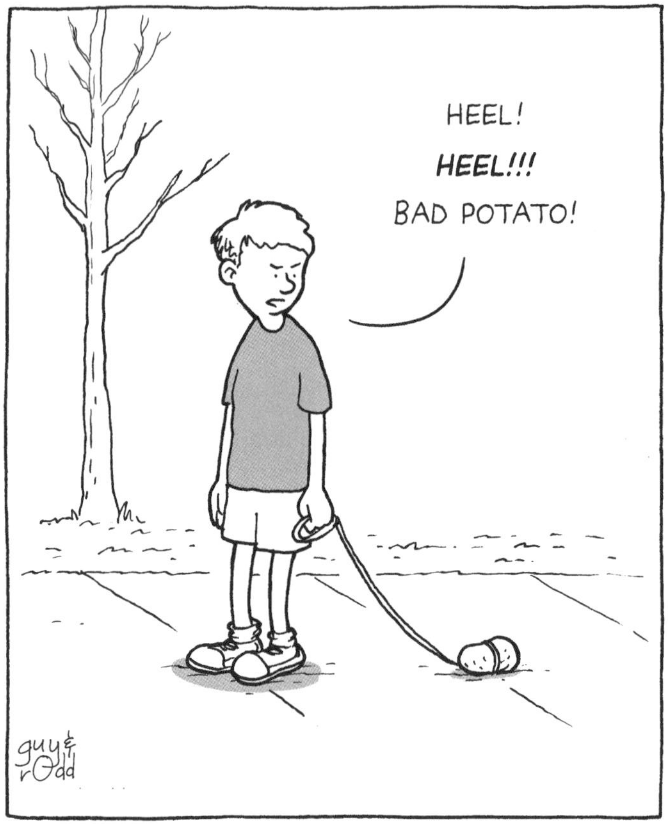
HEEL!
HEEL!!!
BAD POTATO!
guy & rodd

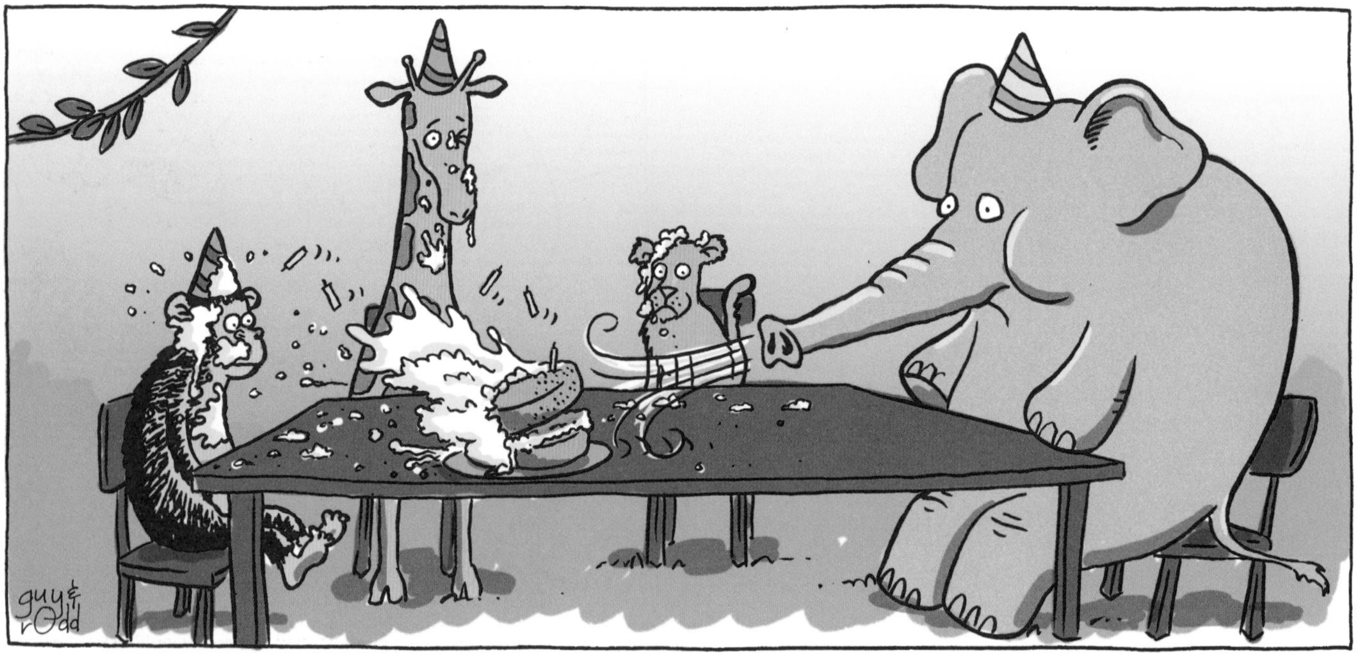
guy & rodd

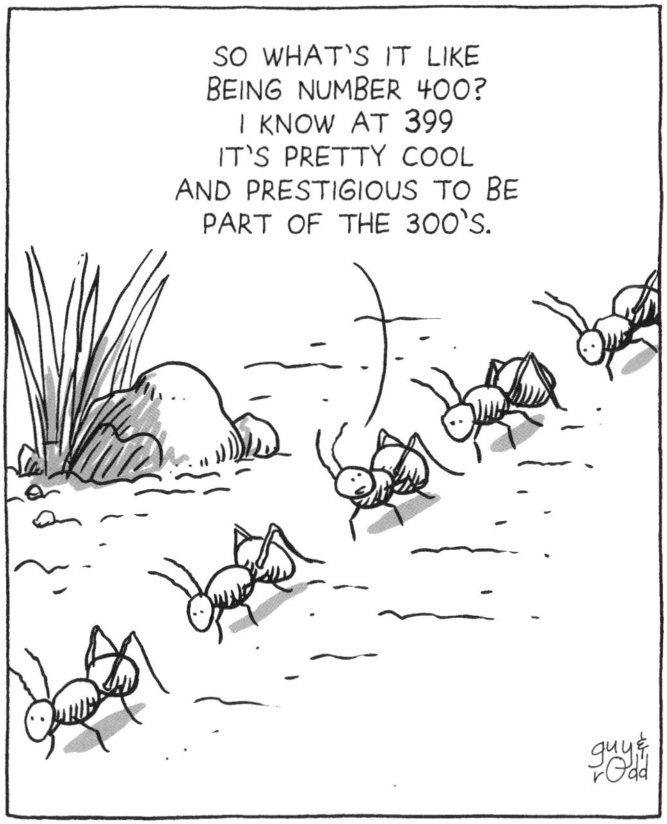
SO WHAT'S IT LIKE BEING NUMBER 400? I KNOW AT 399 IT'S PRETTY COOL AND PRESTIGIOUS TO BE PART OF THE 300'S.
guy & rodd

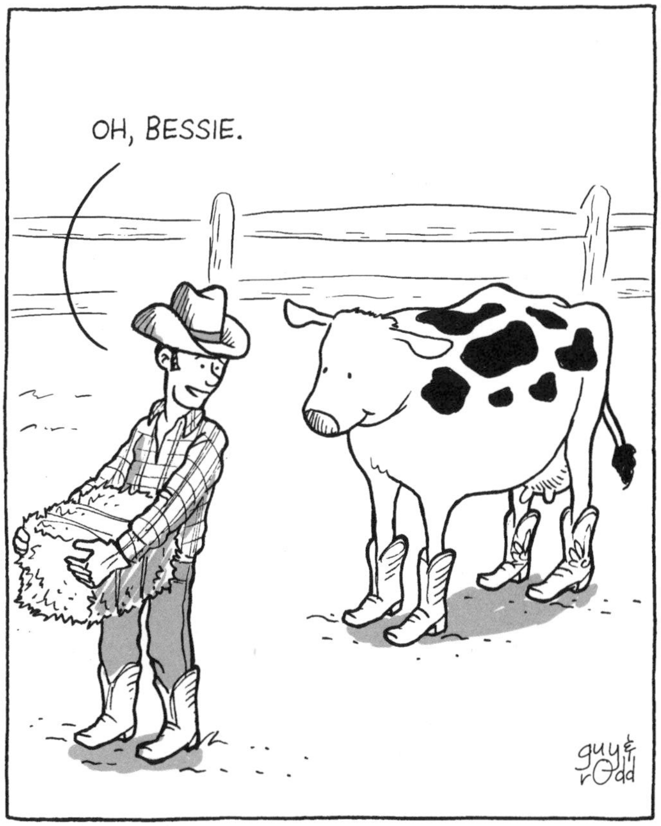
OH, BESSIE.
guy & rodd

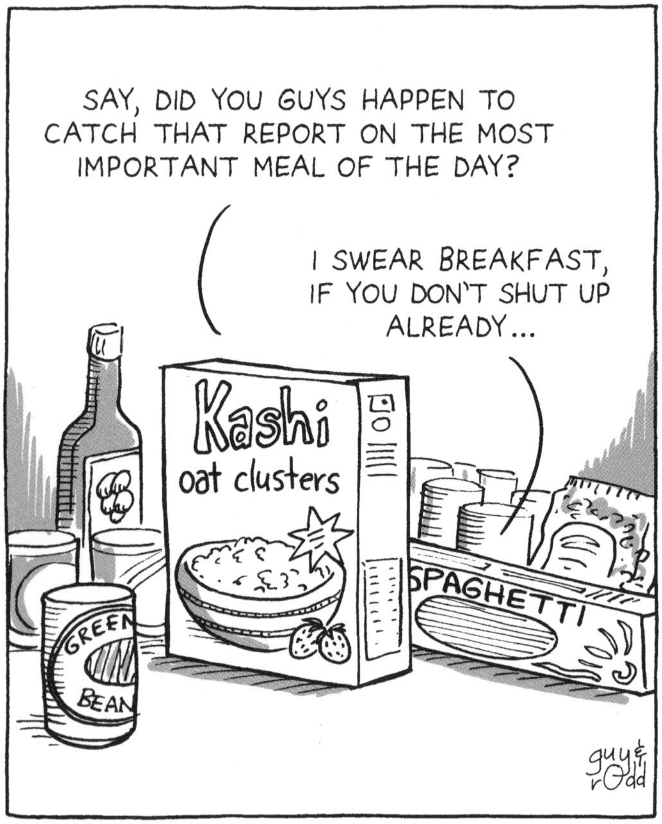
SAY, DID YOU GUYS HAPPEN TO CATCH THAT REPORT ON THE MOST IMPORTANT MEAL OF THE DAY?
I SWEAR BREAKFAST, IF YOU DON'T SHUT UP ALREADY...
Kashi
oat clusters
SPAGHETTI
GREEN
BEAN
guy & rOdd

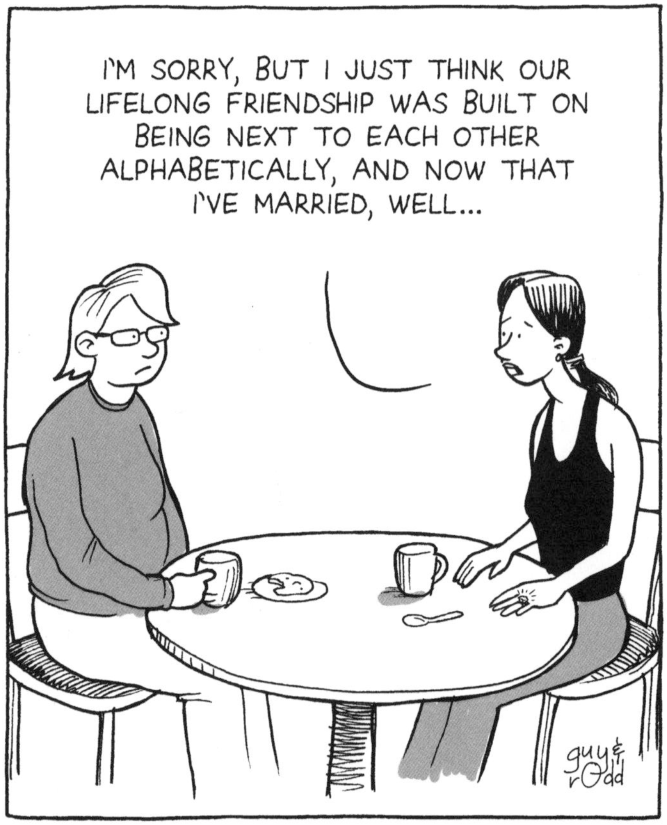
I'M SORRY, BUT I JUST THINK OUR LIFELONG FRIENDSHIP WAS BUILT ON BEING NEXT TO EACH OTHER ALPHABETICALLY, AND NOW THAT I'VE MARRIED, WELL...
guy & rOdd

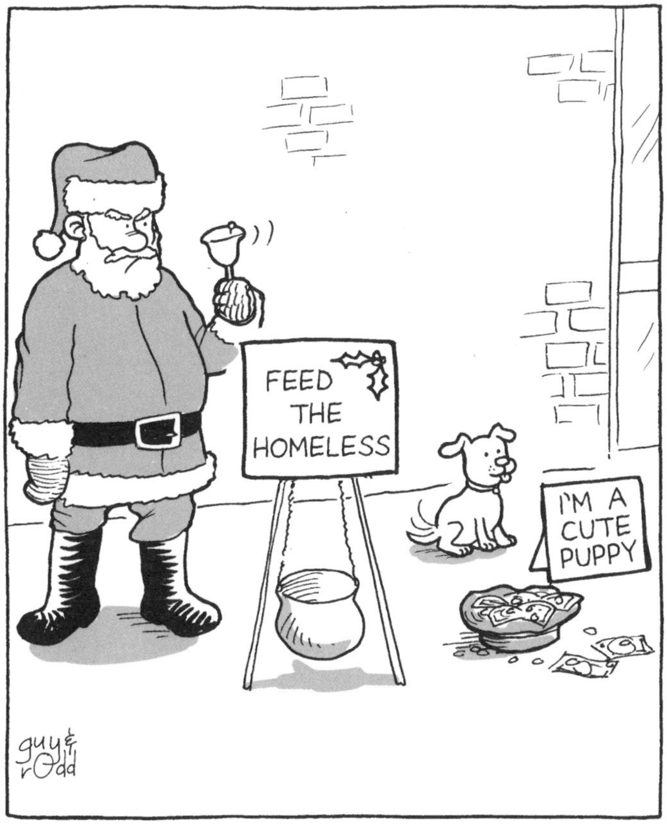
FEED THE HOMELESS
I'M A CUTE PUPPY
guy & rOdd

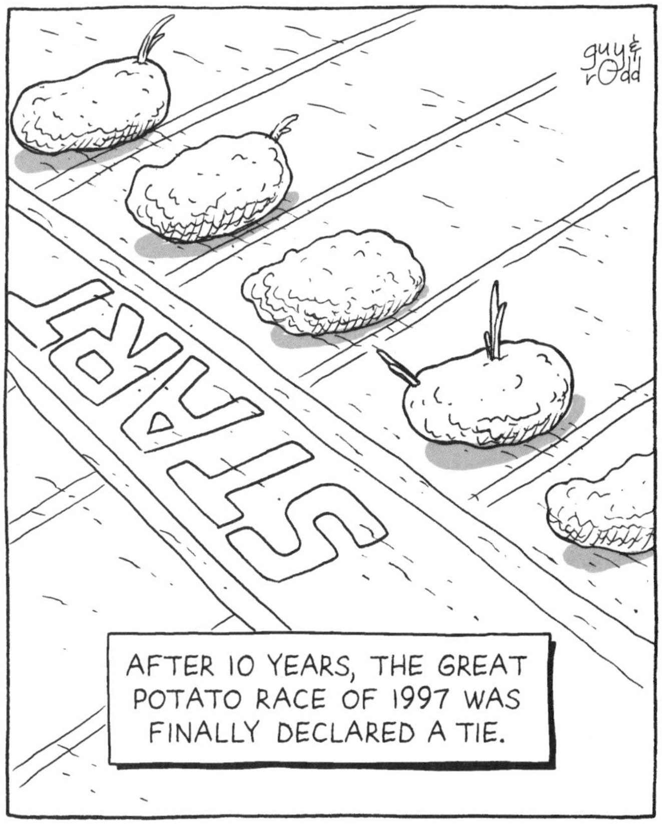
START
guy & rOdd

AFTER 10 YEARS, THE GREAT POTATO RACE OF 1997 WAS FINALLY DECLARED A TIE.

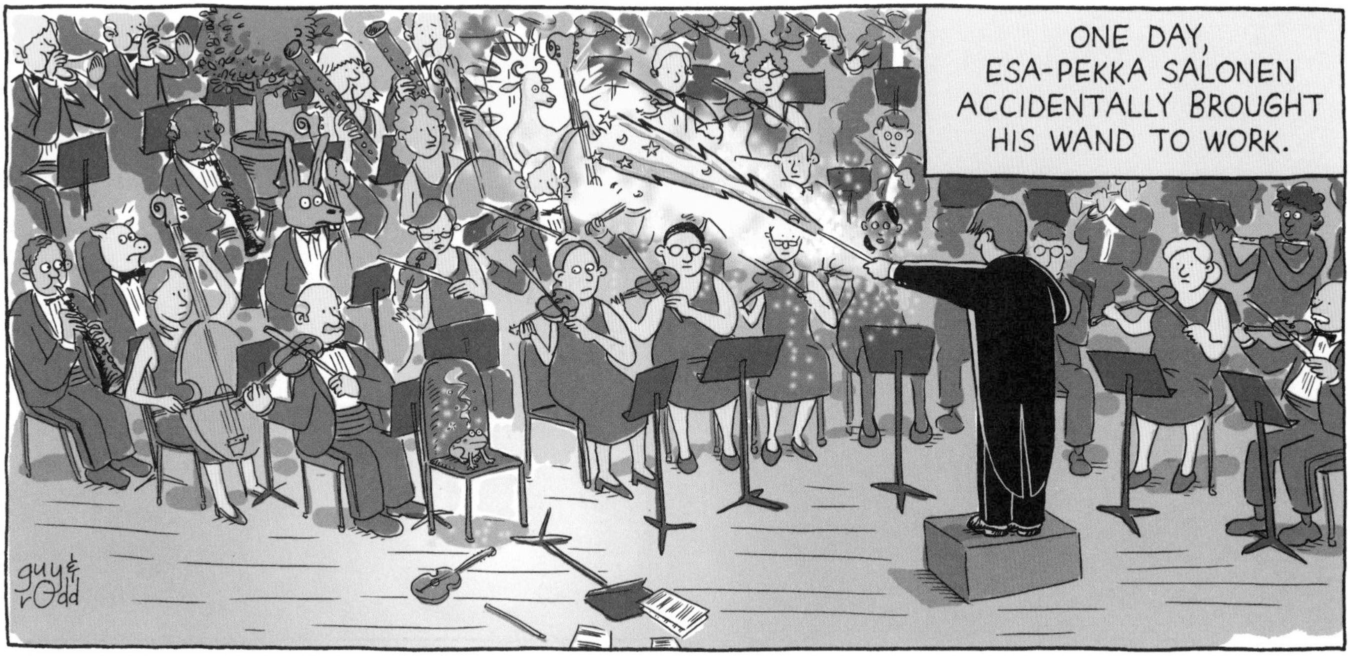
guy & rOdd

ONE DAY, ESA-PEKKA SALONEN ACCIDENTALLY BROUGHT HIS WAND TO WORK.

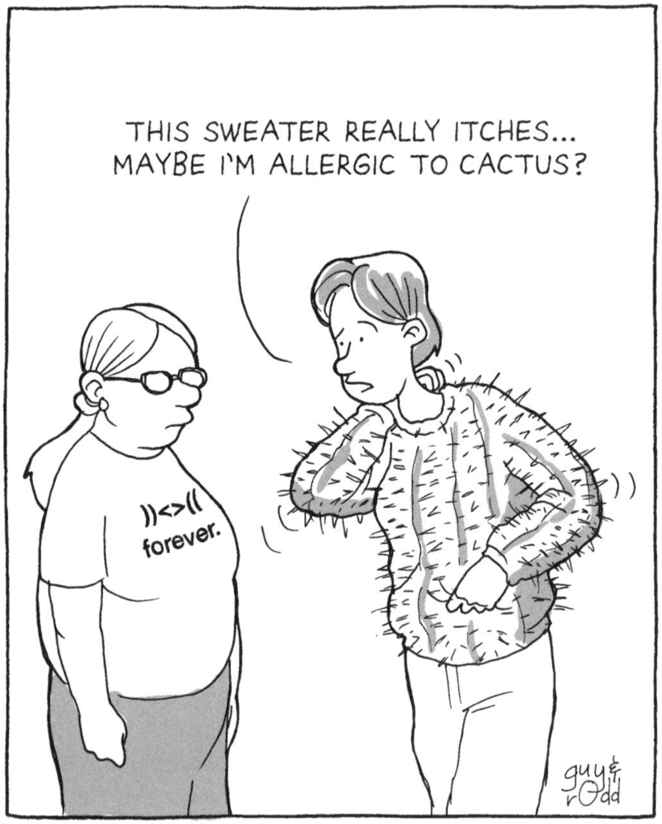
THIS SWEATER REALLY ITCHES...
MAYBE I'M ALLERGIC TO CACTUS?
))<>((
forever.
guy & rOdd

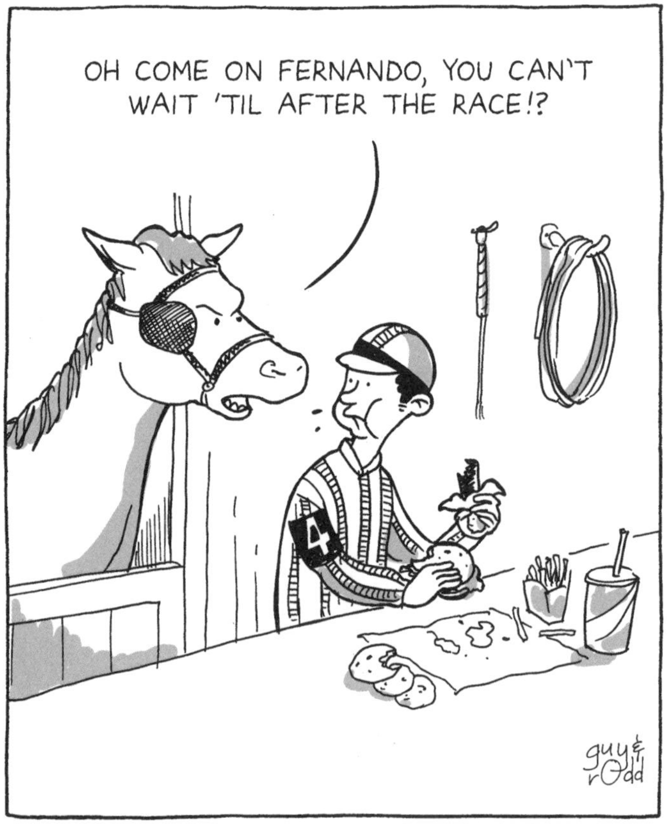
OH COME ON FERNANDO, YOU CAN'T
WAIT 'TIL AFTER THE RACE!?
4
guy & rOdd

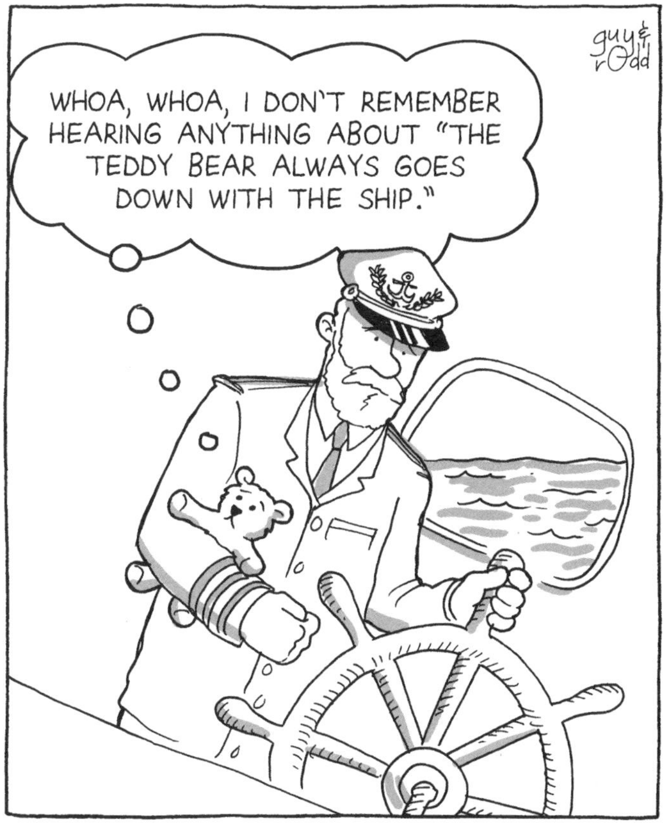
guy & rOdd
WHOA, WHOA, I DON'T REMEMBER HEARING ANYTHING ABOUT "THE TEDDY BEAR ALWAYS GOES DOWN WITH THE SHIP."

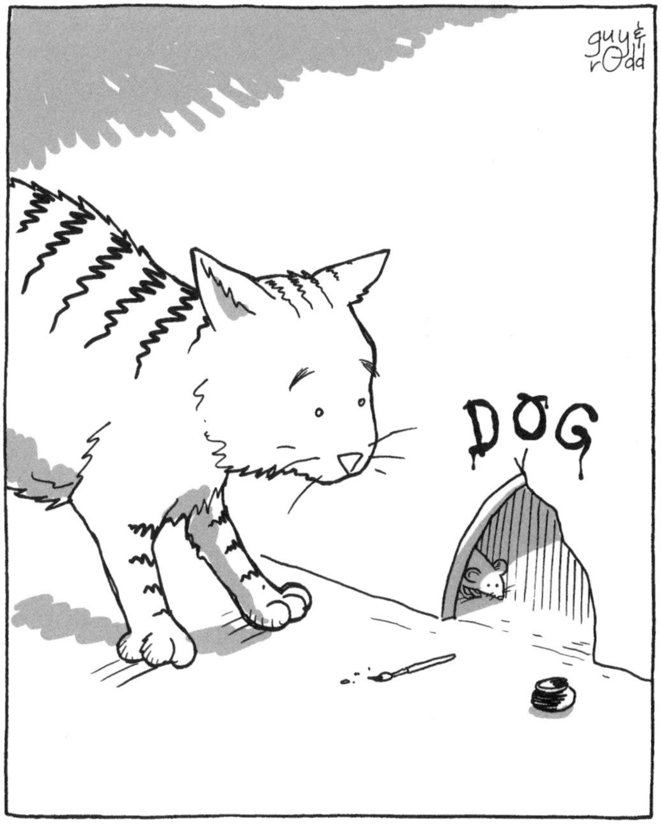
guy & rOdd
DOG

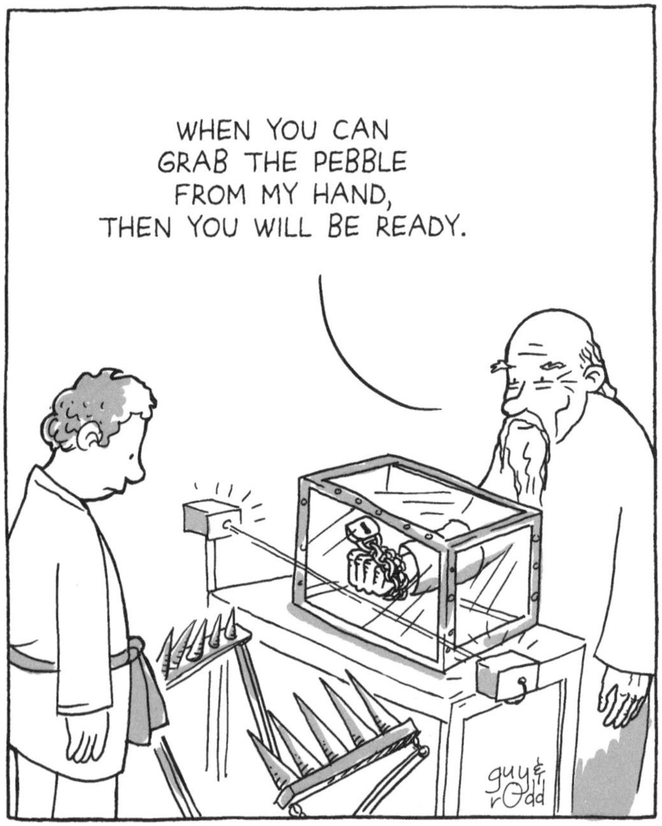
WHEN YOU CAN GRAB THE PEBBLE FROM MY HAND, THEN YOU WILL BE READY.
guy & rOdd

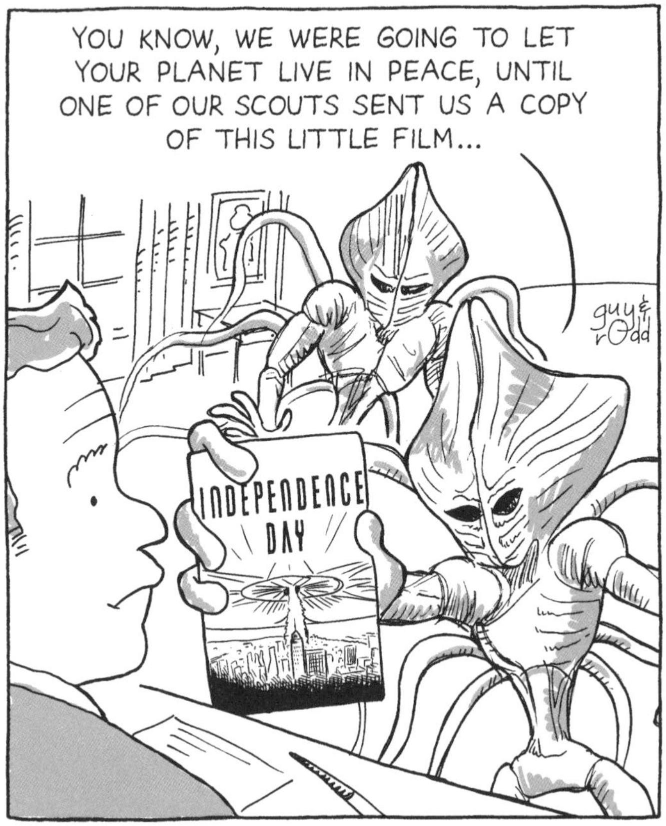
YOU KNOW, WE WERE GOING TO LET YOUR PLANET LIVE IN PEACE, UNTIL ONE OF OUR SCOUTS SENT US A COPY OF THIS LITTLE FILM...
INDEPENDENCE DAY
guy & rOdd

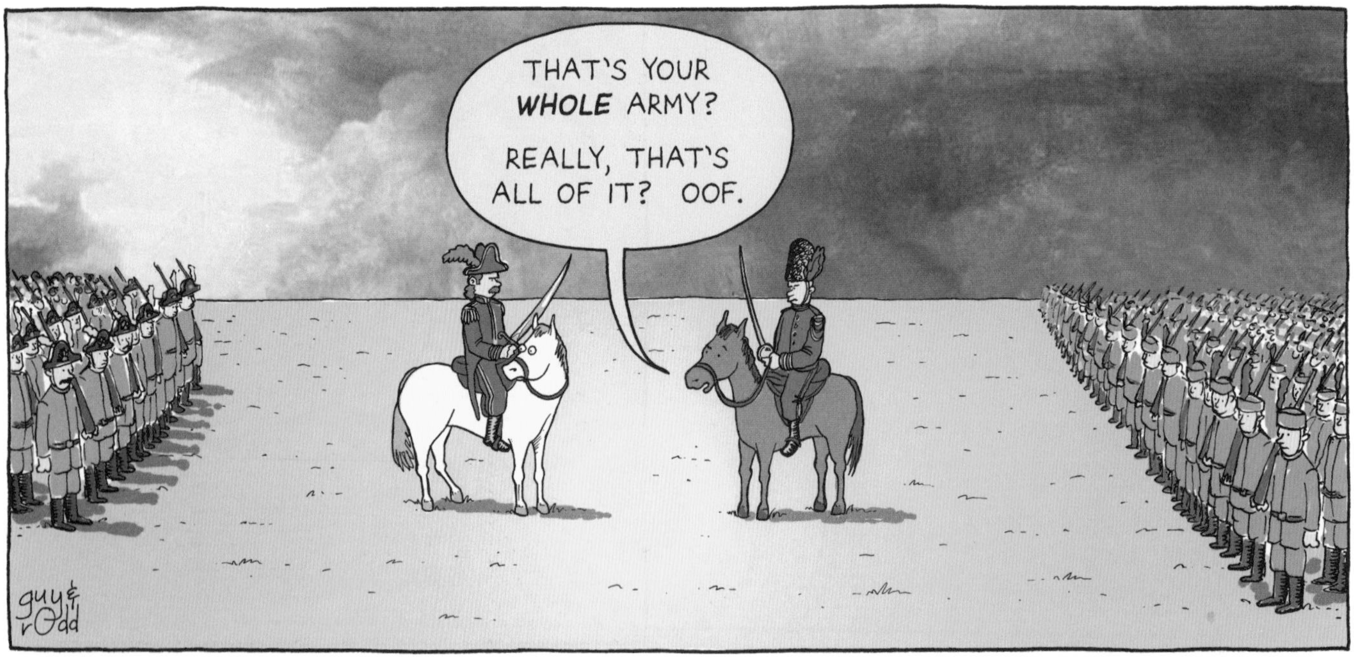
THAT'S YOUR *WHOLE* ARMY?
REALLY, THAT'S ALL OF IT? OOF.
guy & rOdd

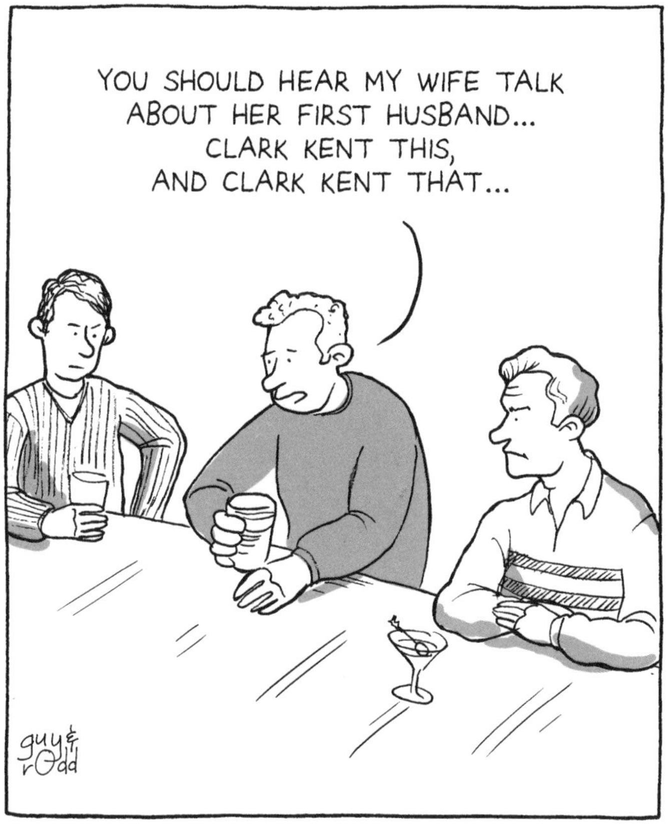
YOU SHOULD HEAR MY WIFE TALK ABOUT HER FIRST HUSBAND... CLARK KENT THIS, AND CLARK KENT THAT...
guy & rOdd

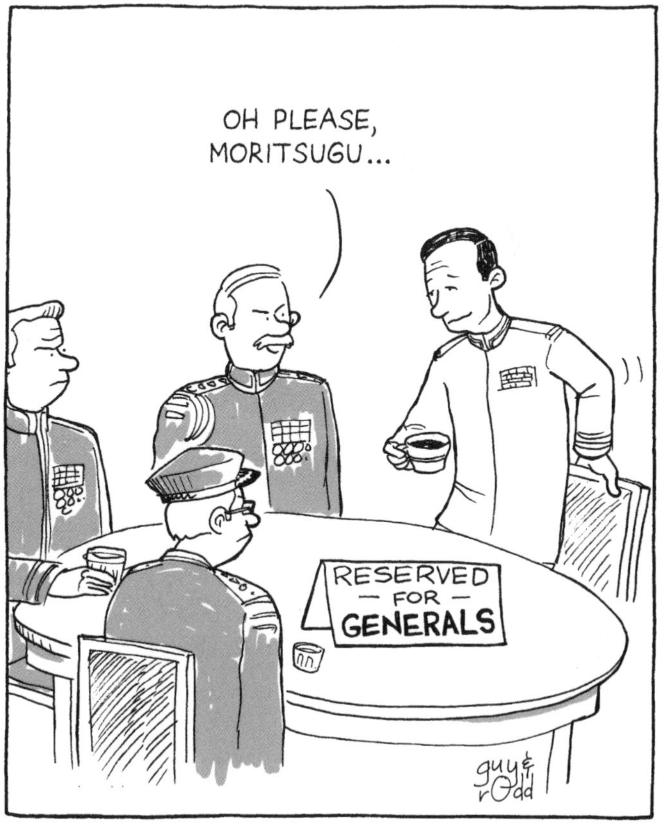
OH PLEASE, MORITSUGU...
RESERVED — FOR — GENERALS
guy & rOdd

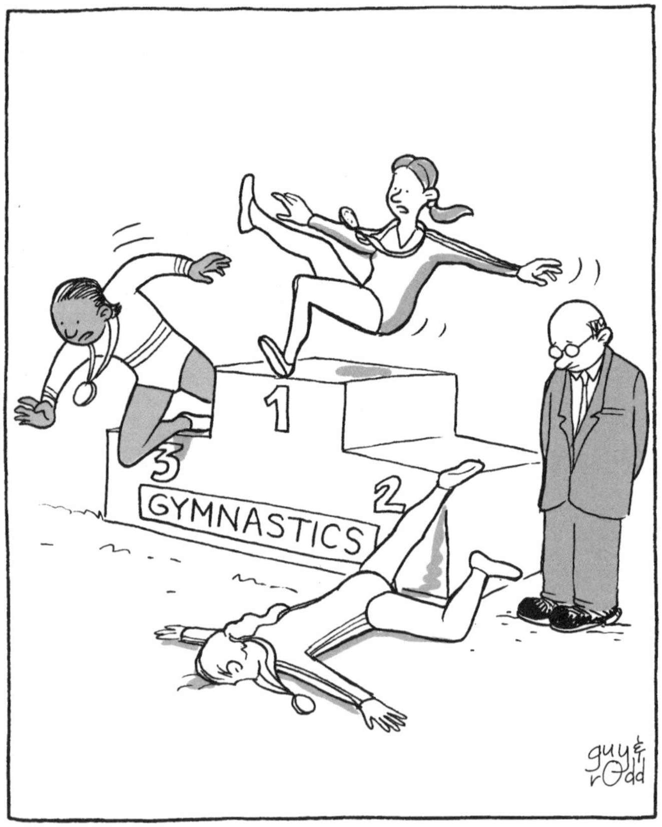
1
2
3
GYMNASTICS
guy & rodd

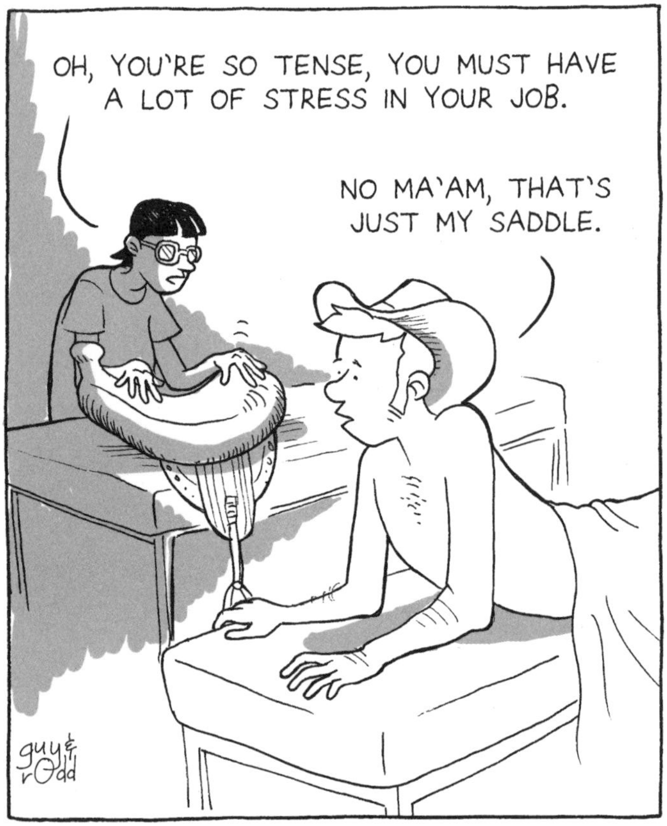
OH, YOU'RE SO TENSE, YOU MUST HAVE A LOT OF STRESS IN YOUR JOB.
NO MA'AM, THAT'S JUST MY SADDLE.
guy & rodd

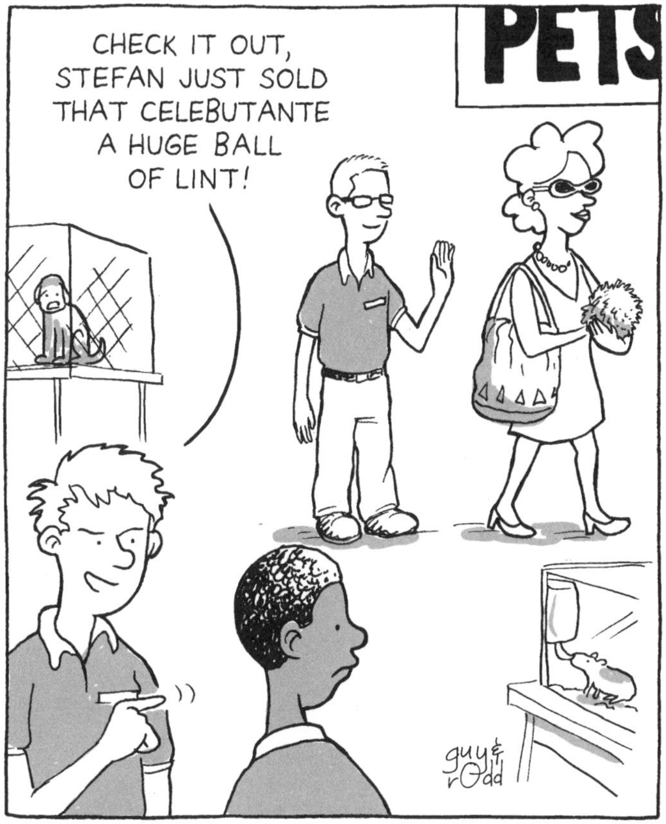
PETS
CHECK IT OUT, STEFAN JUST SOLD THAT CELEBUTANTE A HUGE BALL OF LINT!

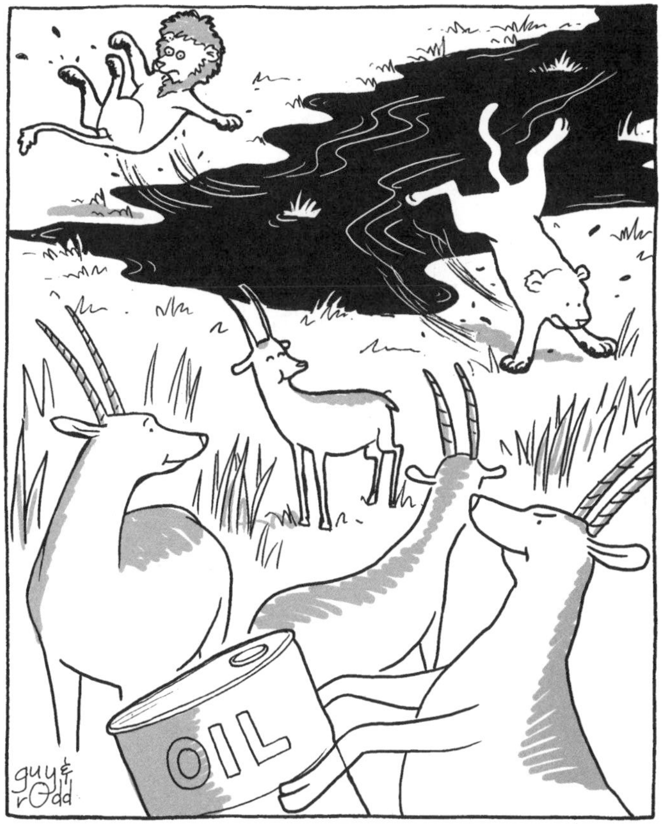
OIL

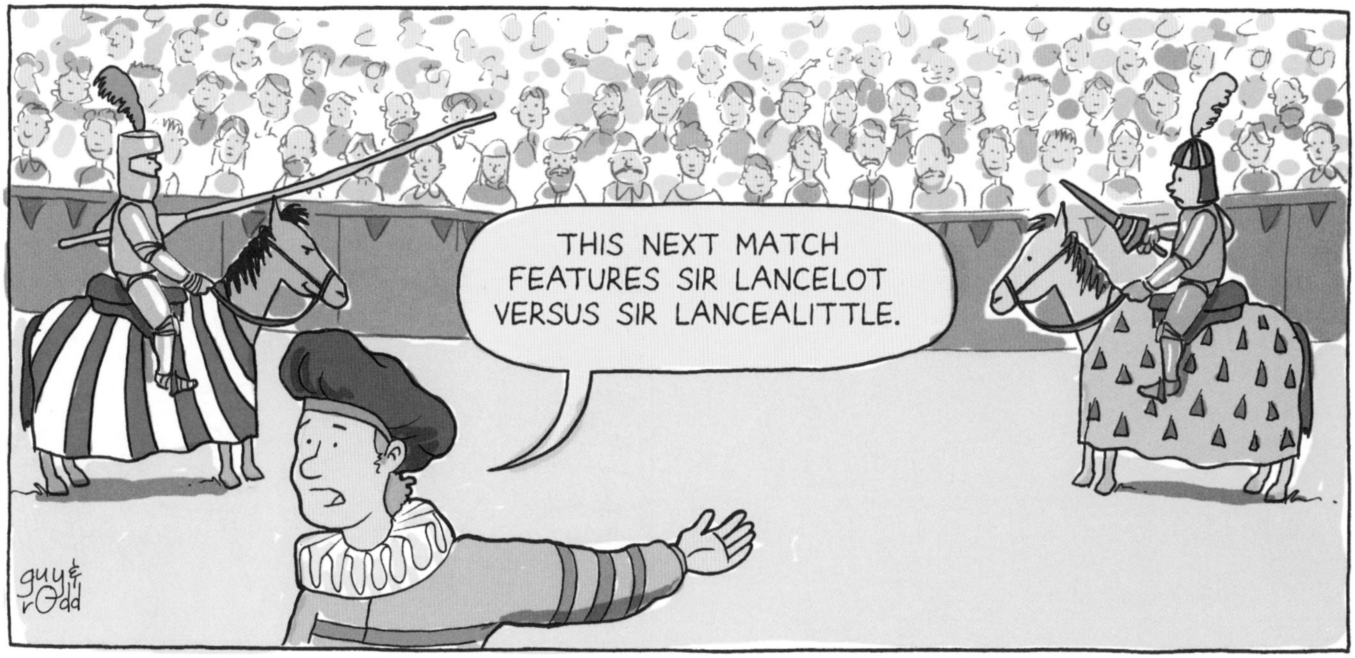
THIS NEXT MATCH FEATURES SIR LANCELOT VERSUS SIR LANCEALITTLE.

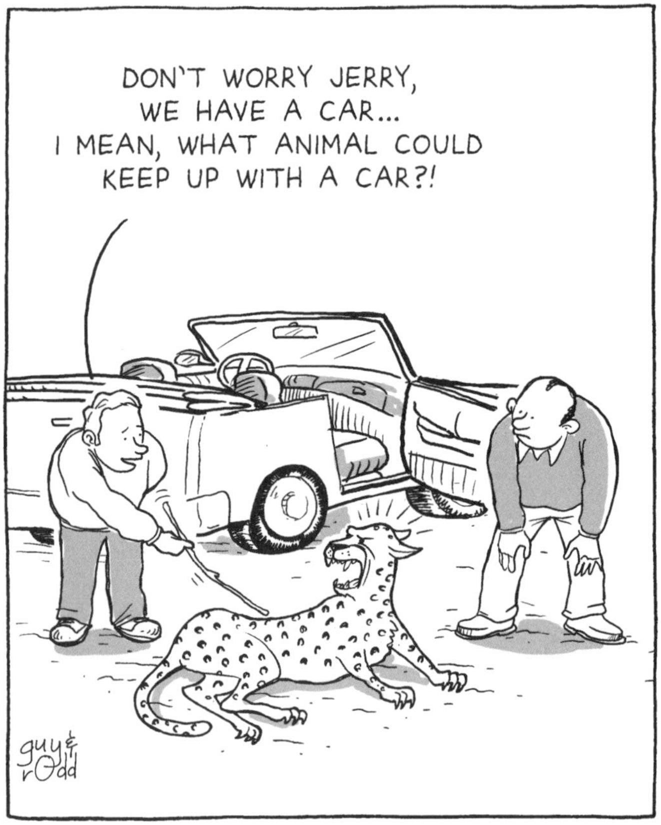
DON'T WORRY JERRY, WE HAVE A CAR... I MEAN, WHAT ANIMAL COULD KEEP UP WITH A CAR?!
guy & rodd

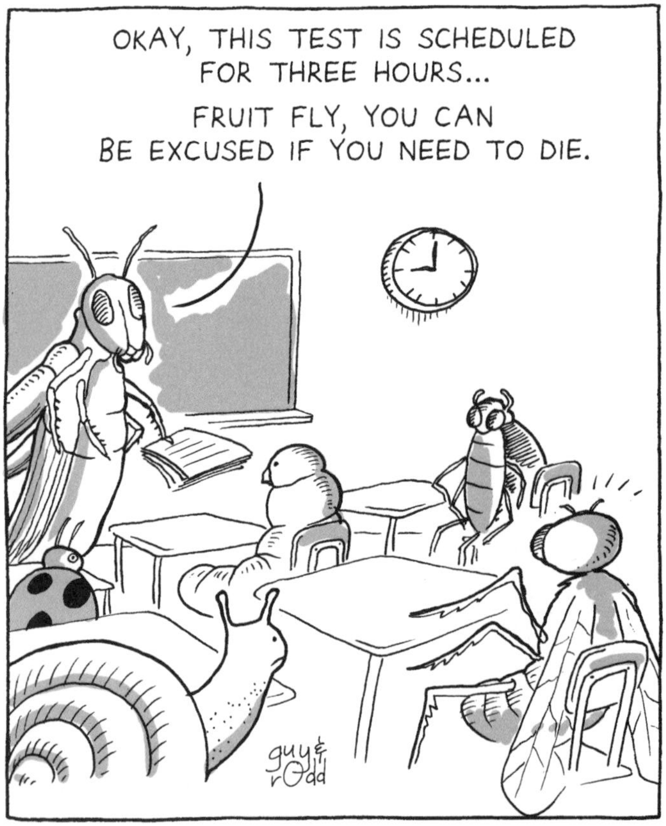
OKAY, THIS TEST IS SCHEDULED FOR THREE HOURS...
FRUIT FLY, YOU CAN BE EXCUSED IF YOU NEED TO DIE.
guy & rodd

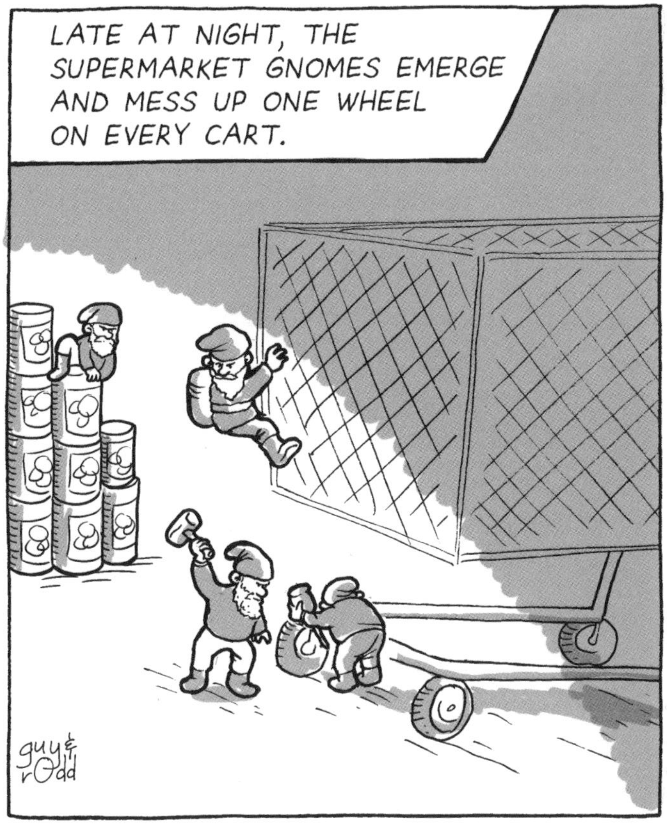
LATE AT NIGHT, THE SUPERMARKET GNOMES EMERGE AND MESS UP ONE WHEEL ON EVERY CART.
guy & rOdd

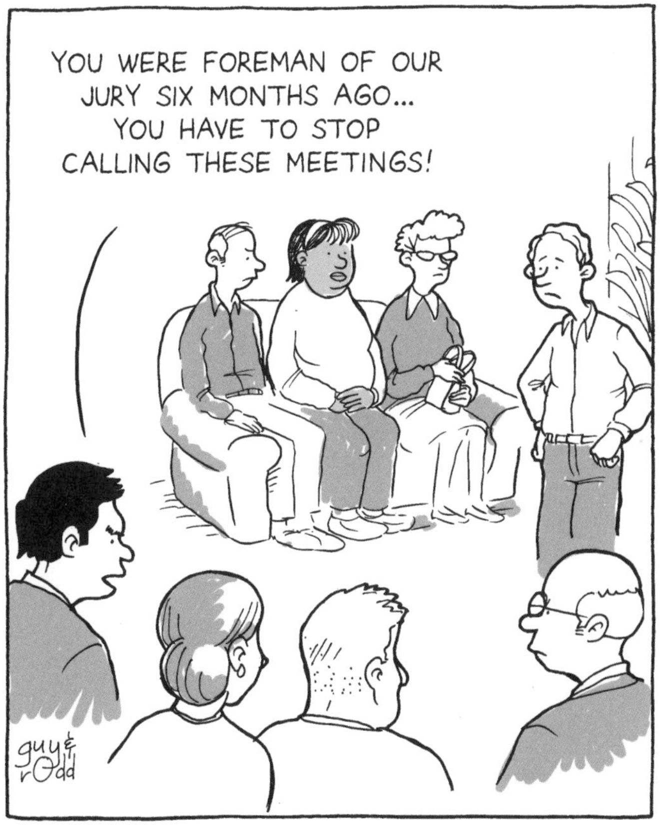
YOU WERE FOREMAN OF OUR JURY SIX MONTHS AGO... YOU HAVE TO STOP CALLING THESE MEETINGS!
guy & rOdd

MAN, WE'RE NEVER GONNA GET ANY LADIES WITH THAT GUY AROUND.

YOU KNOW IT'S TRUE WHAT THEY SAY, LARRY: "HELL HATH NO FURY LIKE A POTATO SCORNED."

PHONE

PHONE

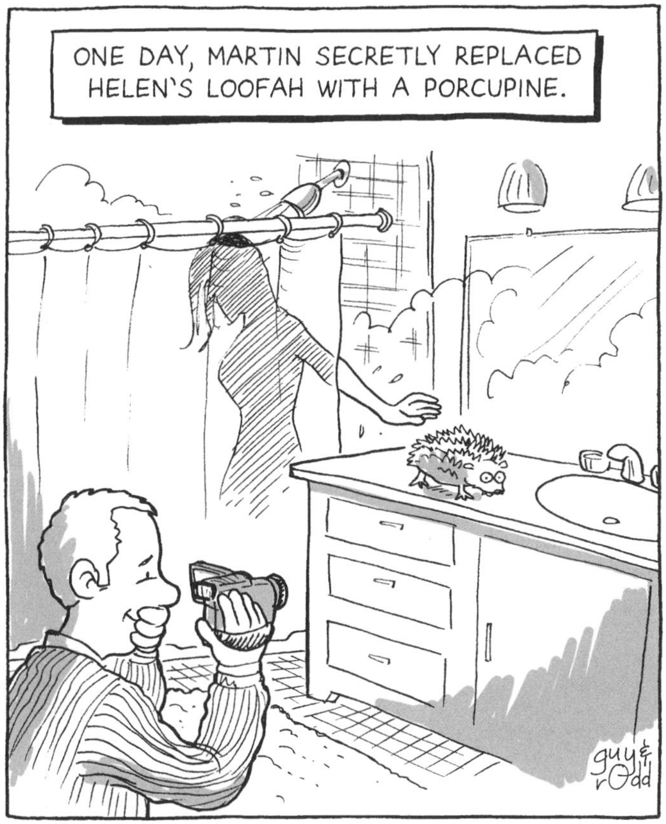
ONE DAY, MARTIN SECRETLY REPLACED HELEN'S LOOFAH WITH A PORCUPINE.
guy & rOdd

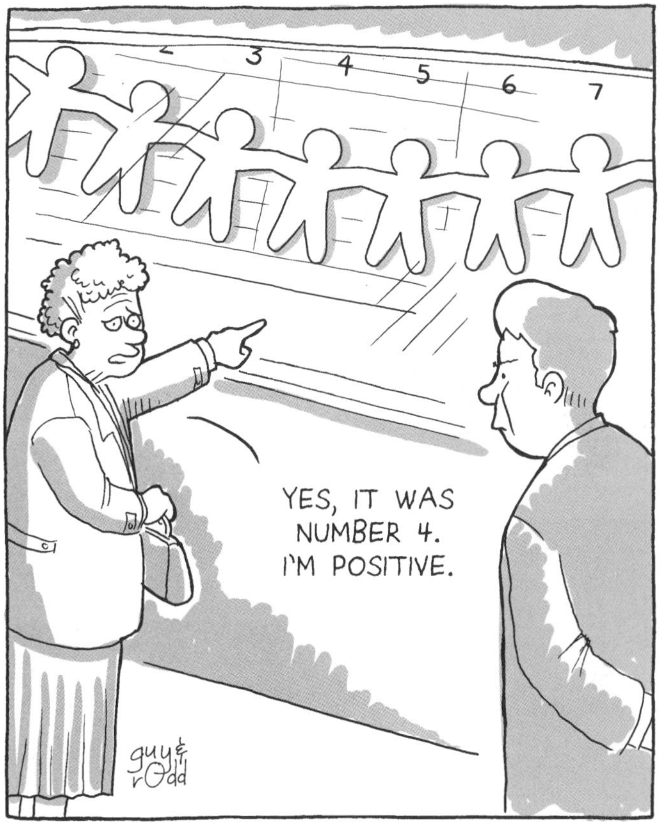
2
3
4
5
6
7
YES, IT WAS NUMBER 4. I'M POSITIVE.
guy & rOdd

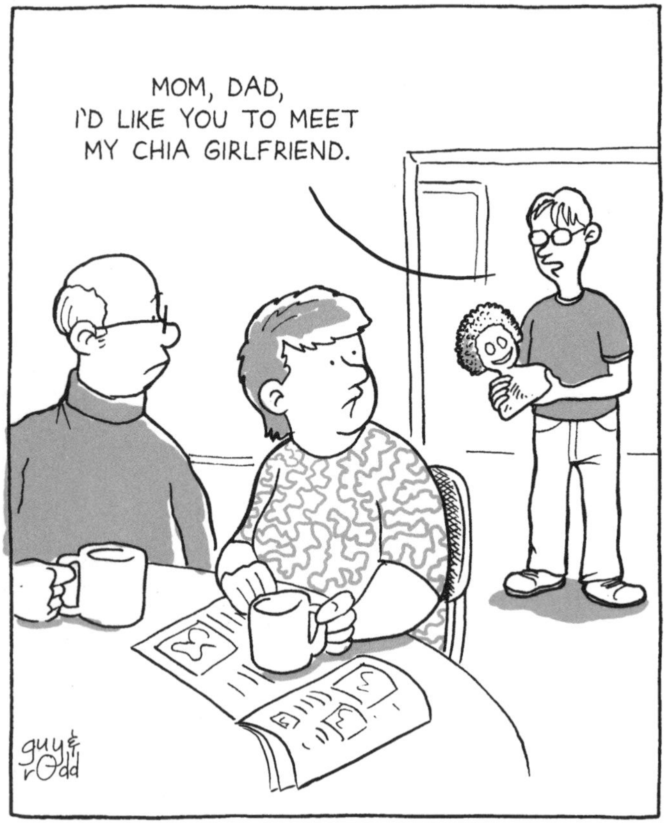
MOM, DAD,
I'D LIKE YOU TO MEET
MY CHIA GIRLFRIEND.
guy & rodd

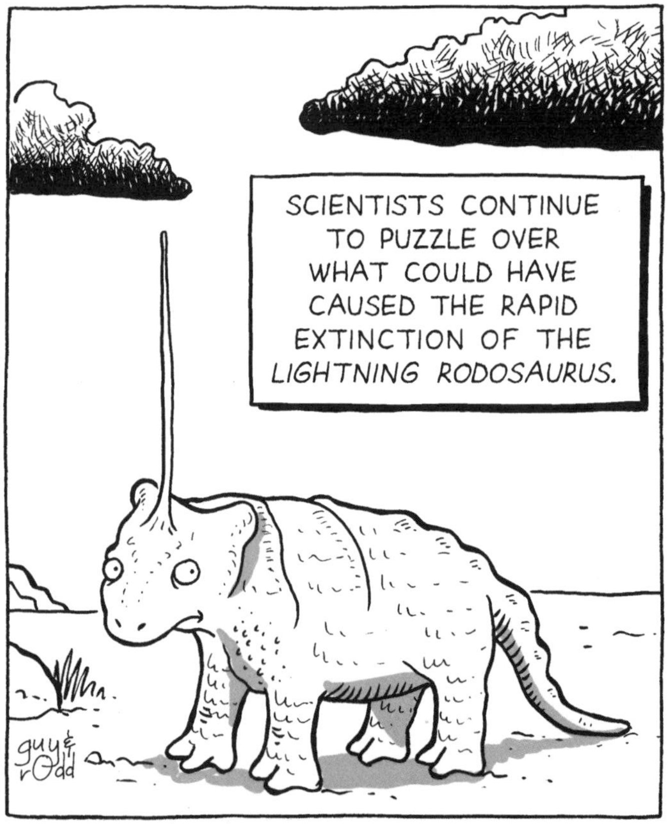
SCIENTISTS CONTINUE
TO PUZZLE OVER
WHAT COULD HAVE
CAUSED THE RAPID
EXTINCTION OF THE
LIGHTNING RODOSAURUS.
guy & rodd

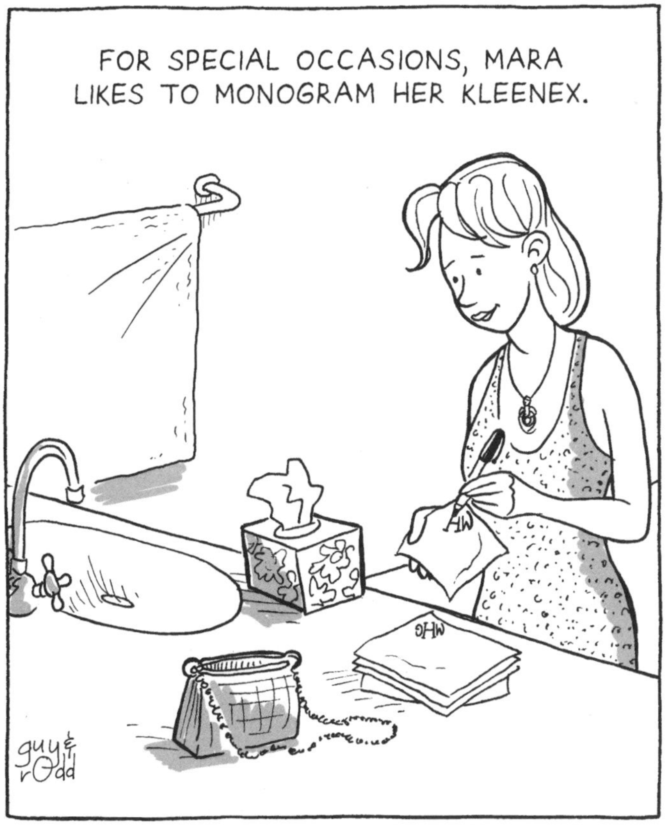
FOR SPECIAL OCCASIONS, MARA LIKES TO MONOGRAM HER KLEENEX.
MHG
guy & rodd

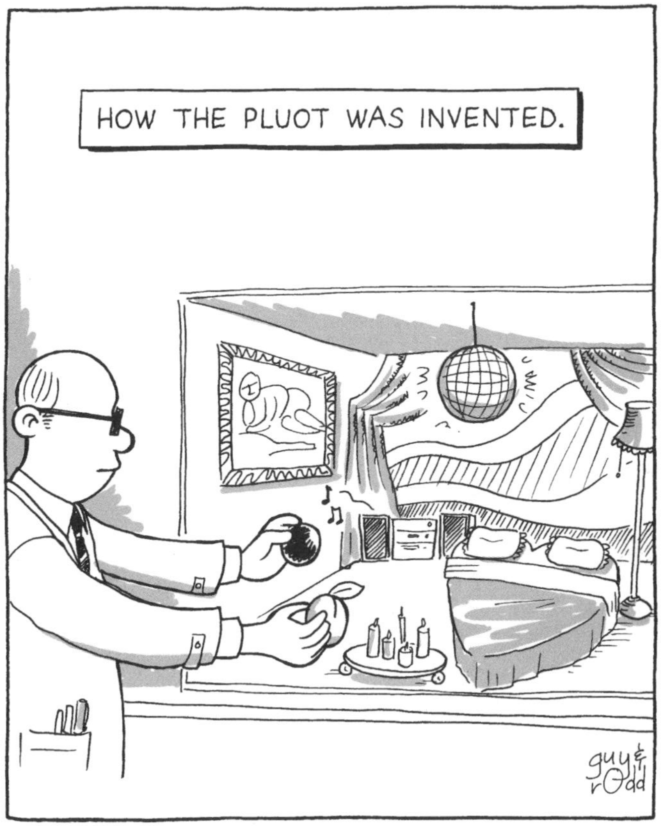
HOW THE PLUOT WAS INVENTED.
guy & rodd

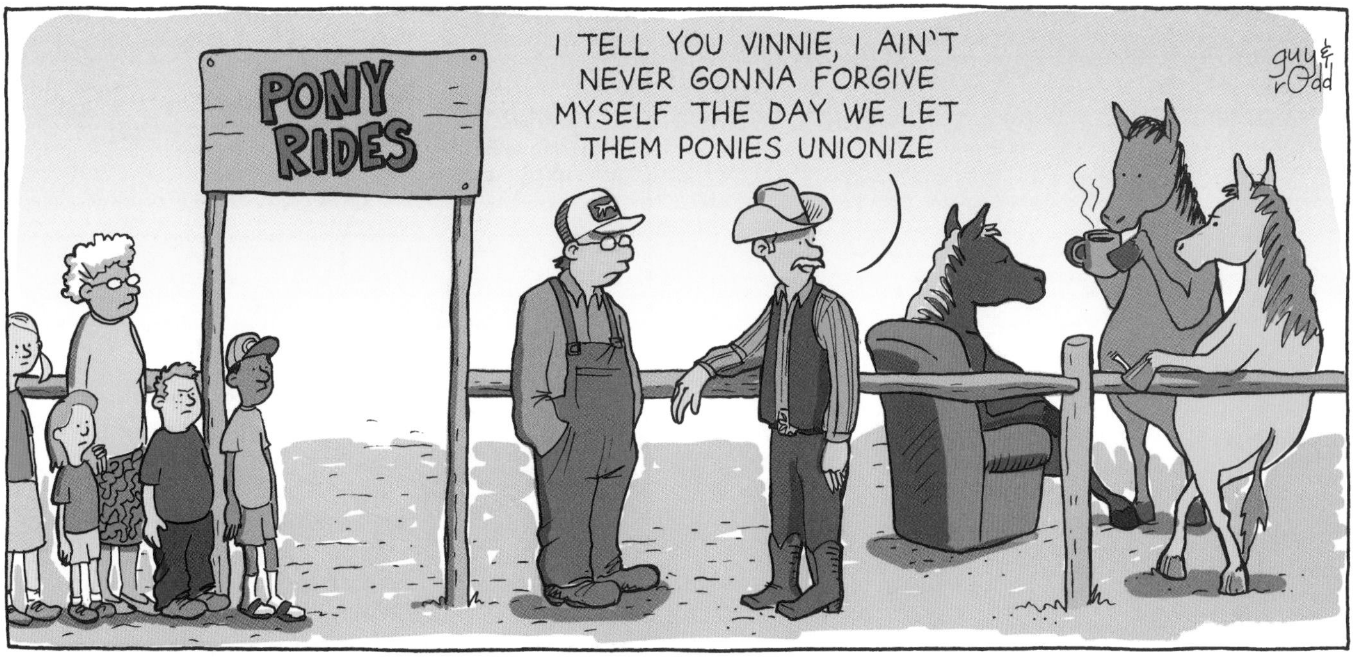
PONY RIDES
I TELL YOU VINNIE, I AIN'T NEVER GONNA FORGIVE MYSELF THE DAY WE LET THEM PONIES UNIONIZE
guy & rodd

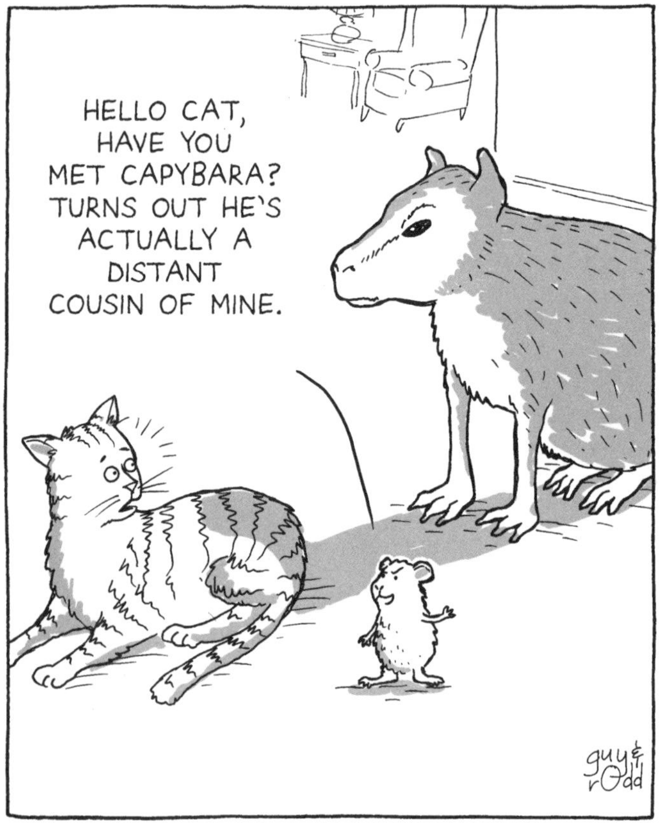
HELLO CAT, HAVE YOU MET CAPYBARA? TURNS OUT HE'S ACTUALLY A DISTANT COUSIN OF MINE.
guy & rOdd

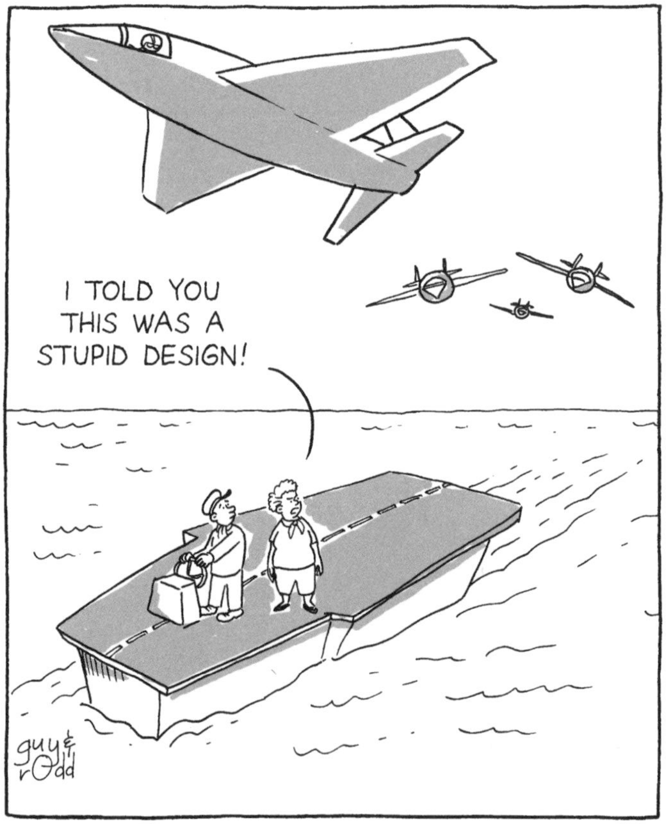
I TOLD YOU THIS WAS A STUPID DESIGN!
guy & rOdd

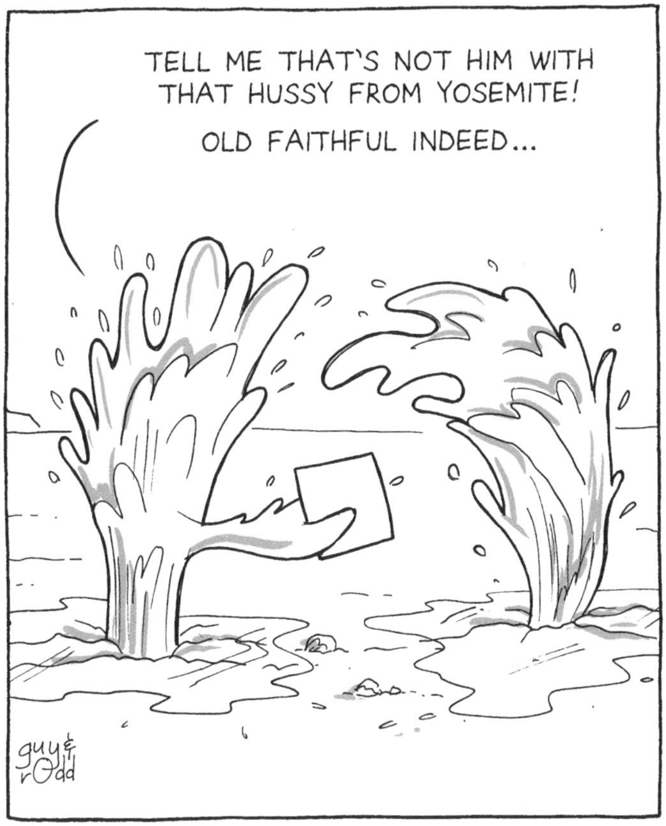
TELL ME THAT'S NOT HIM WITH THAT HUSSY FROM YOSEMITE!
OLD FAITHFUL INDEED...

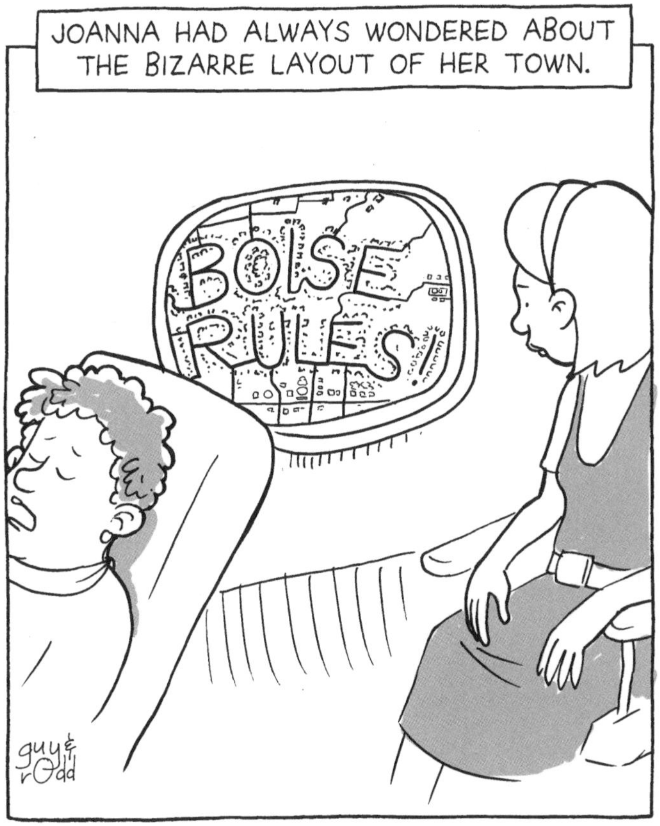
JOANNA HAD ALWAYS WONDERED ABOUT THE BIZARRE LAYOUT OF HER TOWN.
BOISE RULES!

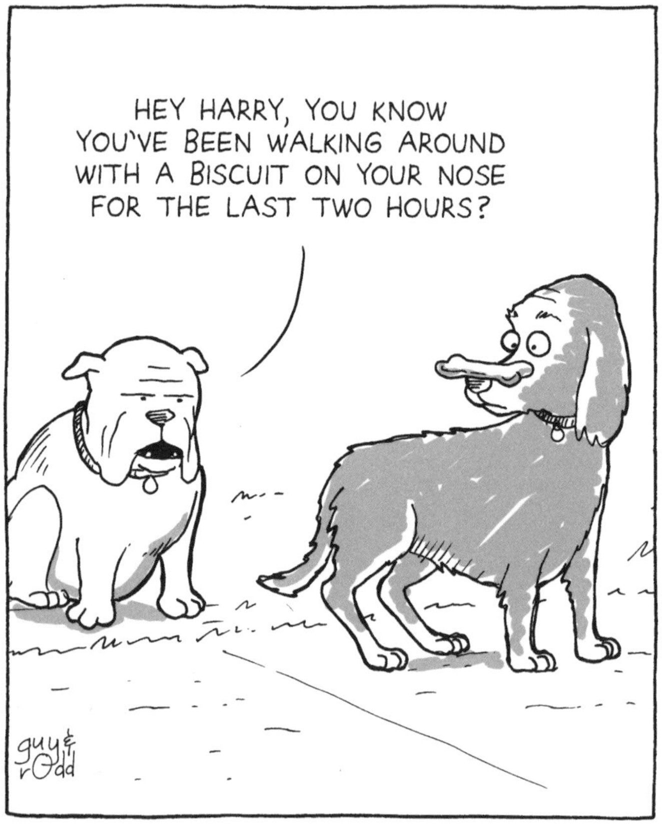
HEY HARRY, YOU KNOW YOU'VE BEEN WALKING AROUND WITH A BISCUIT ON YOUR NOSE FOR THE LAST TWO HOURS?
guy & rOdd

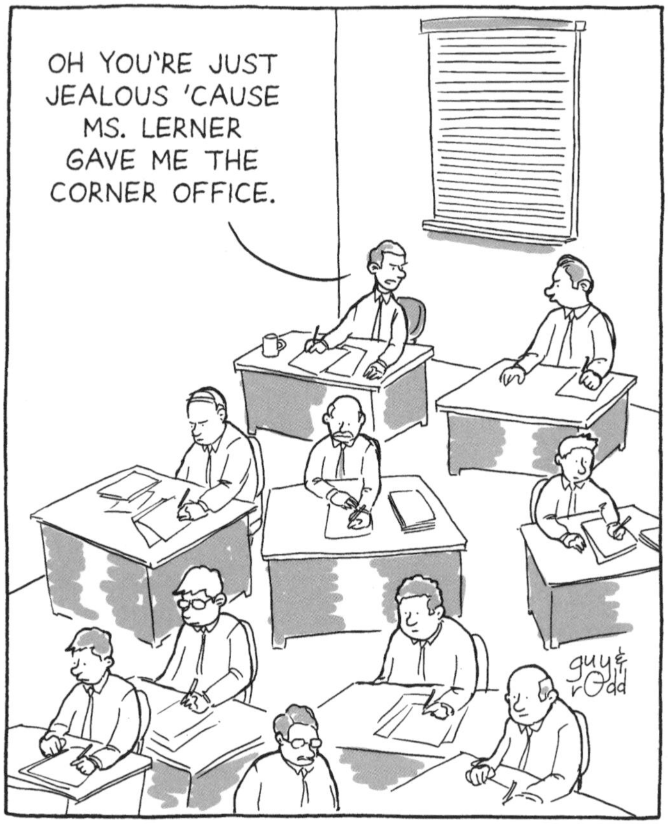
OH YOU'RE JUST JEALOUS 'CAUSE MS. LERNER GAVE ME THE CORNER OFFICE.
guy & rOdd

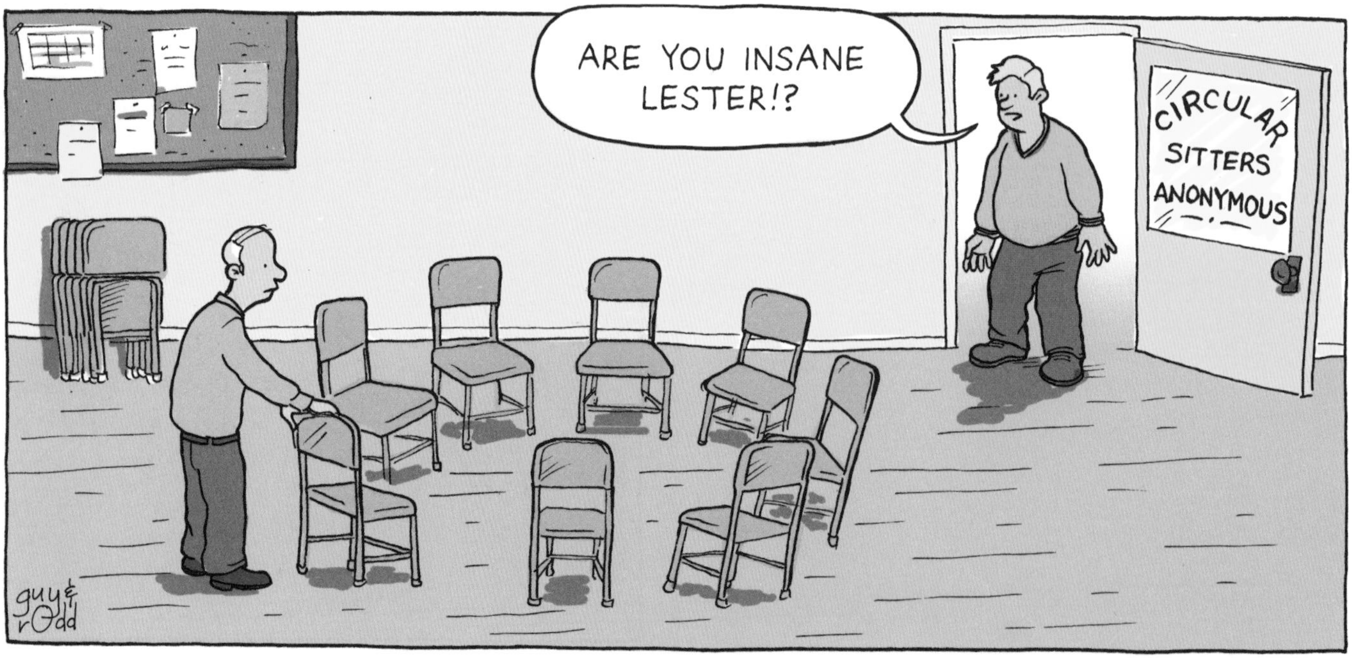
ARE YOU INSANE LESTER!?
CIRCULAR SITTERS ANONYMOUS
guy & rOdd

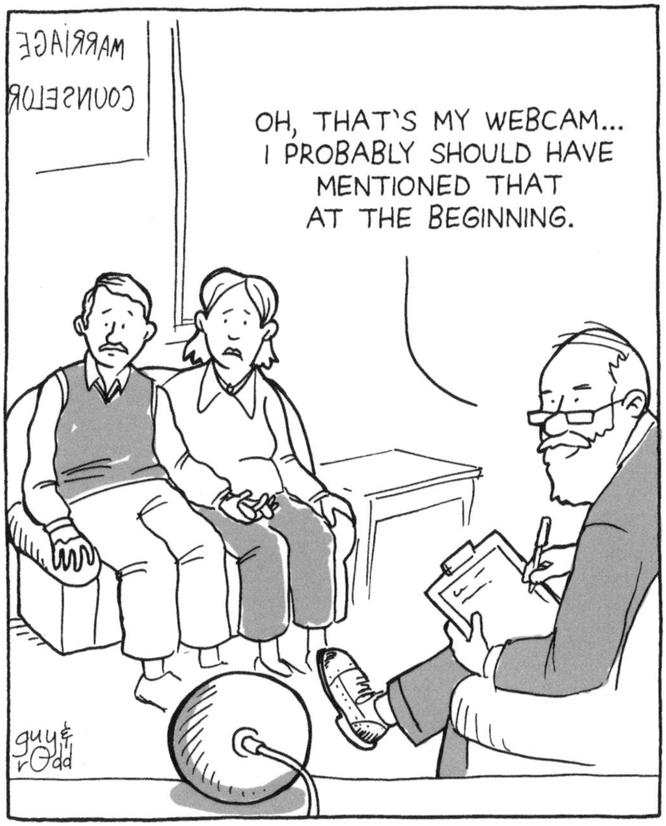
MARRIAGE COUNSELOR
OH, THAT'S MY WEBCAM... I PROBABLY SHOULD HAVE MENTIONED THAT AT THE BEGINNING.
guy & rOdd

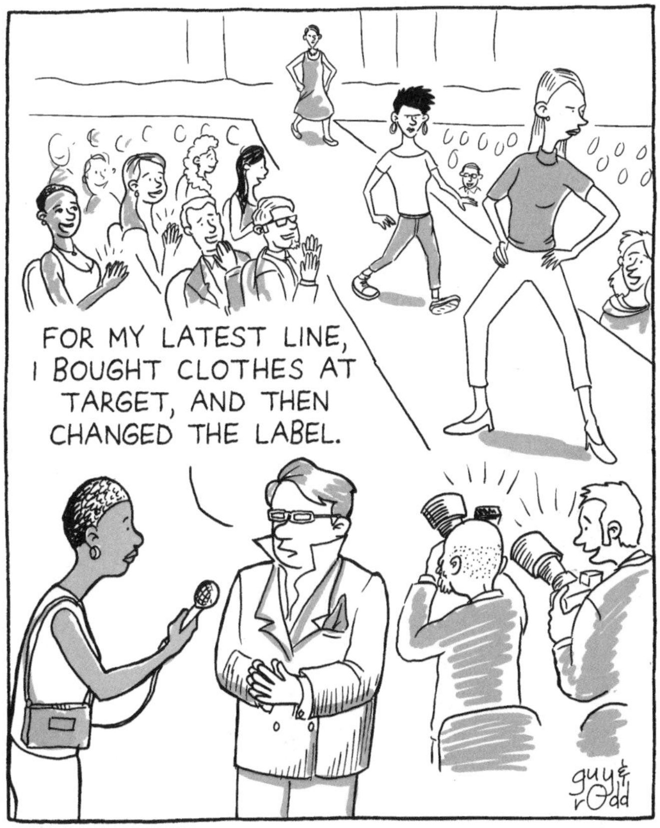
FOR MY LATEST LINE, I BOUGHT CLOTHES AT TARGET, AND THEN CHANGED THE LABEL.
guy & rOdd

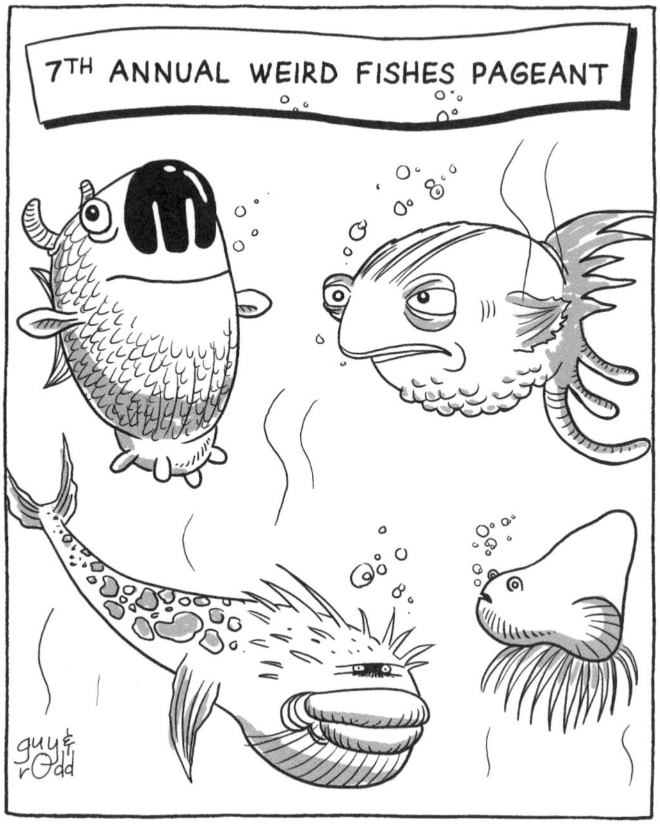
7TH ANNUAL WEIRD FISHES PAGEANT
guy & rOdd

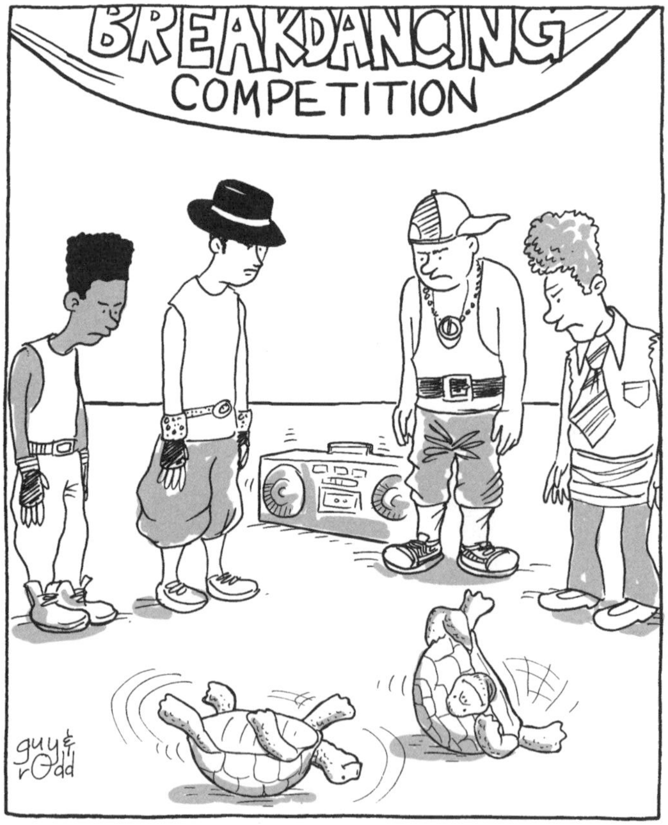
BREAKDANCING
COMPETITION
guy & rOdd

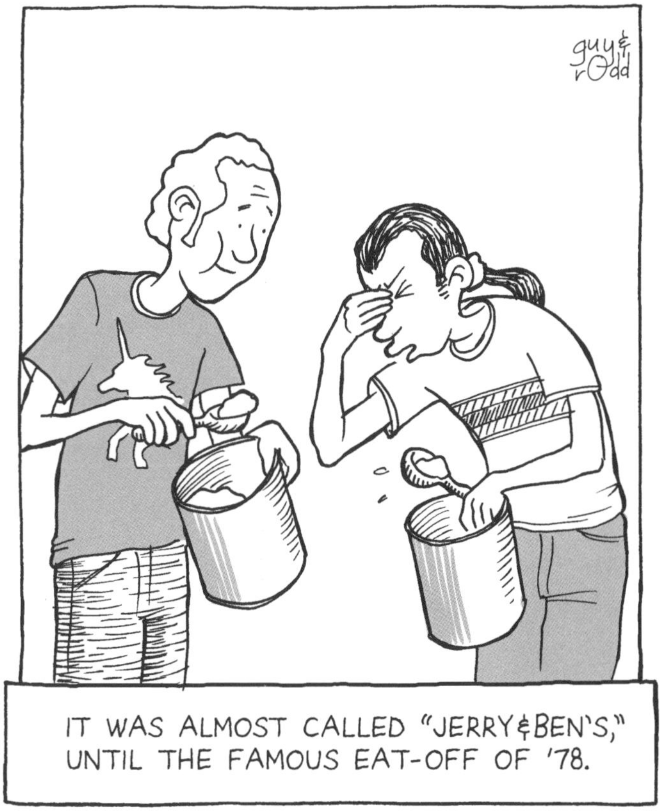
guy & rOdd
IT WAS ALMOST CALLED "JERRY & BEN'S,"
UNTIL THE FAMOUS EAT-OFF OF '78.

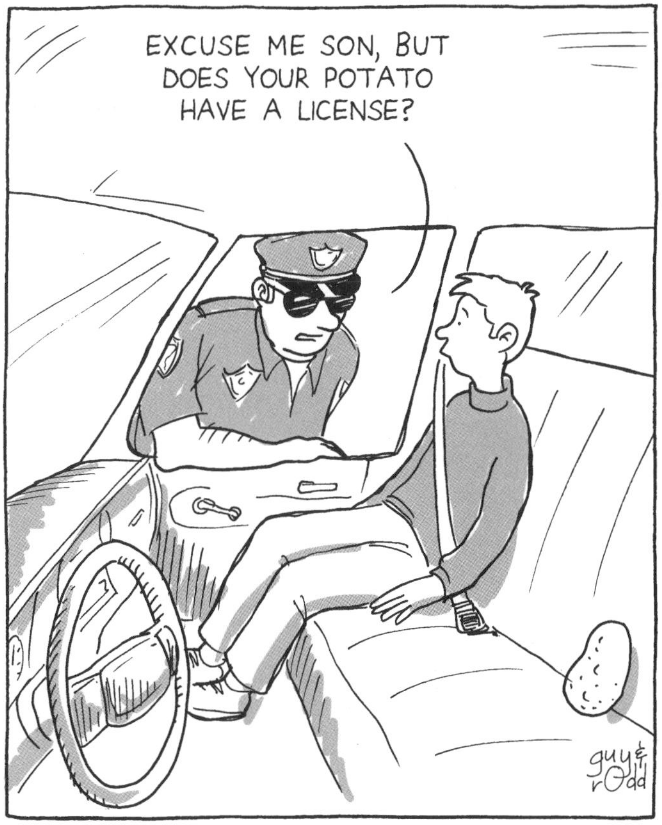
EXCUSE ME SON, BUT DOES YOUR POTATO HAVE A LICENSE?
guy & rOdd

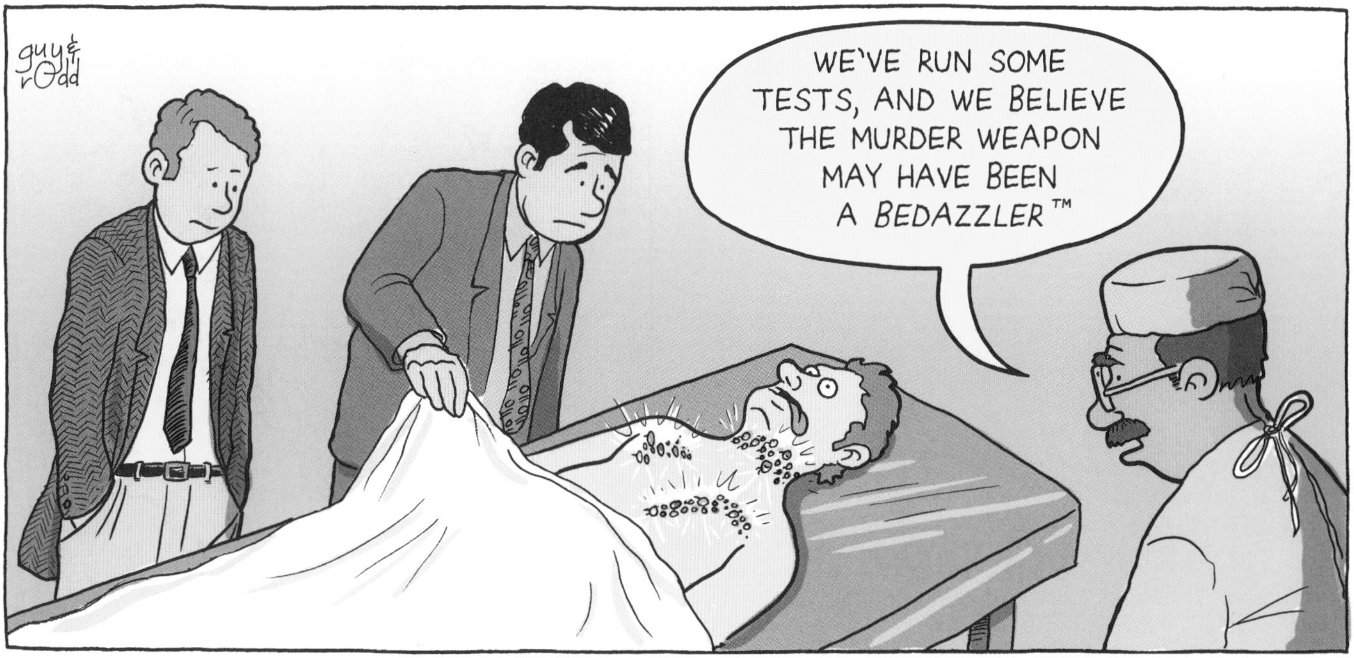
guy & rOdd
WE'VE RUN SOME TESTS, AND WE BELIEVE THE MURDER WEAPON MAY HAVE BEEN A *BEDAZZLER*™

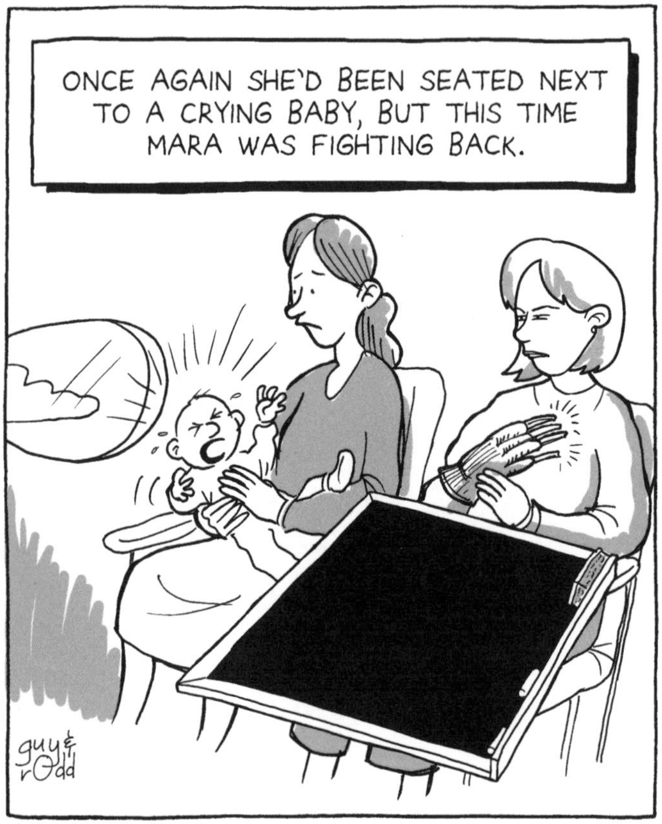
ONCE AGAIN SHE'D BEEN SEATED NEXT TO A CRYING BABY, BUT THIS TIME MARA WAS FIGHTING BACK.
guy & rOdd

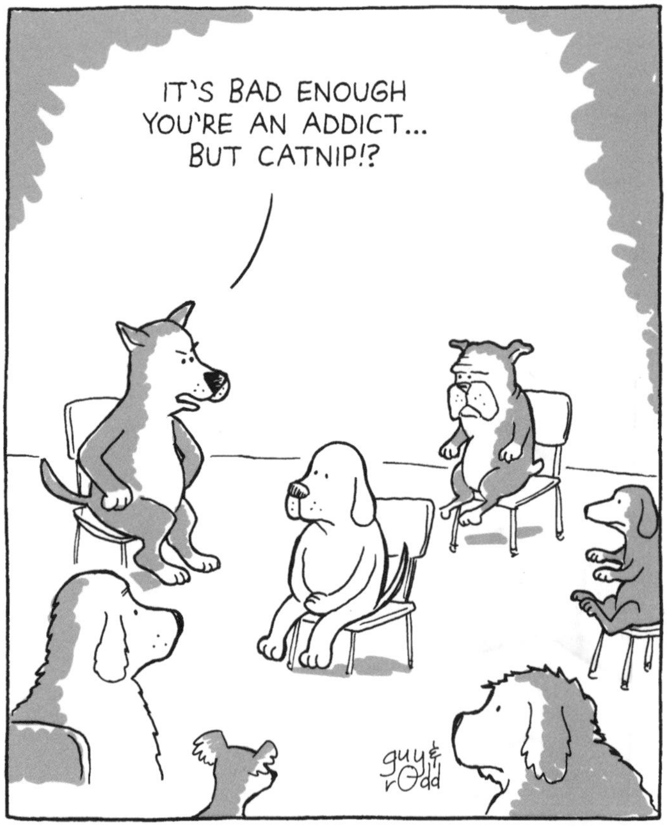
IT'S BAD ENOUGH YOU'RE AN ADDICT... BUT CATNIP!?
guy & rOdd

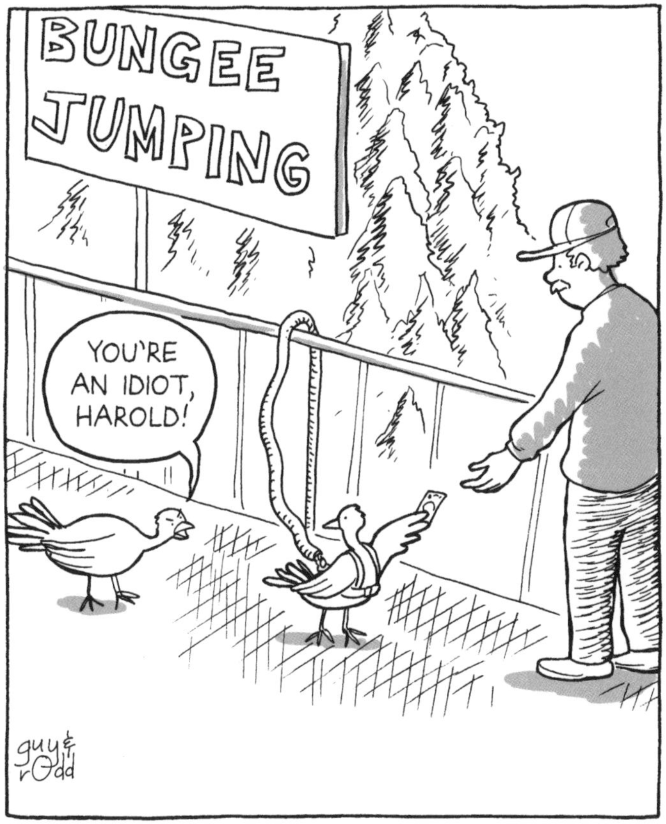
BUNGEE JUMPING
YOU'RE AN IDIOT, HAROLD!
guy & rOdd

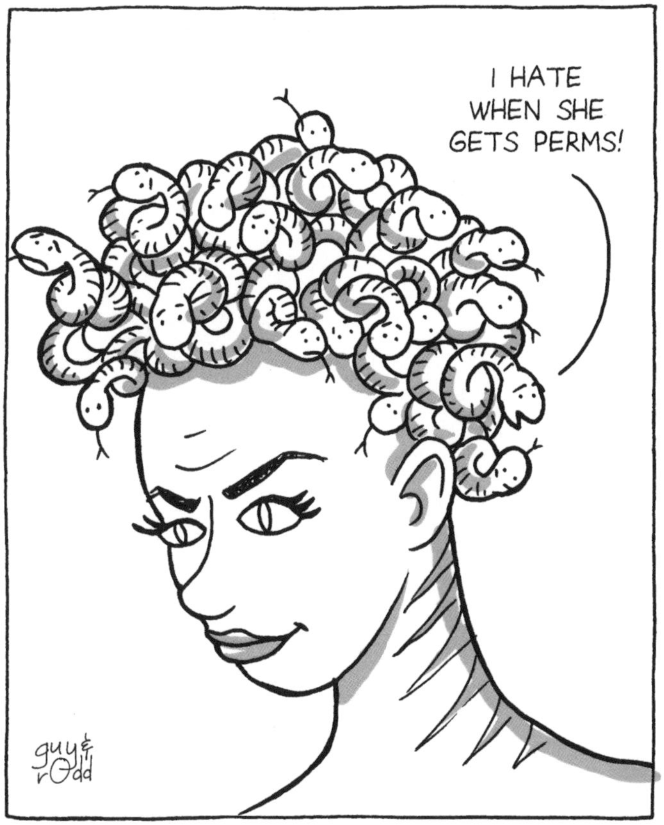
I HATE WHEN SHE GETS PERMS!
guy & rOdd

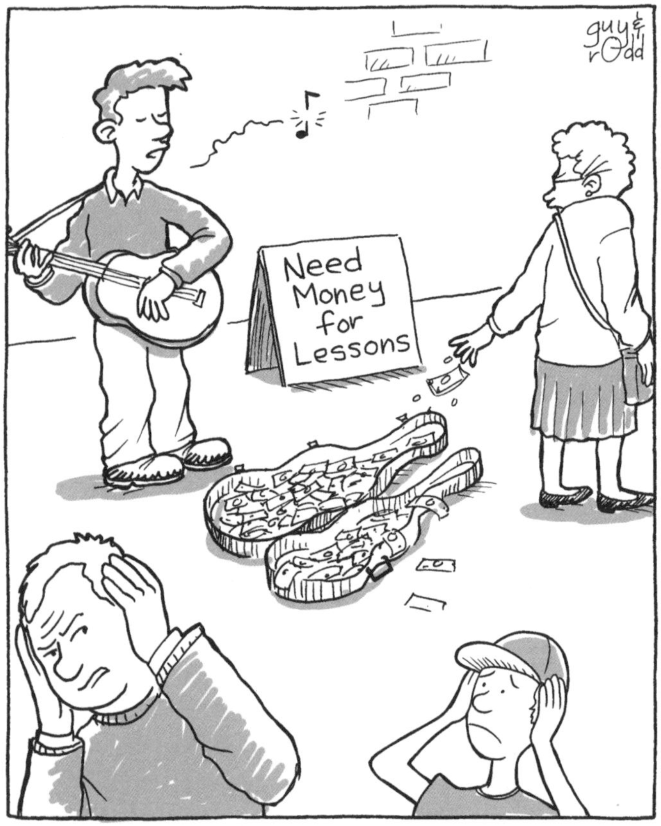
Need Money for Lessons

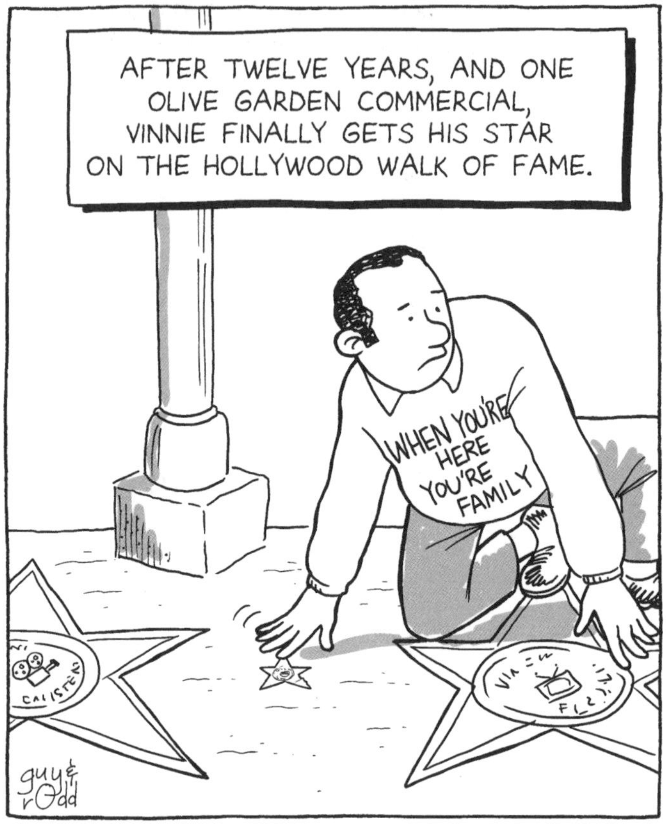
AFTER TWELVE YEARS, AND ONE OLIVE GARDEN COMMERCIAL, VINNIE FINALLY GETS HIS STAR ON THE HOLLYWOOD WALK OF FAME.
WHEN YOU'RE HERE YOU'RE FAMILY

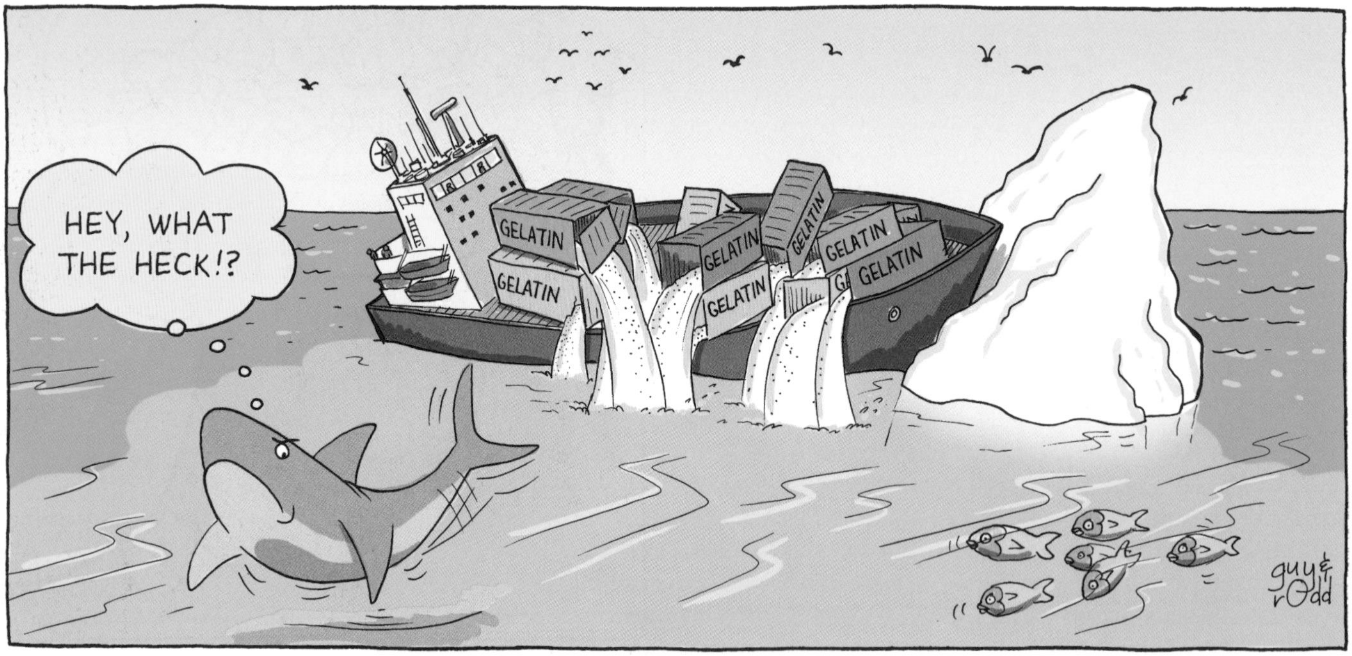
HEY, WHAT THE HECK!?
GELATIN

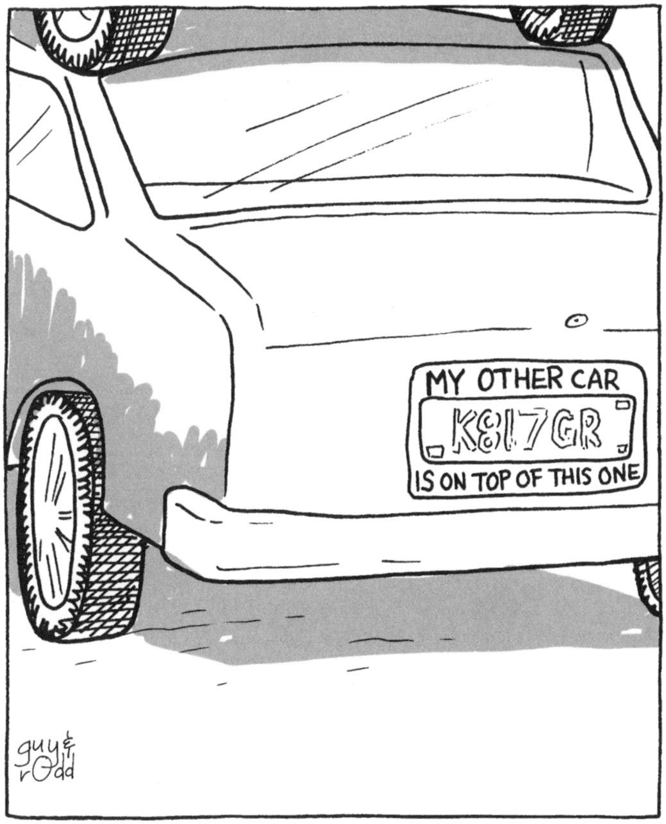
MY OTHER CAR
K817GR
IS ON TOP OF THIS ONE
guy & rOdd

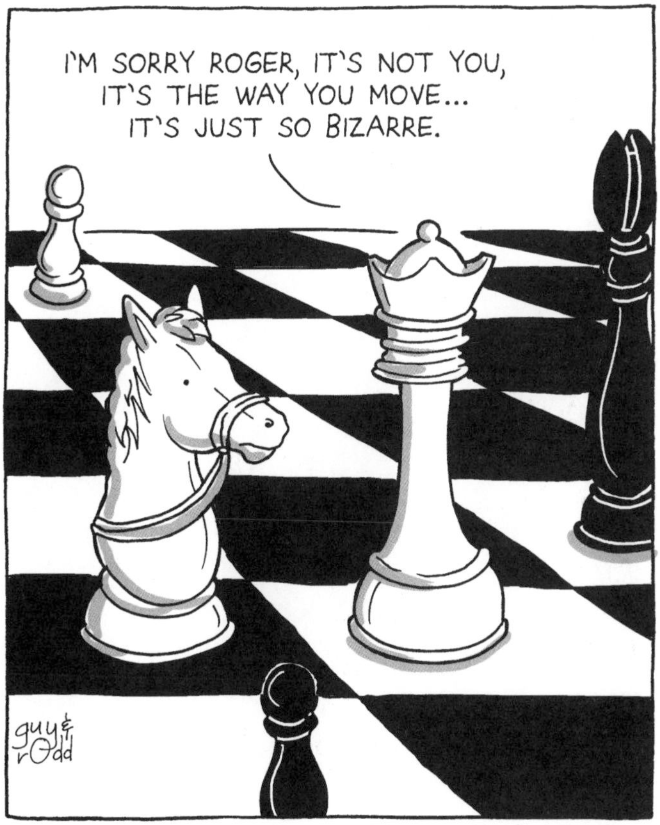
I'M SORRY ROGER, IT'S NOT YOU, IT'S THE WAY YOU MOVE... IT'S JUST SO BIZARRE.
guy & rOdd

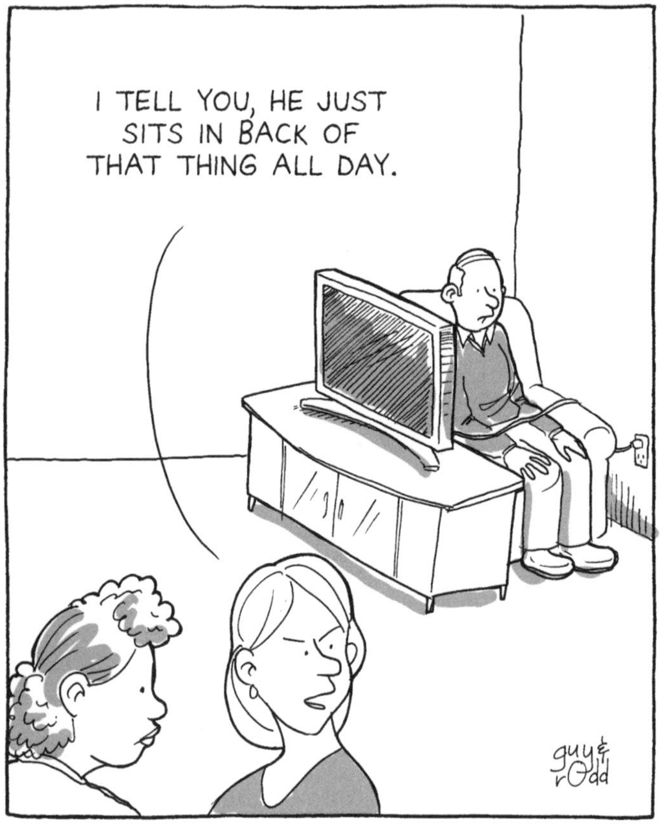
I TELL YOU, HE JUST SITS IN BACK OF THAT THING ALL DAY.
guy & rodd

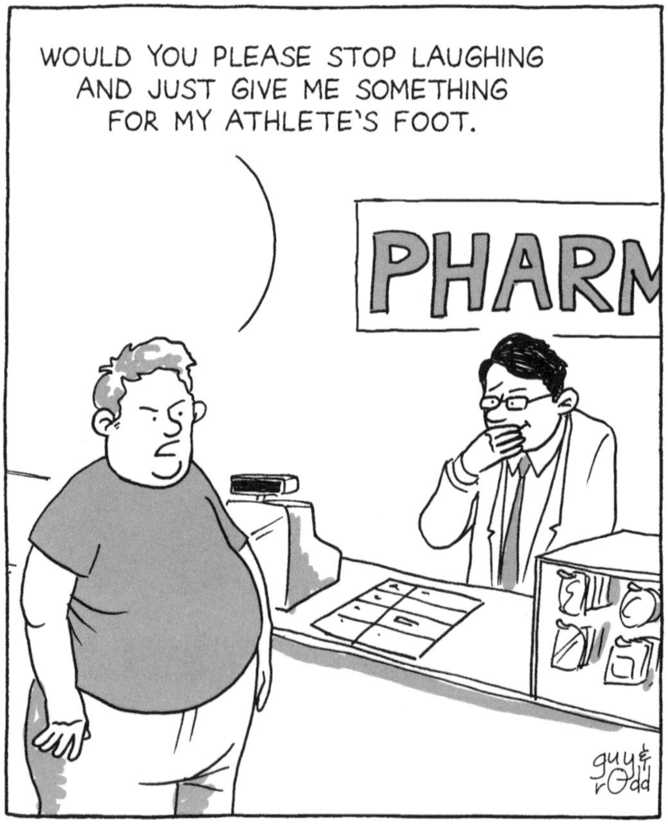
WOULD YOU PLEASE STOP LAUGHING AND JUST GIVE ME SOMETHING FOR MY ATHLETE'S FOOT.
PHARM
guy & rodd

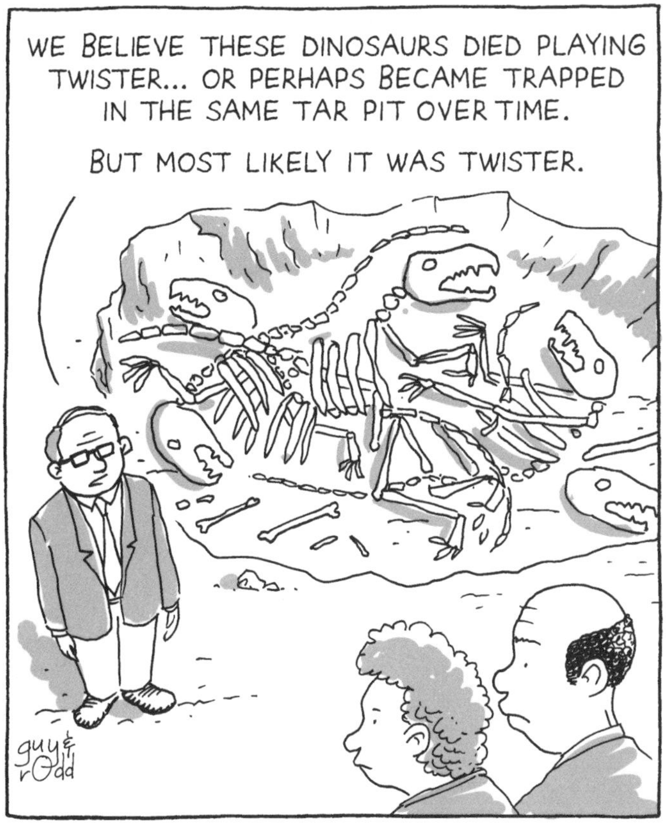
WE BELIEVE THESE DINOSAURS DIED PLAYING TWISTER... OR PERHAPS BECAME TRAPPED IN THE SAME TAR PIT OVER TIME.
BUT MOST LIKELY IT WAS TWISTER.
guy & rOdd

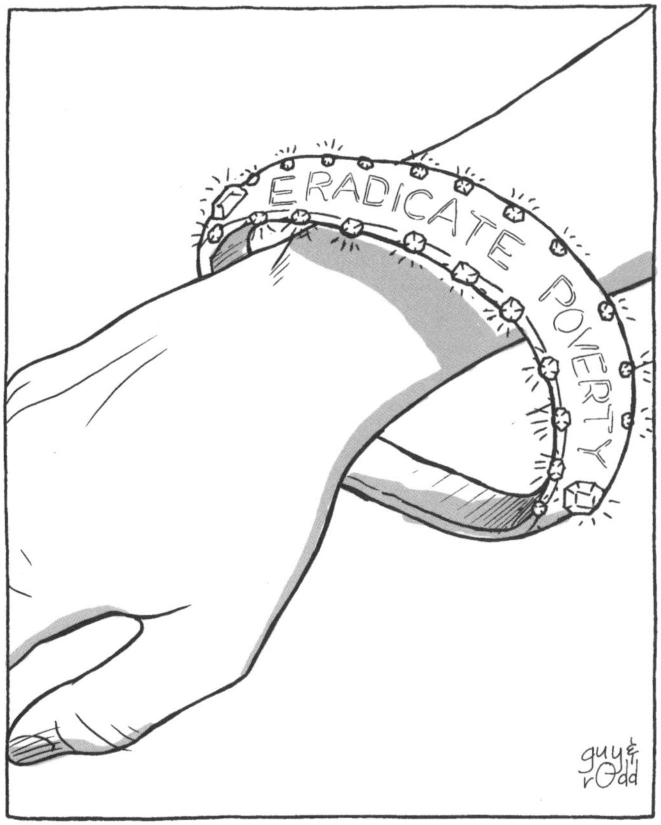
ERADICATE POVERTY
guy & rOdd

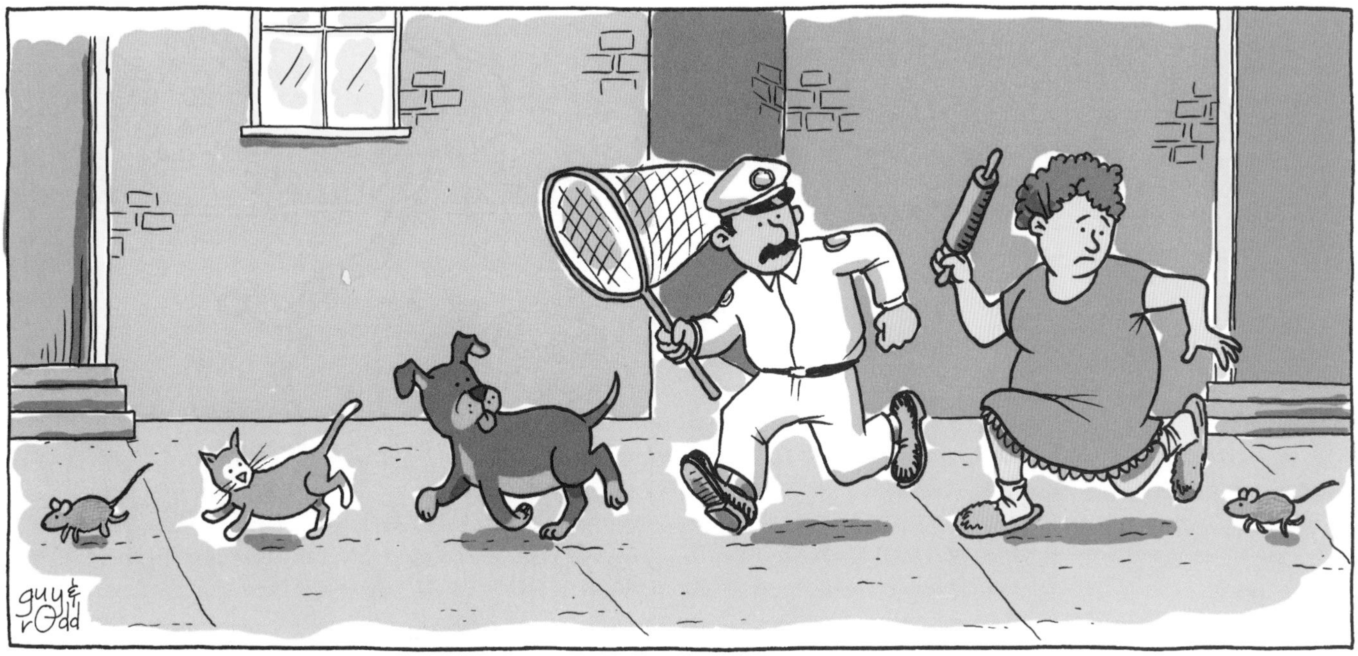
guy & rOdd

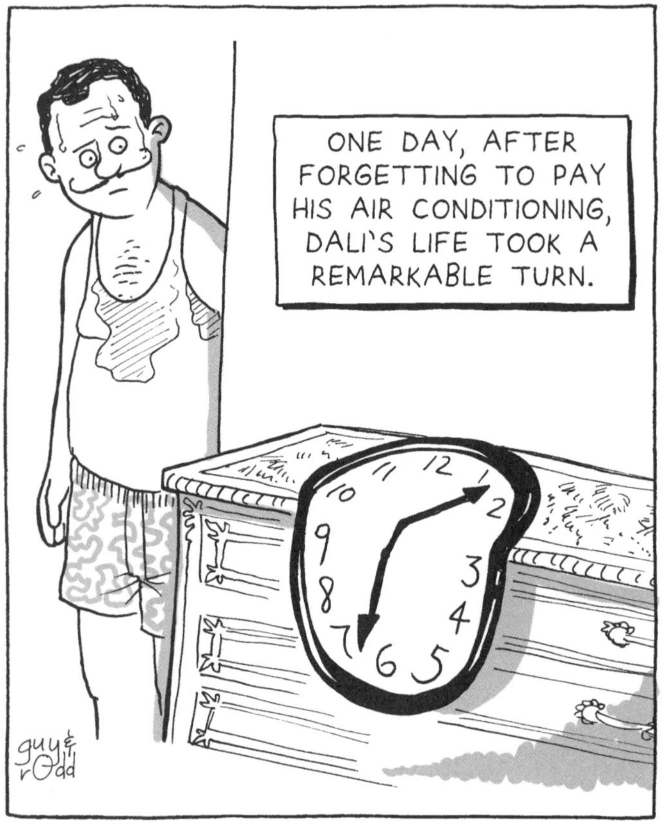
ONE DAY, AFTER FORGETTING TO PAY HIS AIR CONDITIONING, DALI'S LIFE TOOK A REMARKABLE TURN.
guy & rOdd

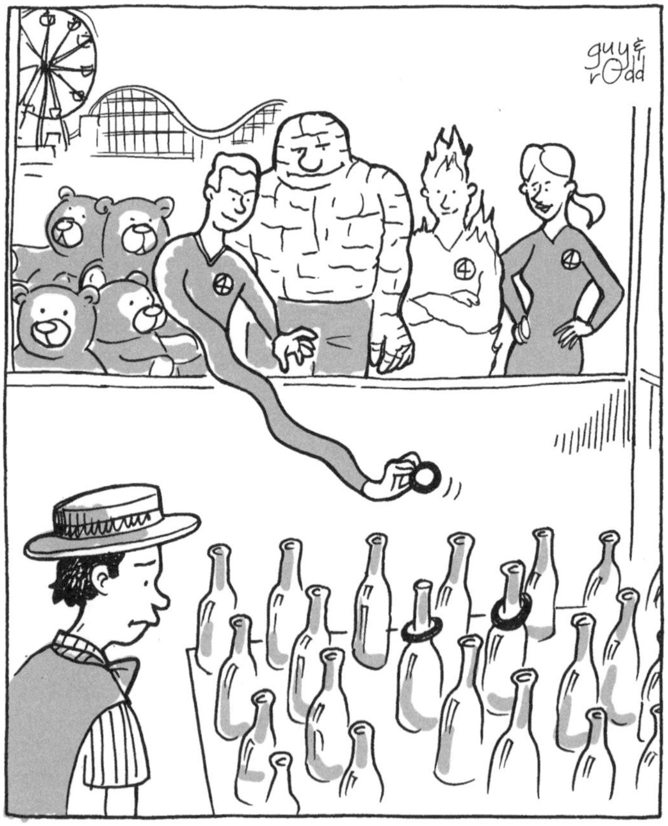
guy & rOdd

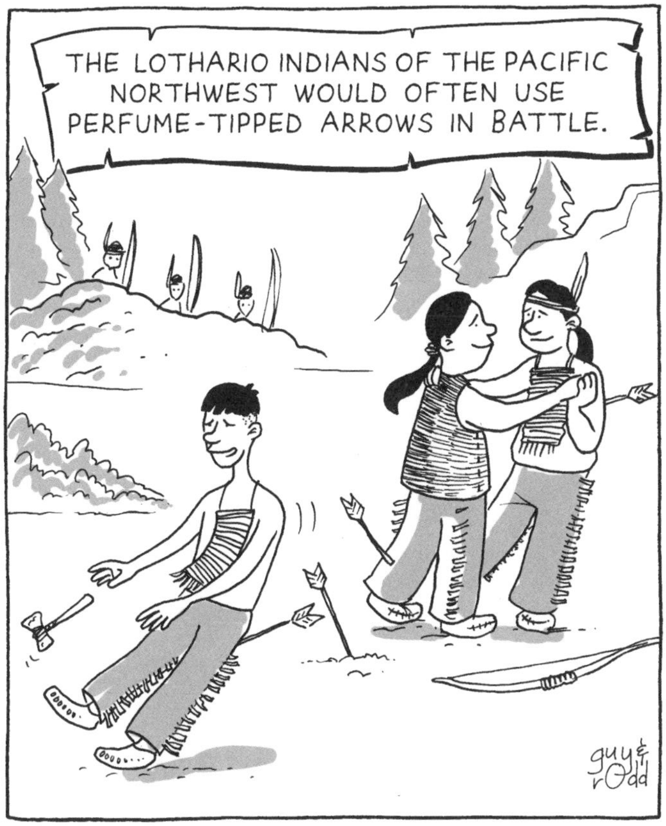
THE LOTHARIO INDIANS OF THE PACIFIC NORTHWEST WOULD OFTEN USE PERFUME-TIPPED ARROWS IN BATTLE.
guy & rodd

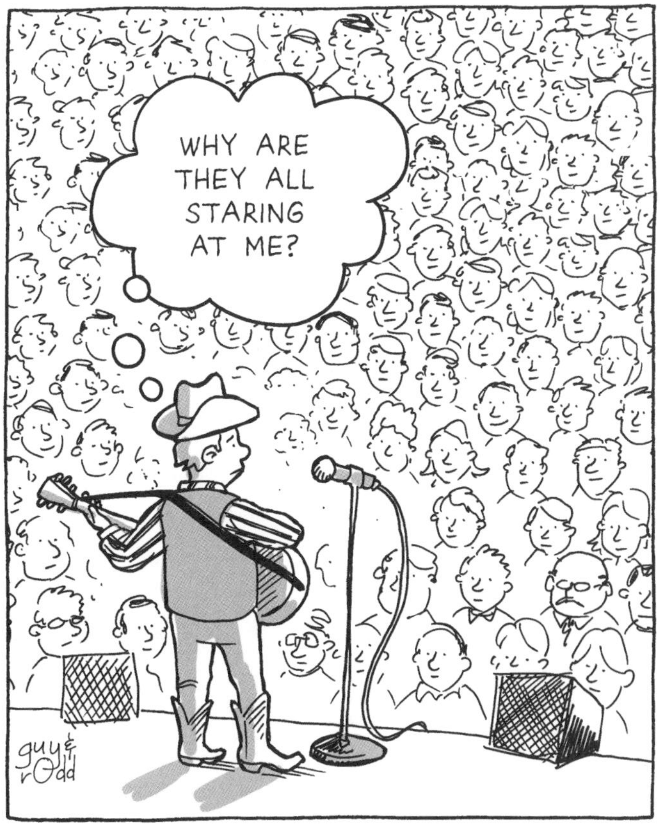
WHY ARE THEY ALL STARING AT ME?
guy & rodd

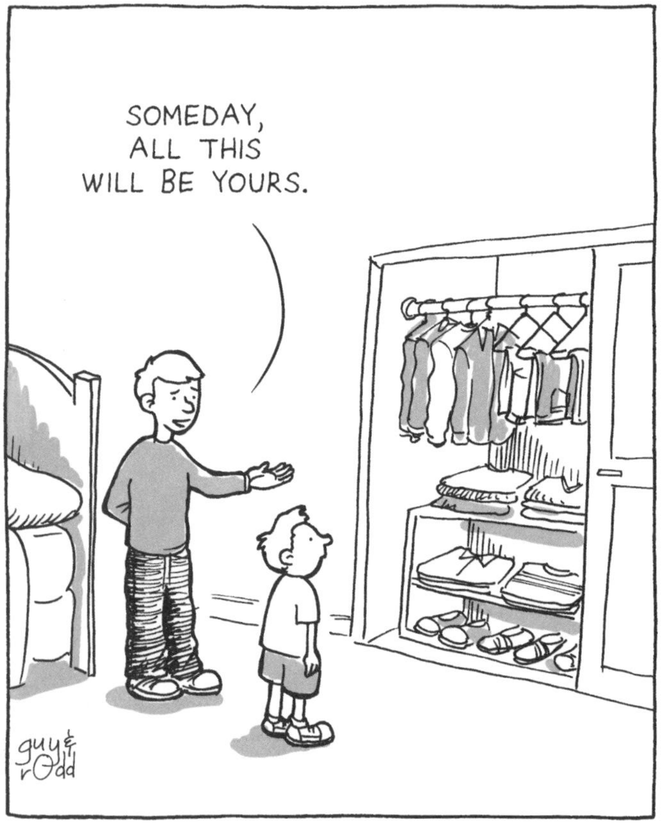
SOMEDAY, ALL THIS WILL BE YOURS.
guy & rOdd

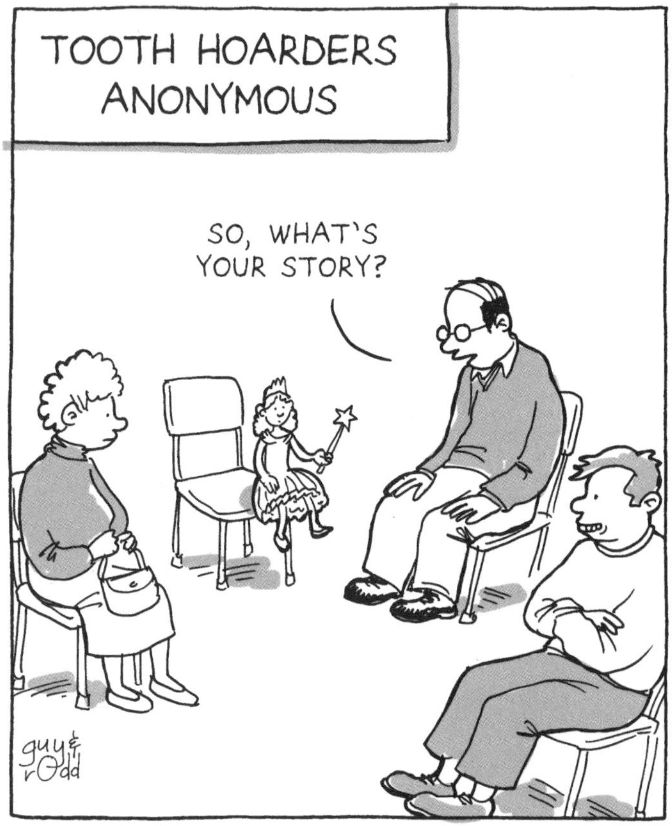
TOOTH HOARDERS ANONYMOUS
SO, WHAT'S YOUR STORY?
guy & rOdd

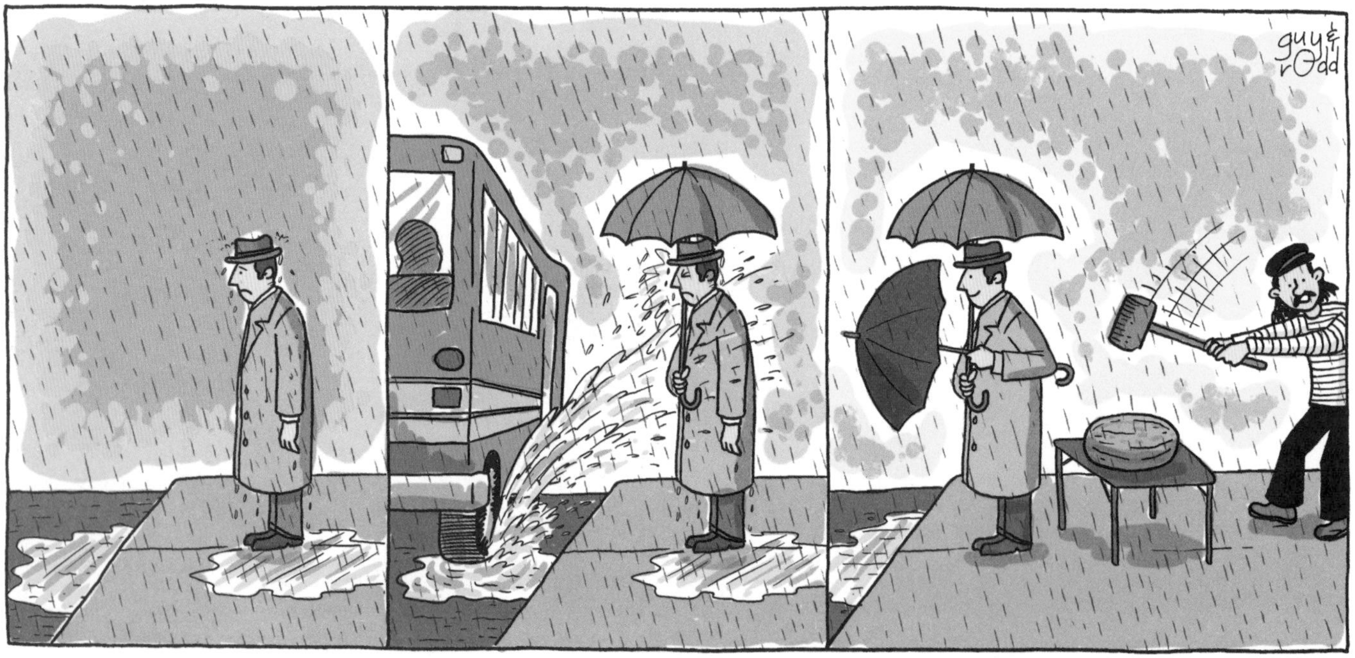
guy & rOdd

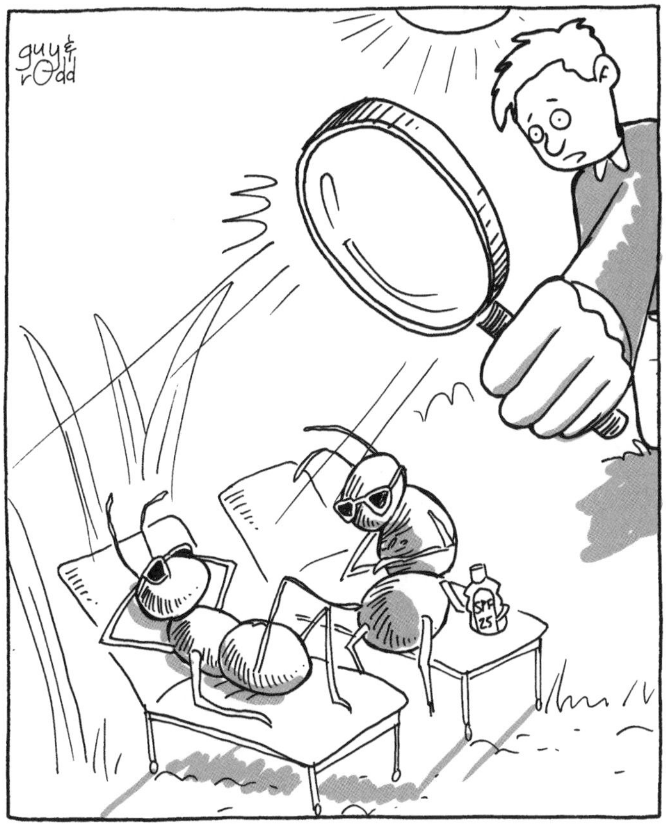
guy & rOdd
SPF 25

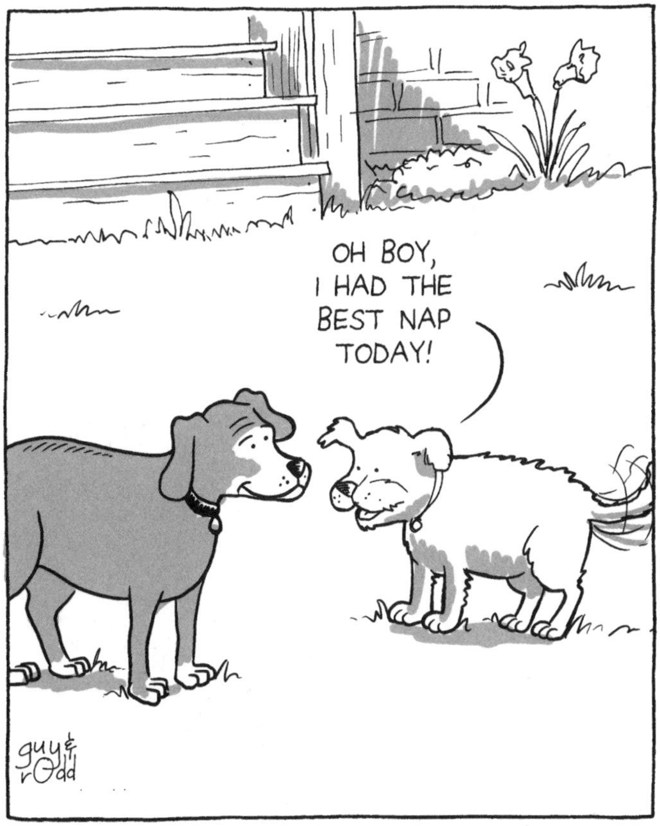
OH BOY,
I HAD THE
BEST NAP
TODAY!
guy & rOdd

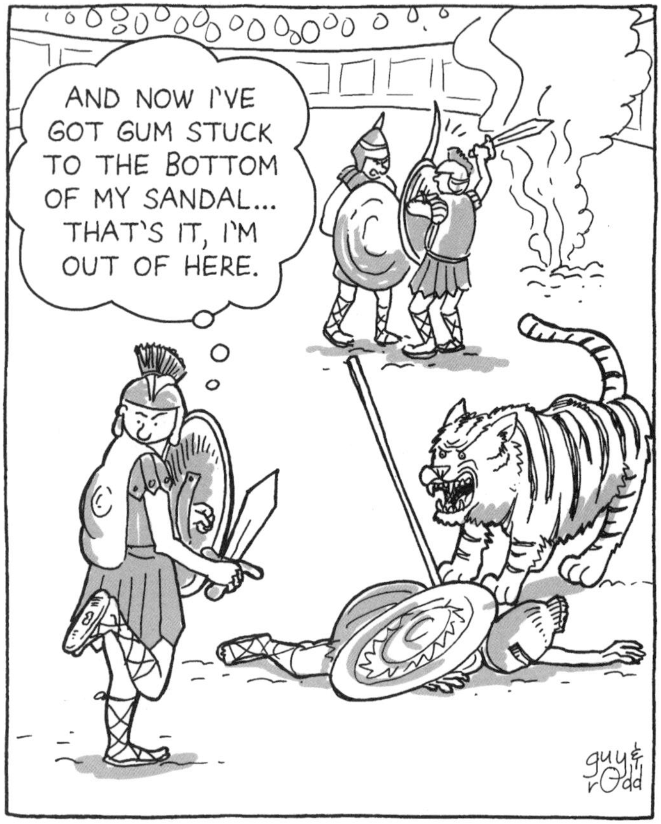
AND NOW I'VE GOT GUM STUCK TO THE BOTTOM OF MY SANDAL... THAT'S IT, I'M OUT OF HERE.
guy & rOdd

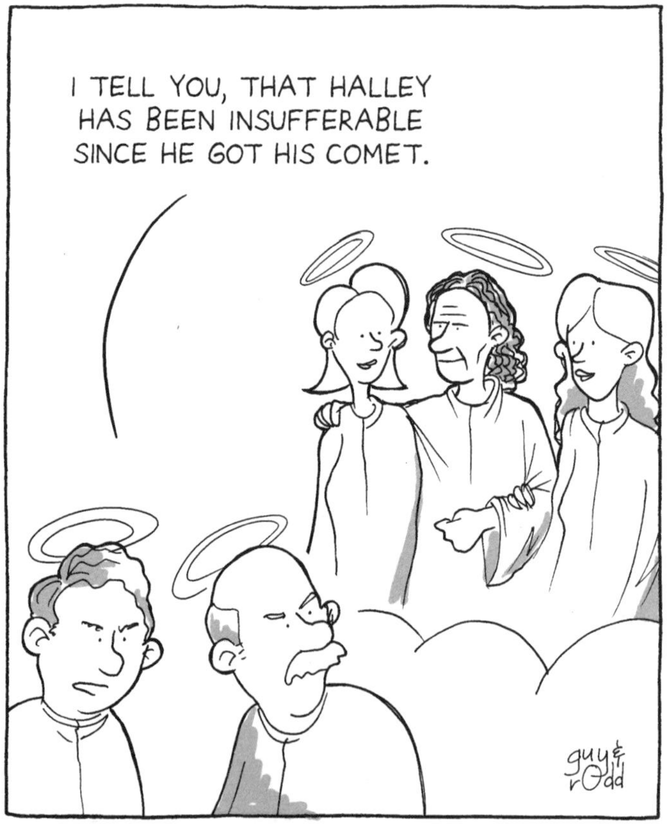
I TELL YOU, THAT HALLEY HAS BEEN INSUFFERABLE SINCE HE GOT HIS COMET.
guy & rOdd

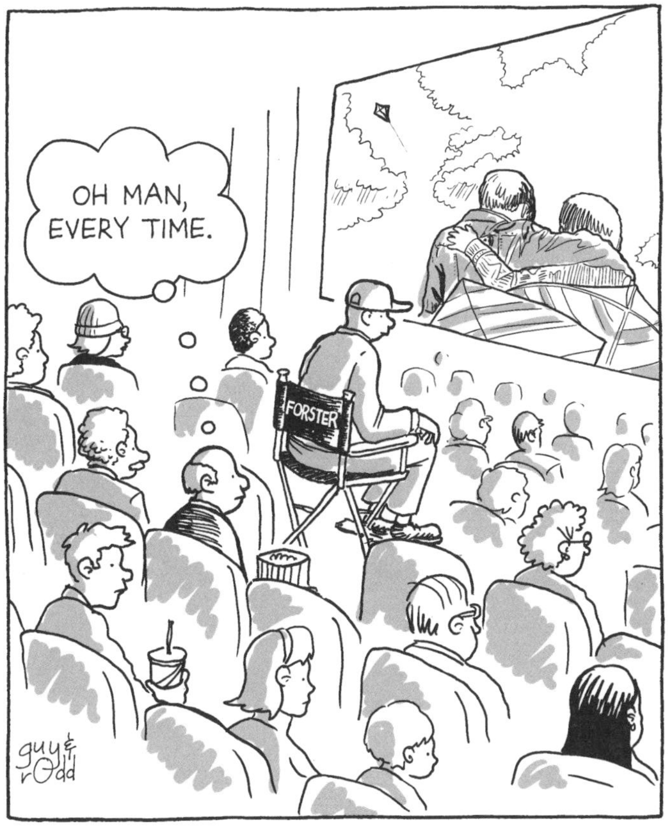
OH MAN, EVERY TIME.
FORSTER
guy & rodd

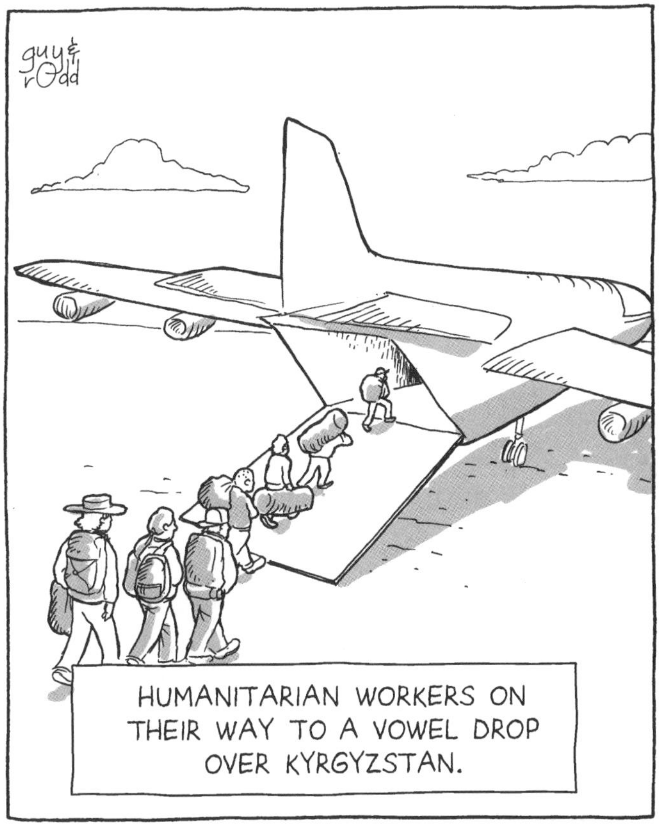
guy & rodd
HUMANITARIAN WORKERS ON THEIR WAY TO A VOWEL DROP OVER KYRGYZSTAN.

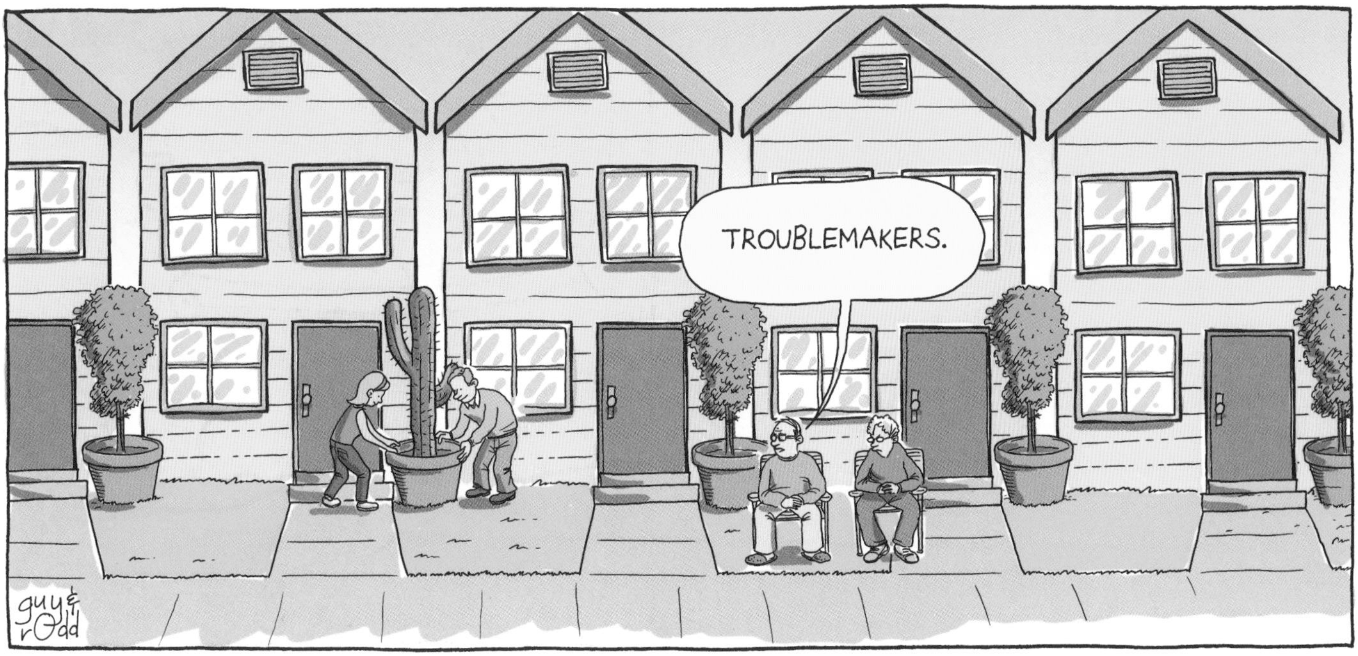
TROUBLEMAKERS.
guy & rodd

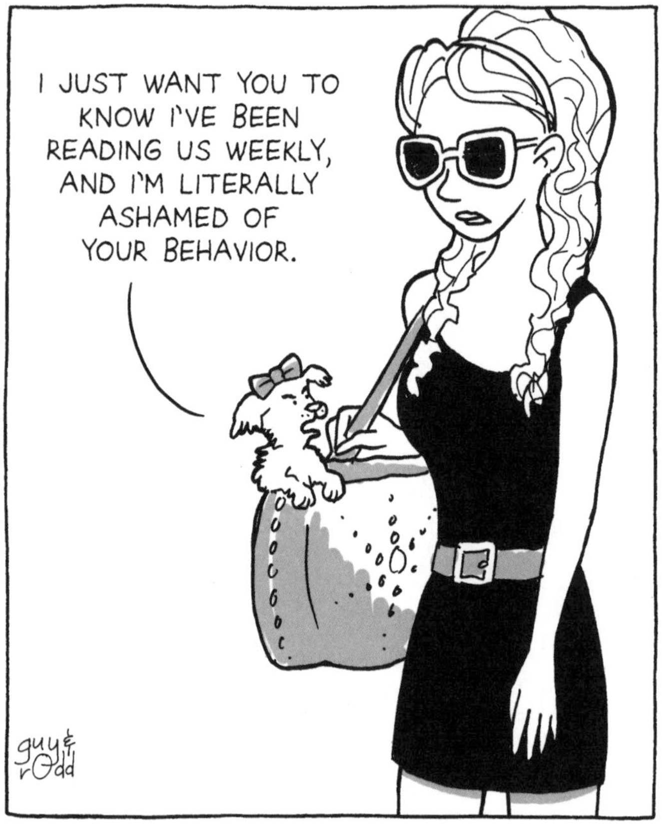
I JUST WANT YOU TO KNOW I'VE BEEN READING US WEEKLY, AND I'M LITERALLY ASHAMED OF YOUR BEHAVIOR.
guy & rOdd

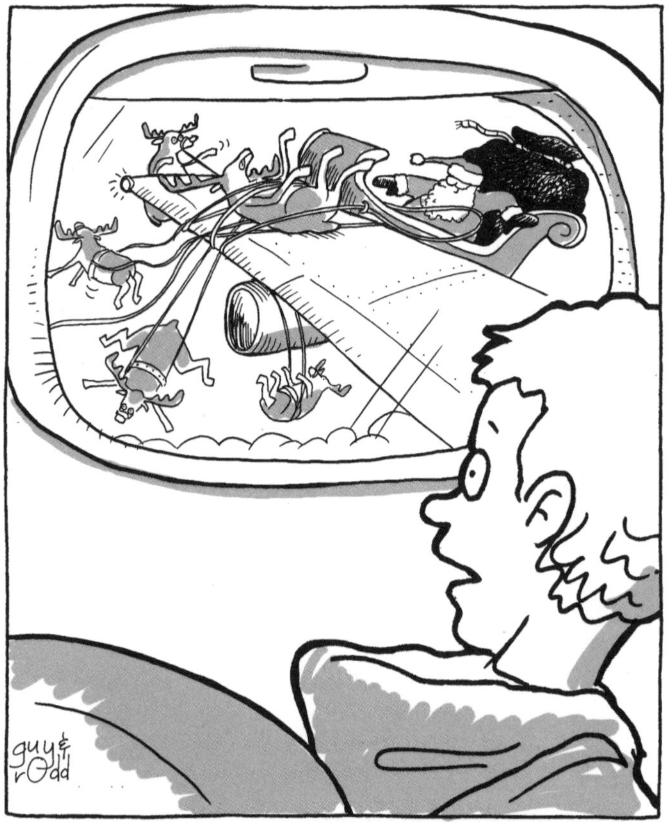
guy & rOdd

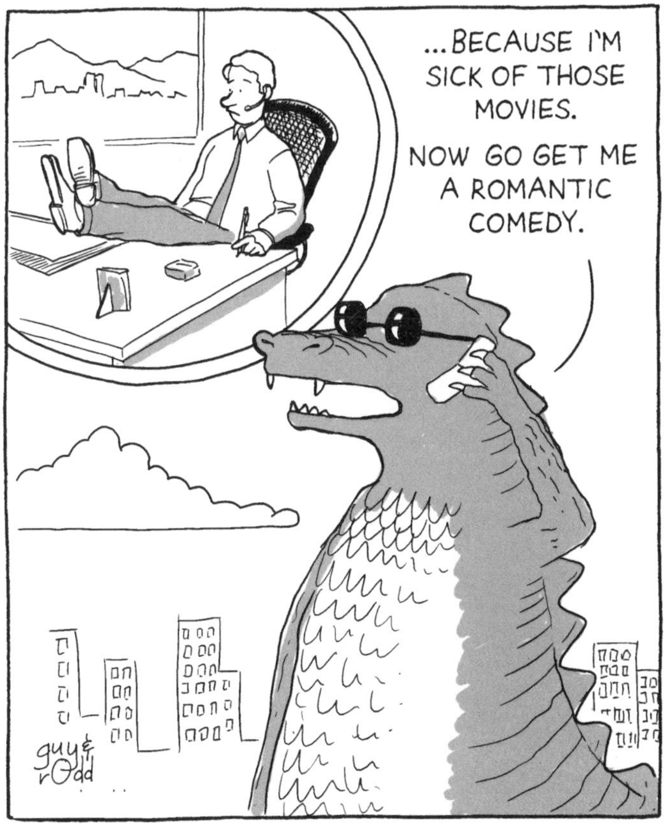
...BECAUSE I'M SICK OF THOSE MOVIES.
NOW GO GET ME A ROMANTIC COMEDY.
guy & rOdd

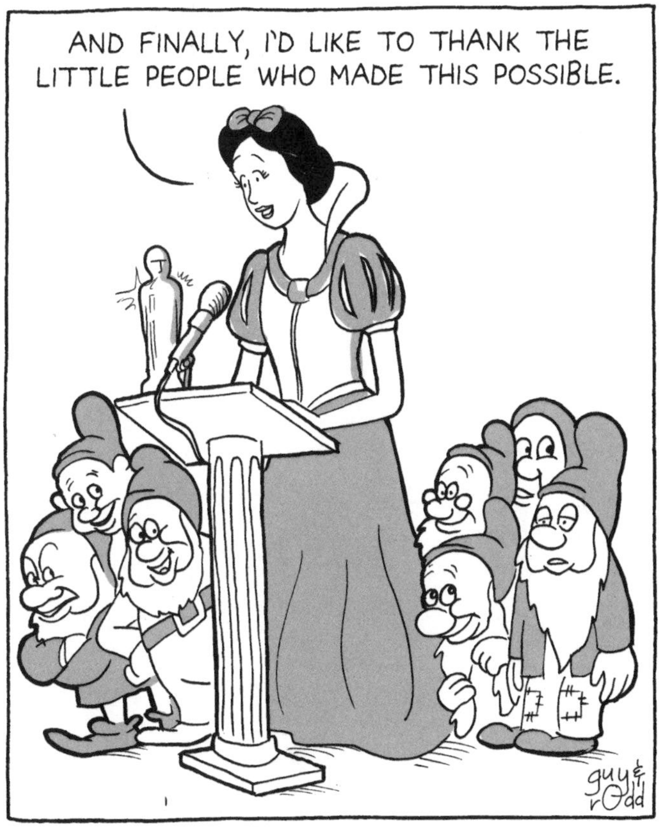
AND FINALLY, I'D LIKE TO THANK THE LITTLE PEOPLE WHO MADE THIS POSSIBLE.
guy & rOdd

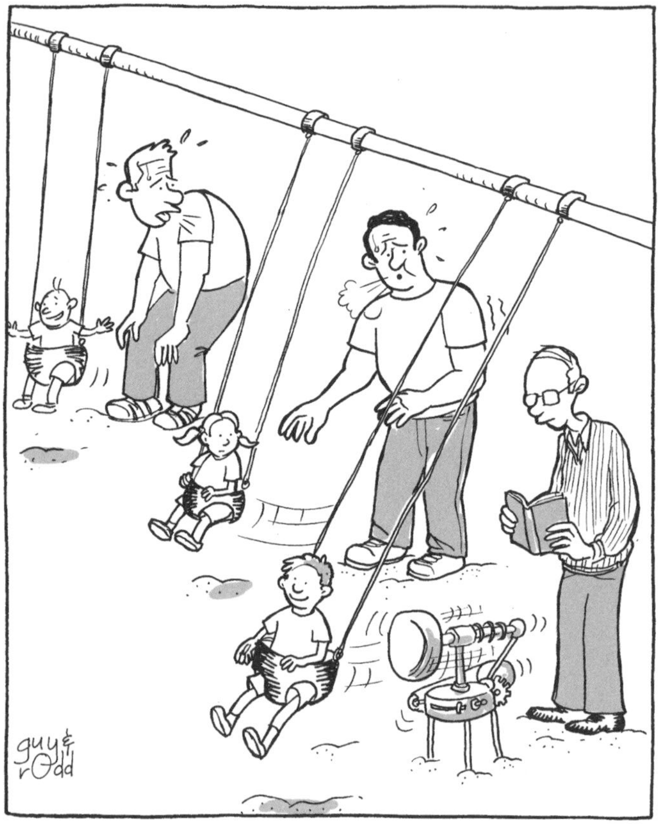

guy & rOdd

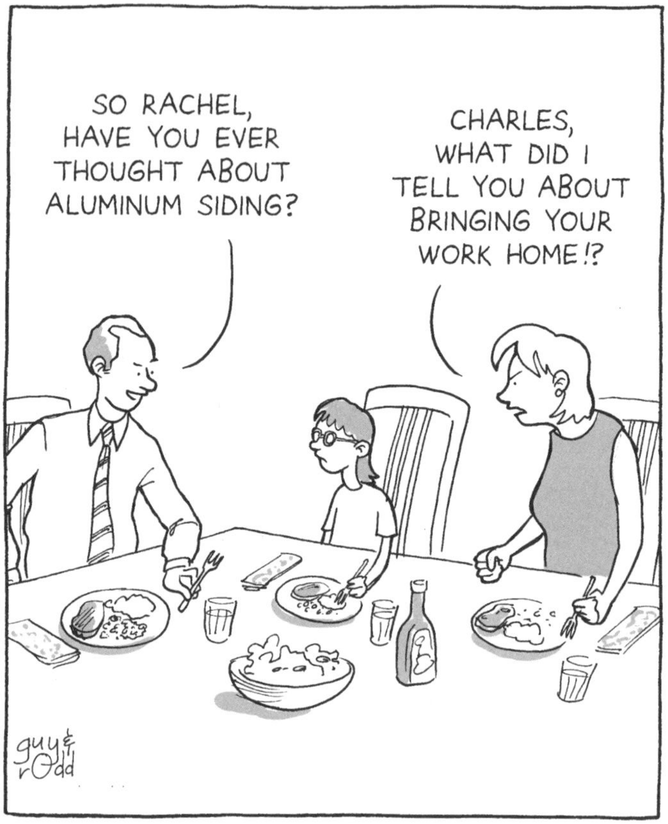

SO RACHEL, HAVE YOU EVER THOUGHT ABOUT ALUMINUM SIDING?
CHARLES, WHAT DID I TELL YOU ABOUT BRINGING YOUR WORK HOME!?
guy & rOdd

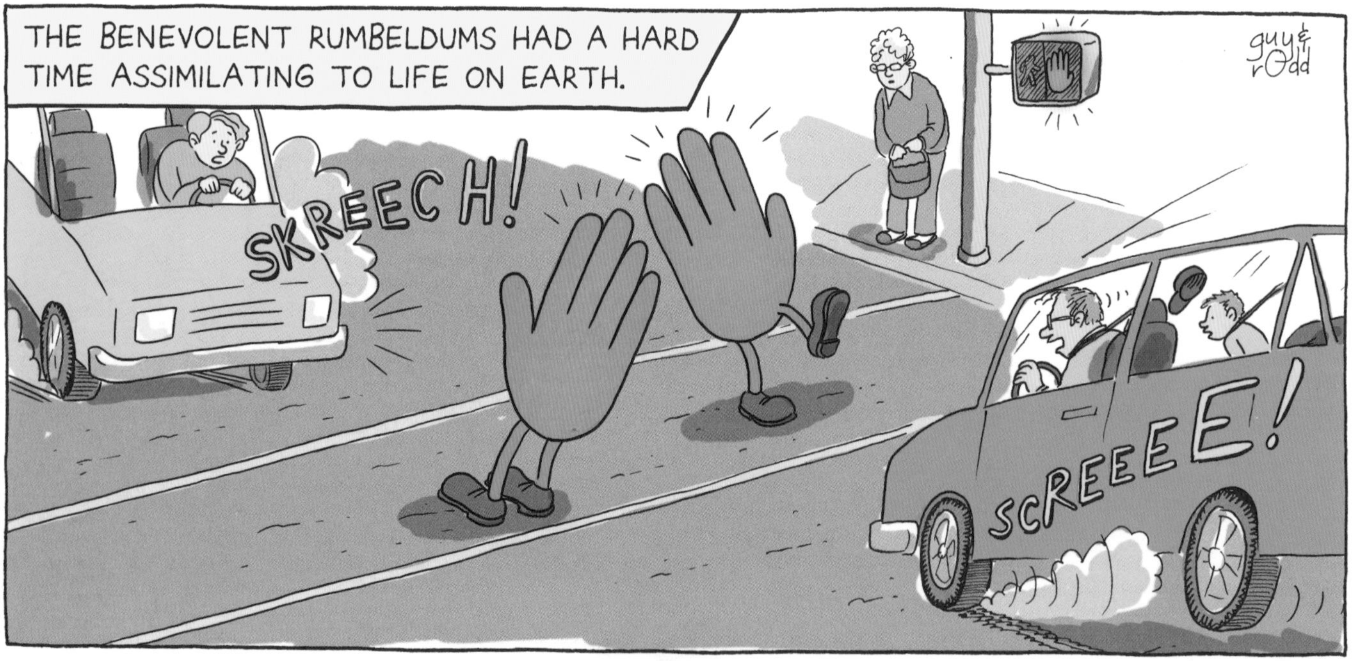

THE BENEVOLENT RUMBELDUMS HAD A HARD TIME ASSIMILATING TO LIFE ON EARTH.
SKREECH!
SCREEEEE!
guy & rOdd

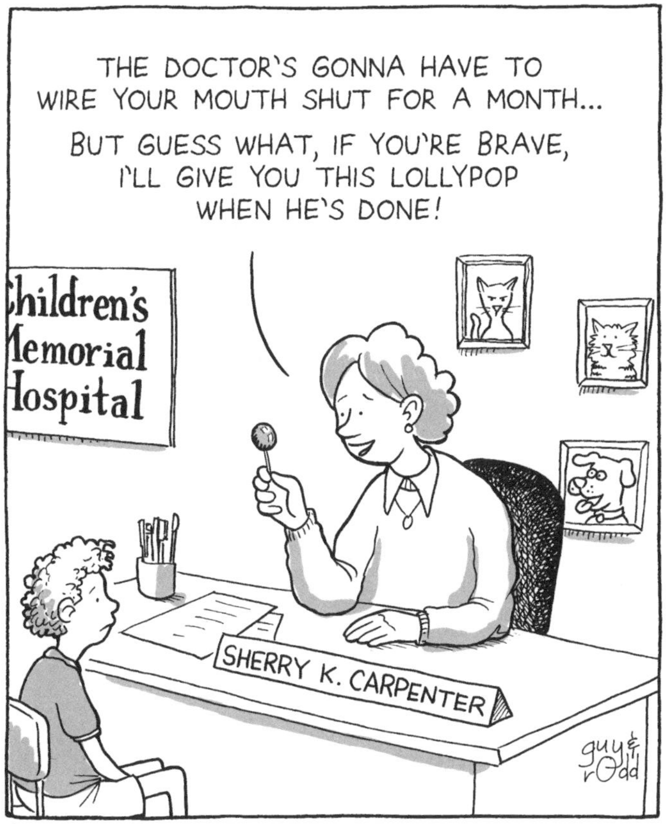
THE DOCTOR'S GONNA HAVE TO WIRE YOUR MOUTH SHUT FOR A MONTH...
BUT GUESS WHAT, IF YOU'RE BRAVE, I'LL GIVE YOU THIS LOLLYPOP WHEN HE'S DONE!
Children's Memorial Hospital
SHERRY K. CARPENTER
guy & rOdd

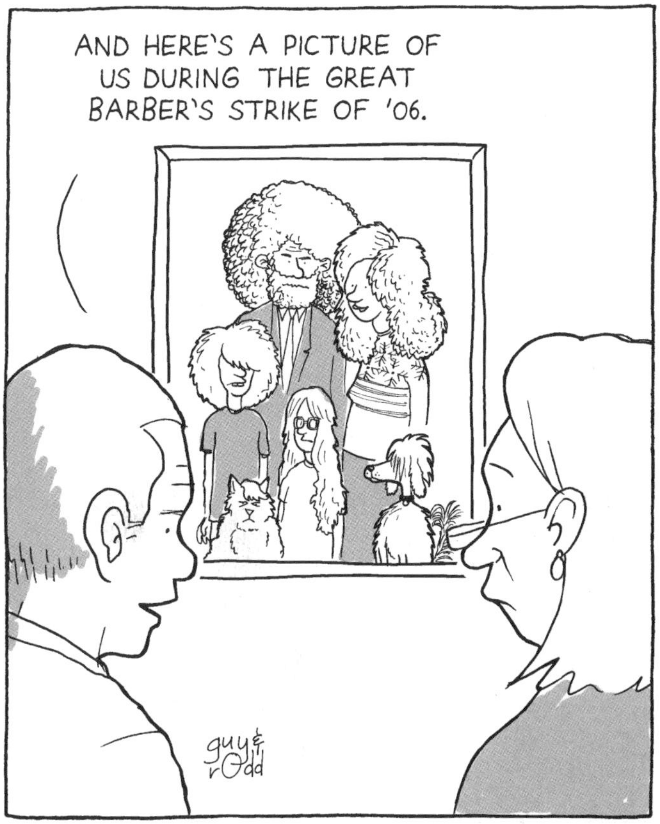
AND HERE'S A PICTURE OF US DURING THE GREAT BARBER'S STRIKE OF '06.
guy & rOdd

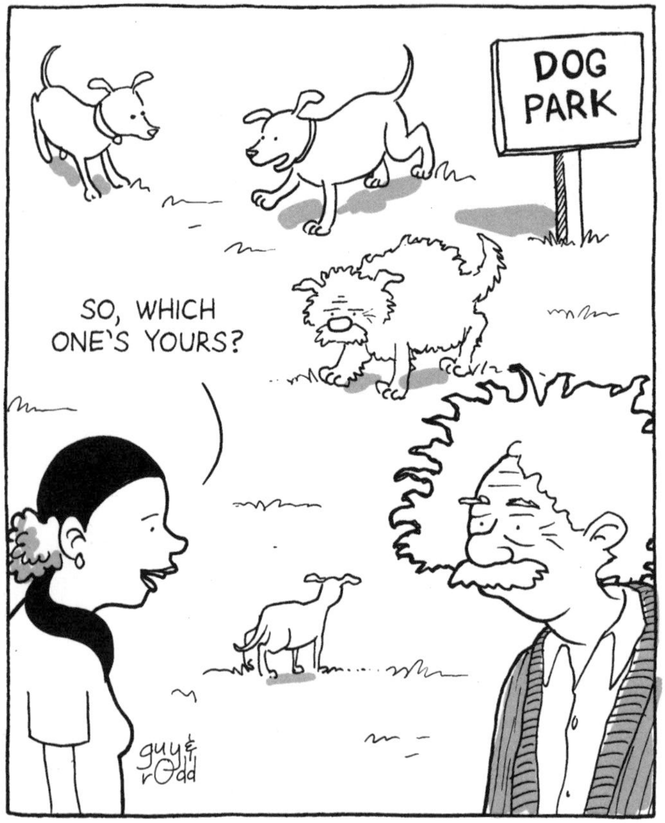
DOG PARK
SO, WHICH ONE'S YOURS?
guy & rOdd

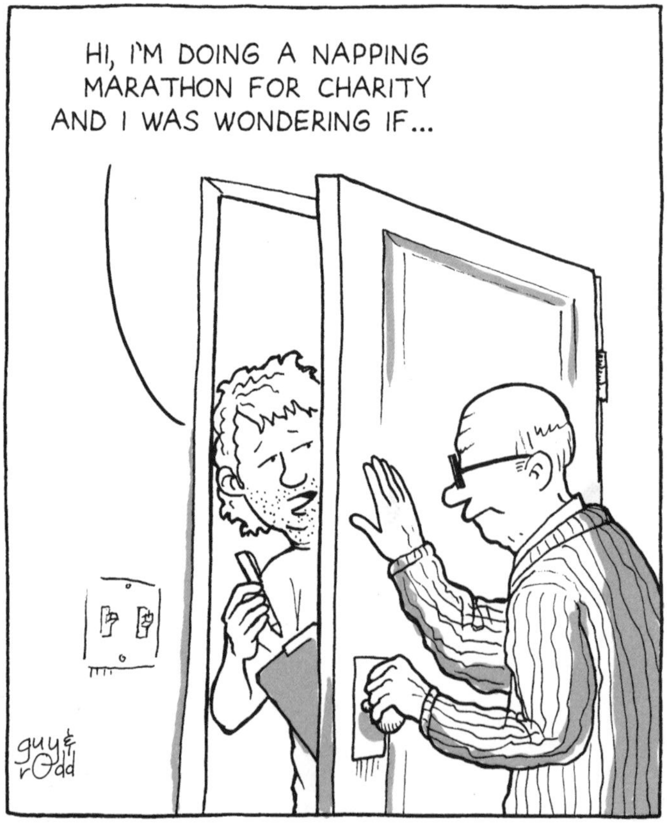
HI, I'M DOING A NAPPING MARATHON FOR CHARITY AND I WAS WONDERING IF...
guy & rOdd

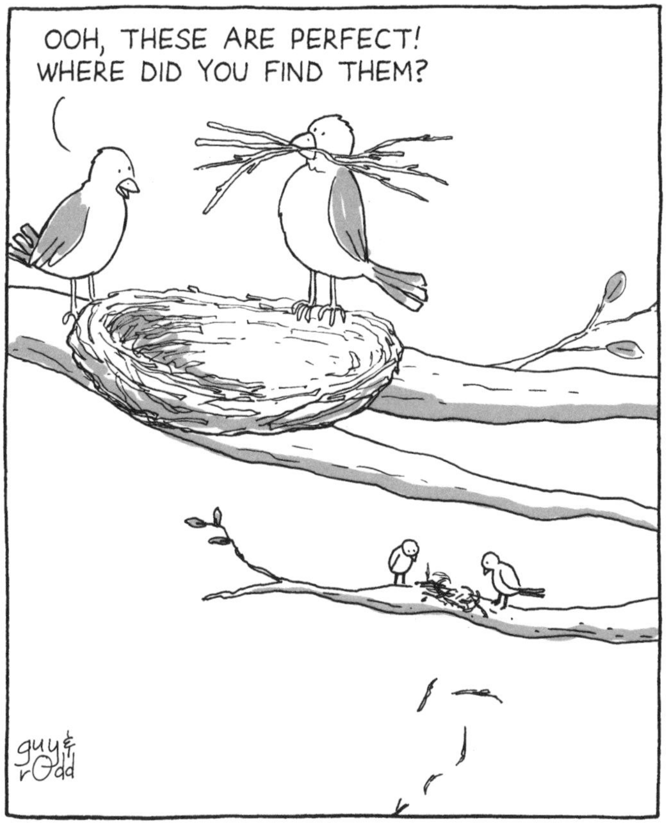
OOH, THESE ARE PERFECT! WHERE DID YOU FIND THEM?

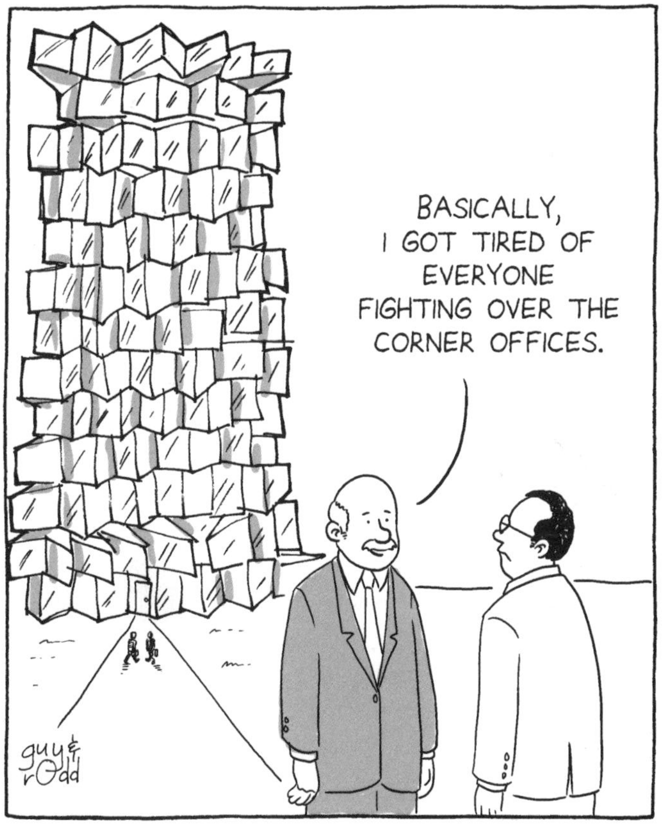
BASICALLY, I GOT TIRED OF EVERYONE FIGHTING OVER THE CORNER OFFICES.

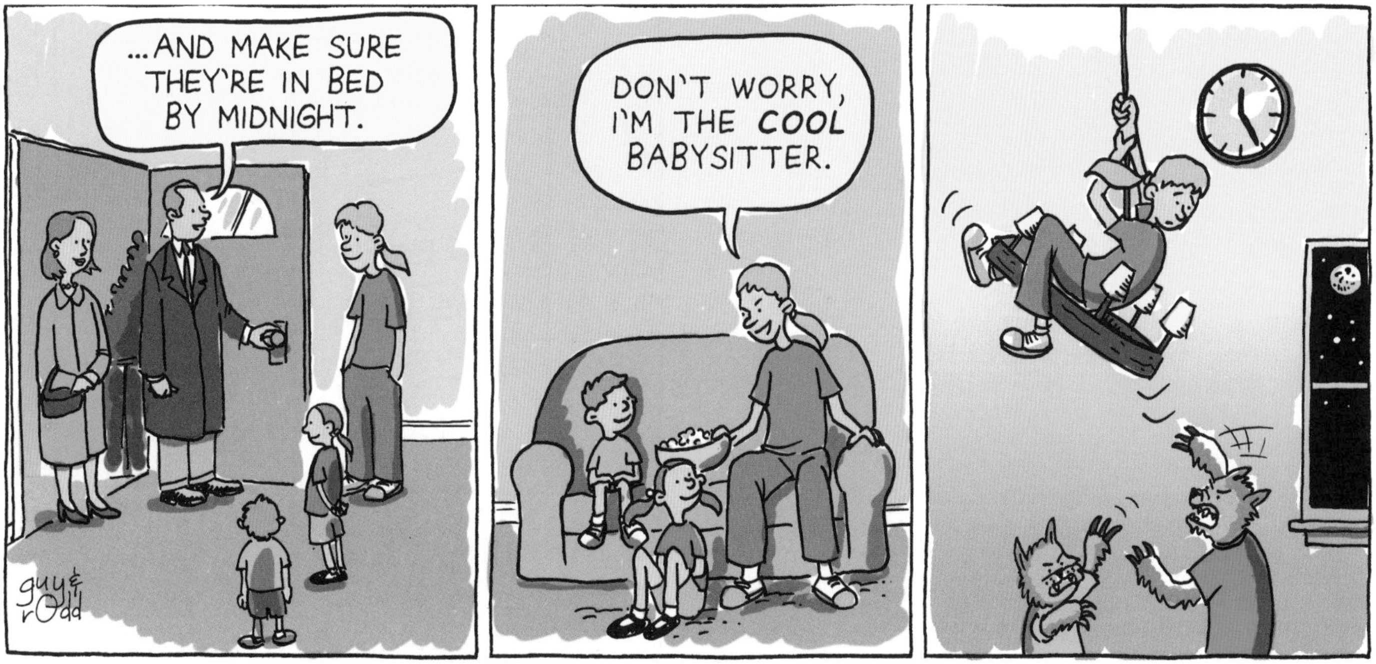
...AND MAKE SURE THEY'RE IN BED BY MIDNIGHT.
DON'T WORRY, I'M THE **COOL** BABYSITTER.

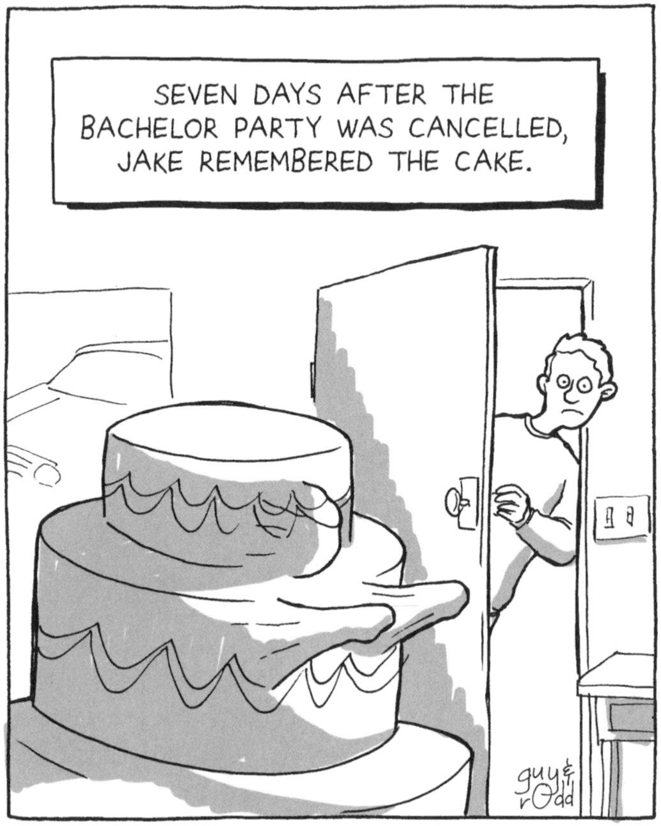
SEVEN DAYS AFTER THE BACHELOR PARTY WAS CANCELLED, JAKE REMEMBERED THE CAKE.
guy & rOdd

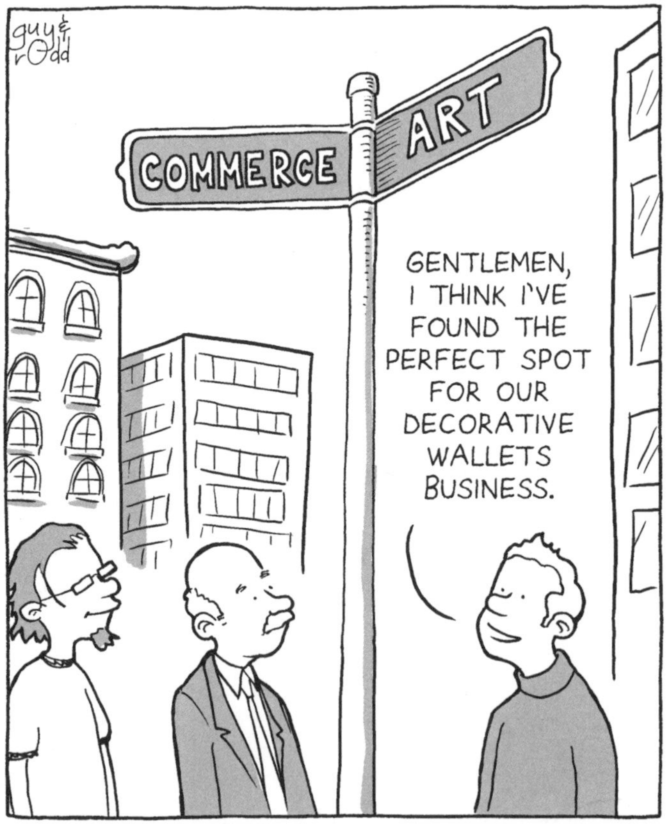
guy & rOdd
COMMERCE
ART
GENTLEMEN, I THINK I'VE FOUND THE PERFECT SPOT FOR OUR DECORATIVE WALLETS BUSINESS.

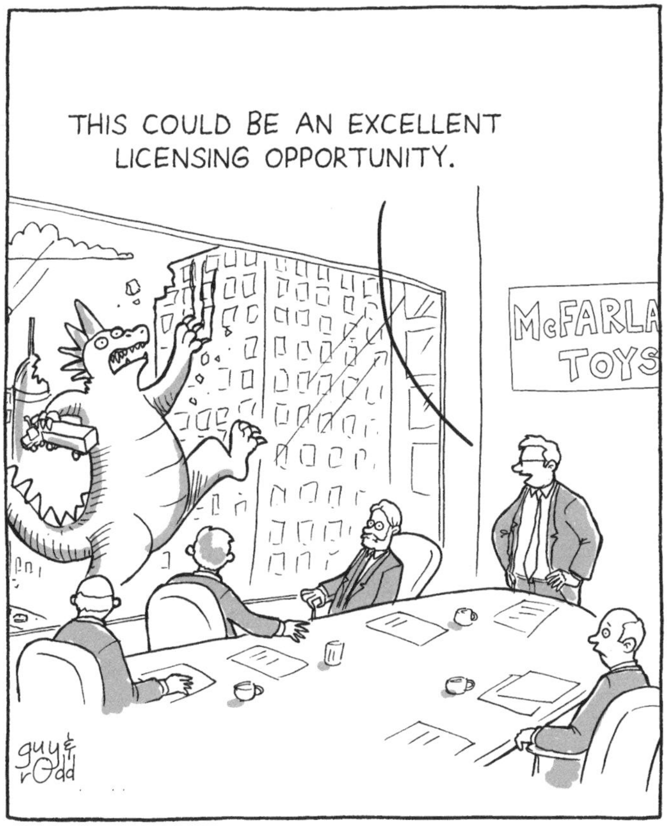
THIS COULD BE AN EXCELLENT LICENSING OPPORTUNITY.
McFARLA
TOYS
guy & rOdd

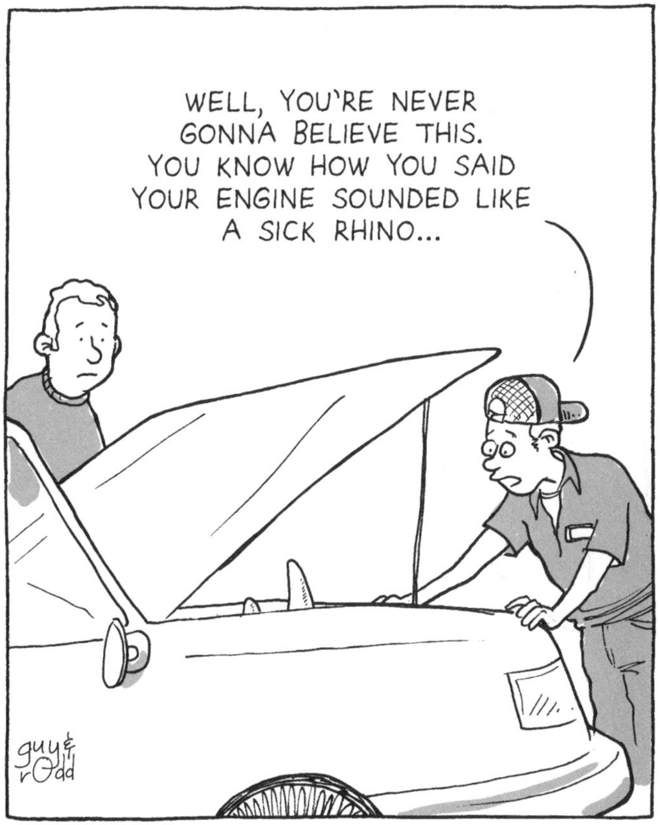
WELL, YOU'RE NEVER GONNA BELIEVE THIS. YOU KNOW HOW YOU SAID YOUR ENGINE SOUNDED LIKE A SICK RHINO...
guy & rOdd

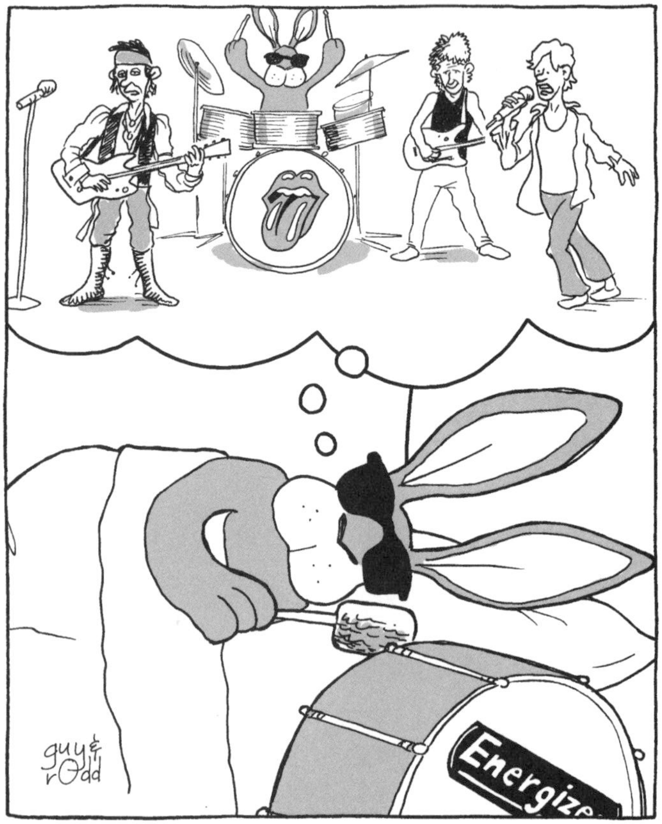
Energize
guy & rOdd

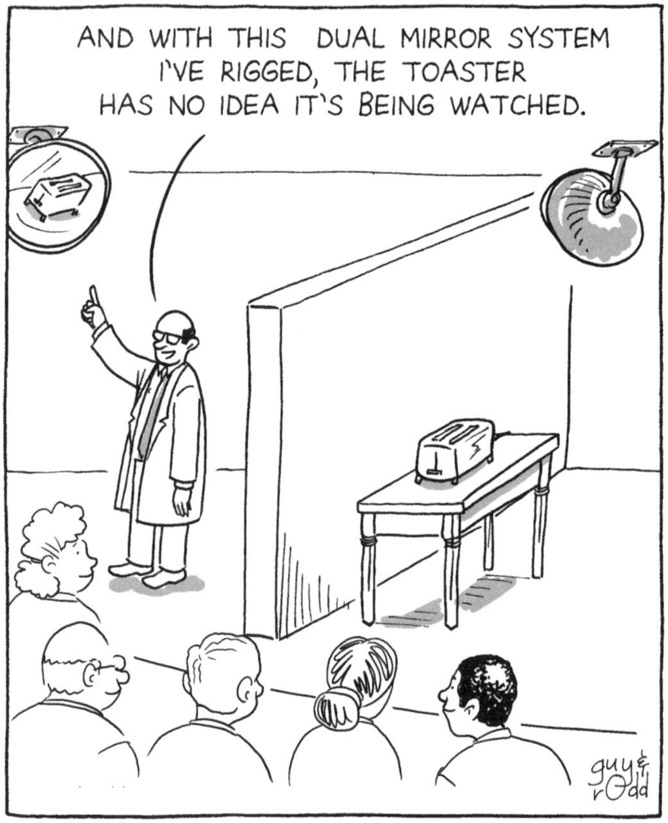
AND WITH THIS DUAL MIRROR SYSTEM I'VE RIGGED, THE TOASTER HAS NO IDEA IT'S BEING WATCHED.
guy & rOdd

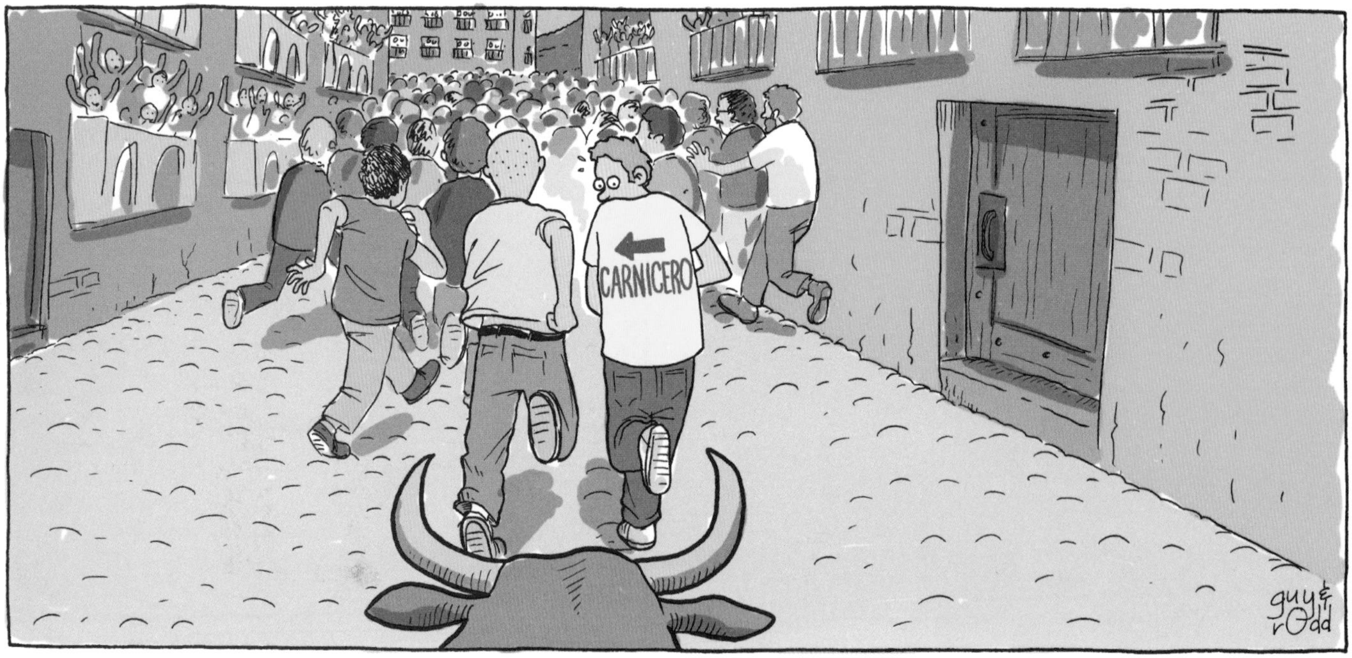
CARNICERO
guy & rOdd

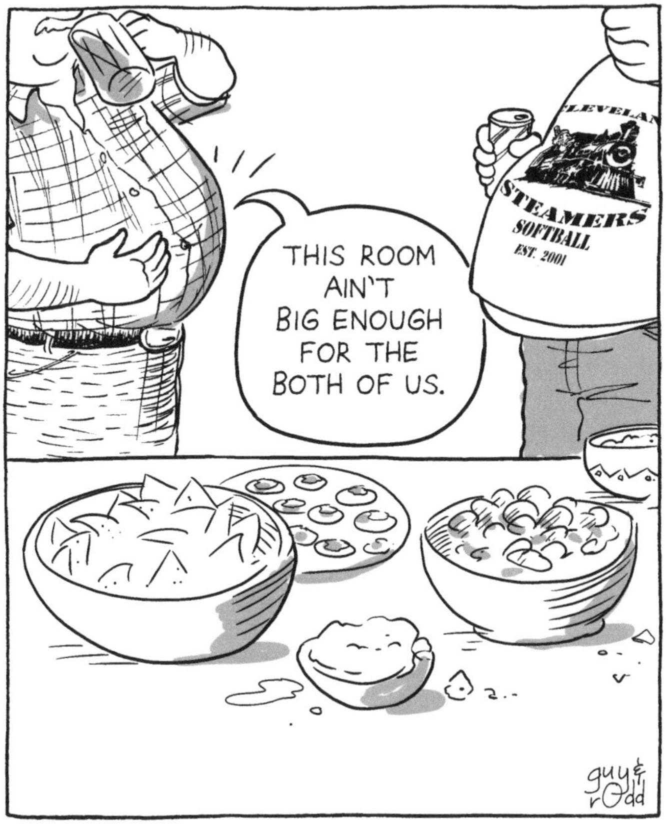
CLEVELAN
STEAMERS
SOFTBALL
EST. 2001
THIS ROOM AIN'T BIG ENOUGH FOR THE BOTH OF US.
guy & rodd

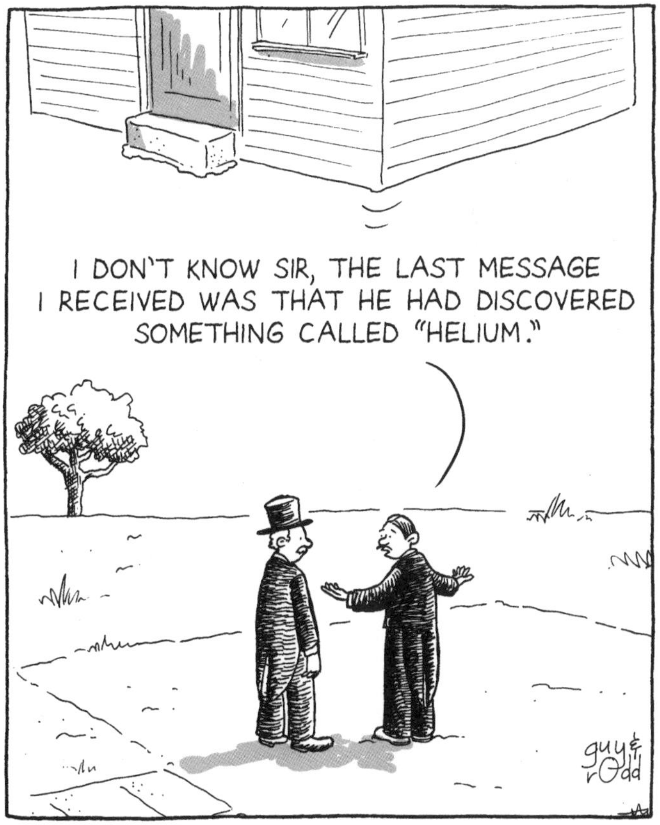
I DON'T KNOW SIR, THE LAST MESSAGE I RECEIVED WAS THAT HE HAD DISCOVERED SOMETHING CALLED "HELIUM."
guy & rodd

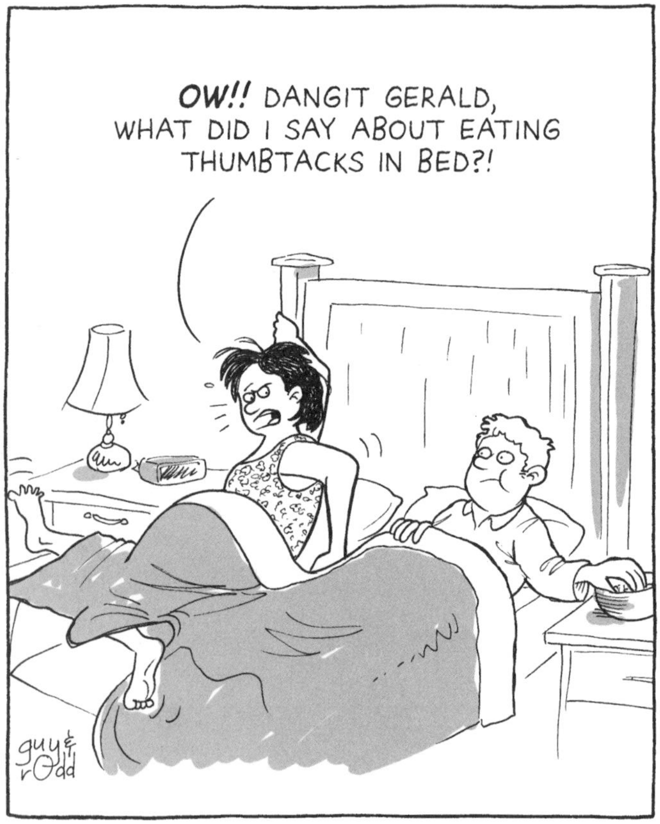
OW!! DANGIT GERALD, WHAT DID I SAY ABOUT EATING THUMBTACKS IN BED?!
guy & rodd

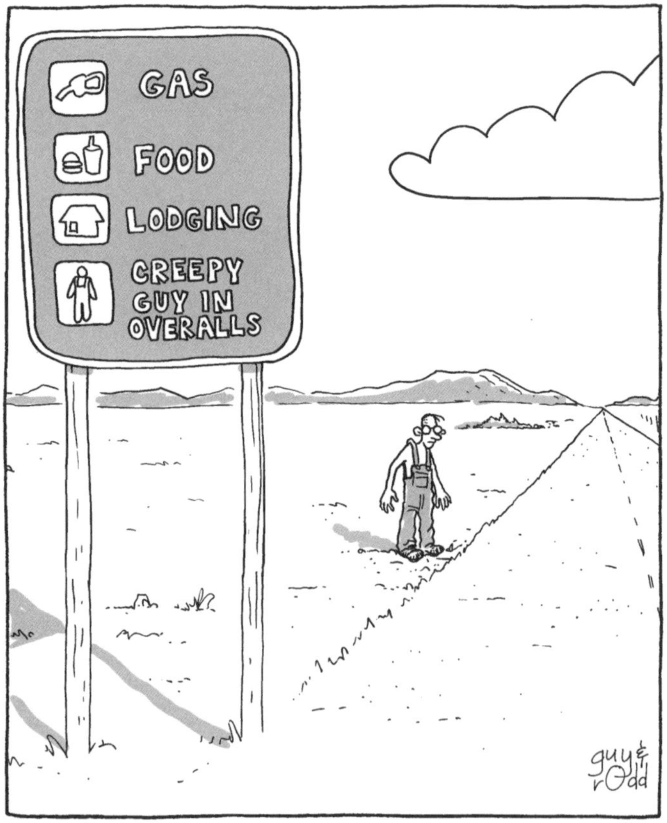
GAS
FOOD
LODGING
CREEPY GUY IN OVERALLS
guy & rodd

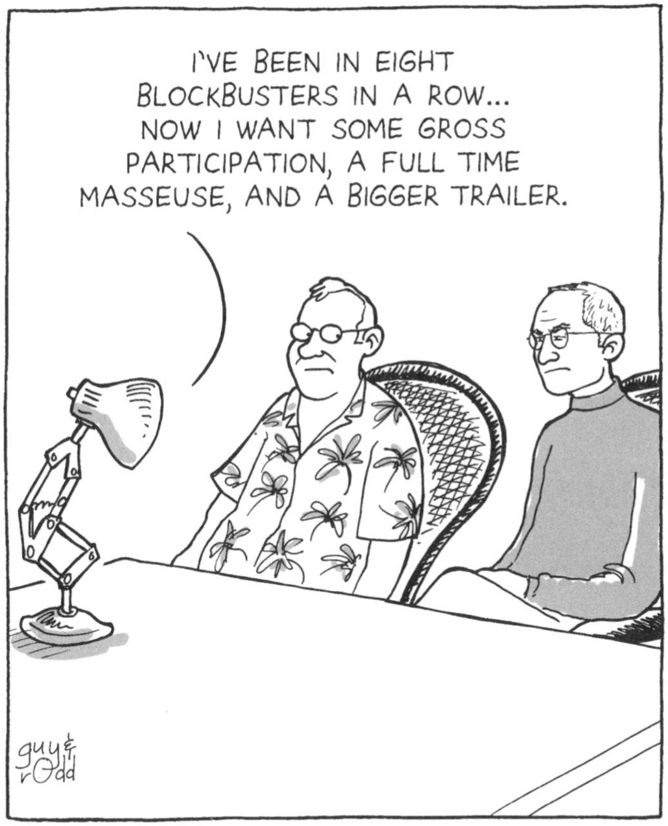
I'VE BEEN IN EIGHT BLOCKBUSTERS IN A ROW... NOW I WANT SOME GROSS PARTICIPATION, A FULL TIME MASSEUSE, AND A BIGGER TRAILER.
guy & rOdd

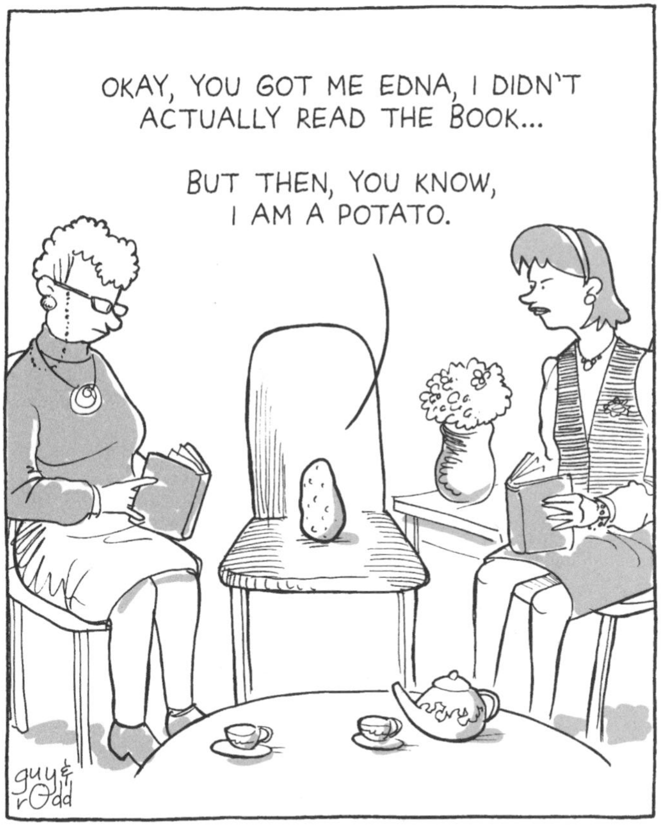
OKAY, YOU GOT ME EDNA, I DIDN'T ACTUALLY READ THE BOOK...
BUT THEN, YOU KNOW, I AM A POTATO.
guy & rOdd

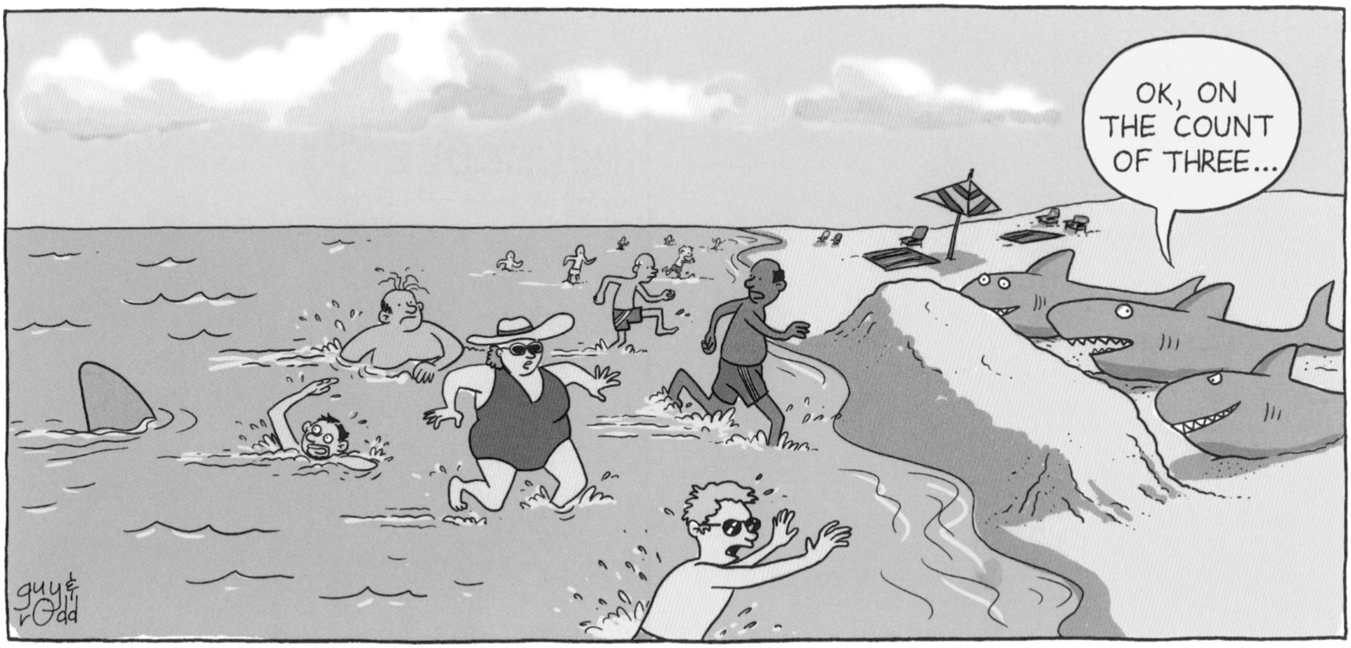
OK, ON THE COUNT OF THREE...
guy & rOdd

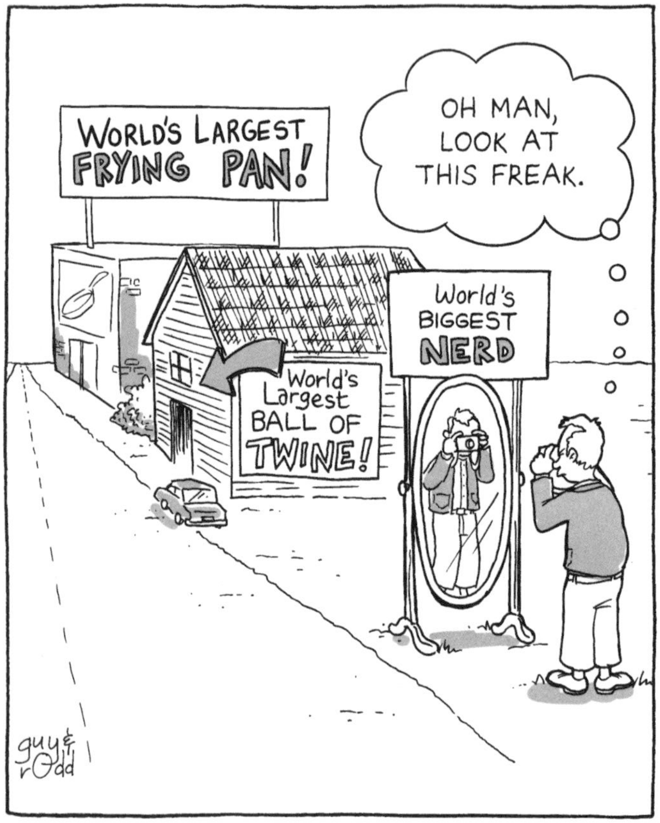
WORLD'S LARGEST FRYING PAN!
OH MAN, LOOK AT THIS FREAK.
World's BIGGEST NERD
World's Largest BALL OF TWINE!
guy & rOdd

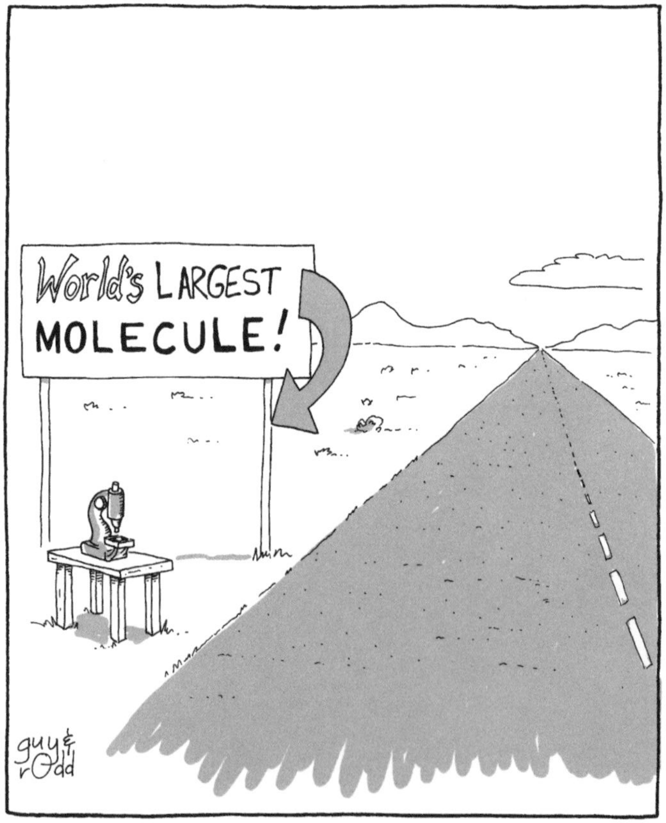
World's LARGEST MOLECULE!
guy & rOdd

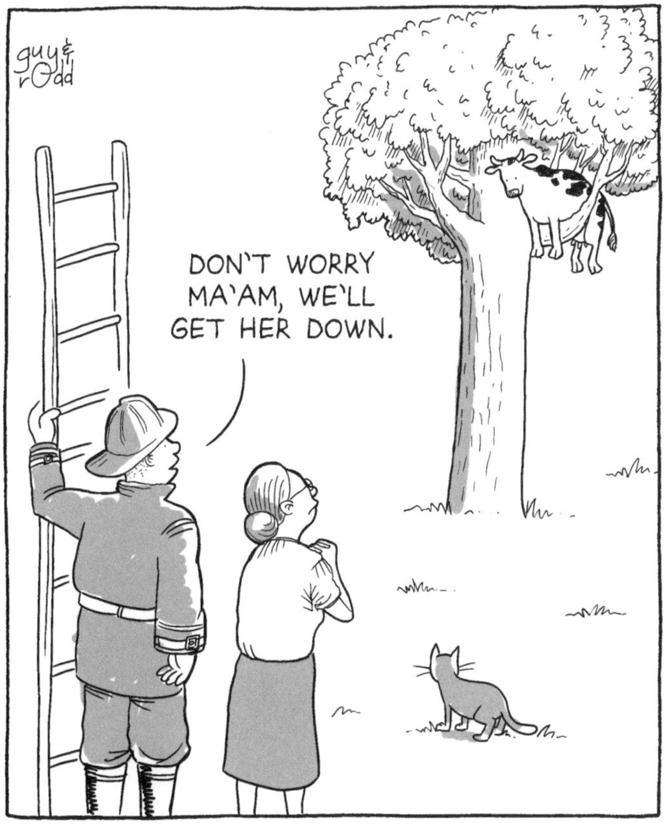
guy & rodd
DON'T WORRY MA'AM, WE'LL GET HER DOWN.

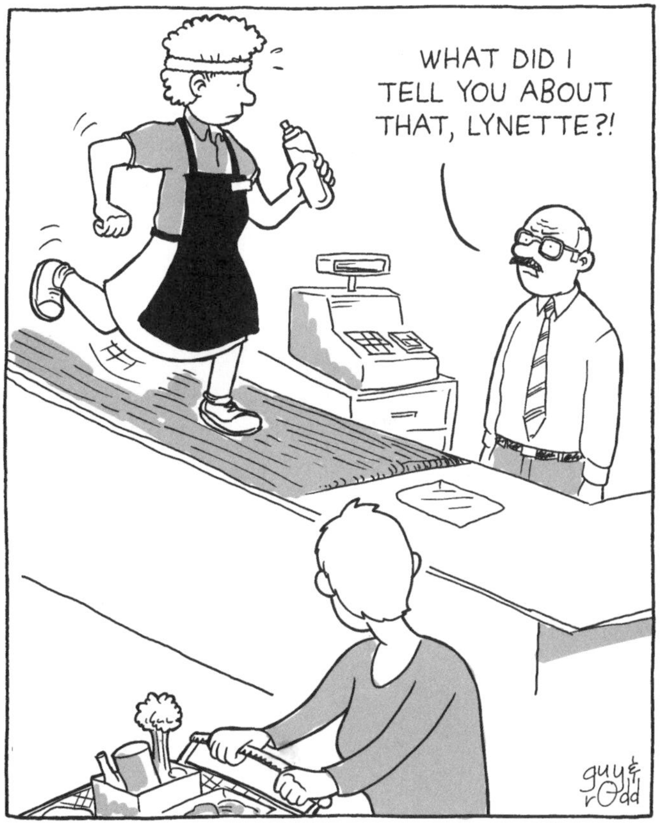
WHAT DID I TELL YOU ABOUT THAT, LYNETTE?!
guy & rodd

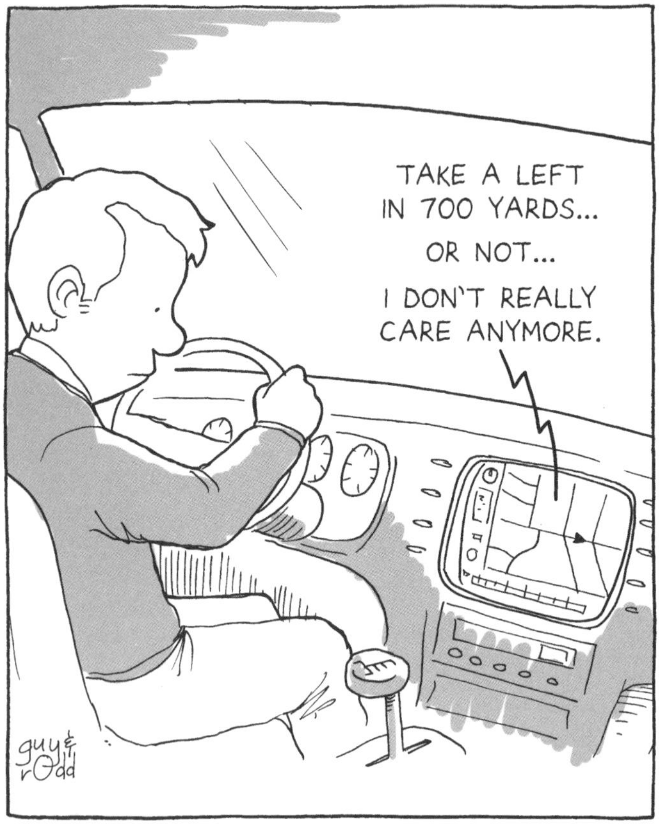
TAKE A LEFT IN 700 YARDS...
OR NOT...
I DON'T REALLY CARE ANYMORE.
guy & rodd

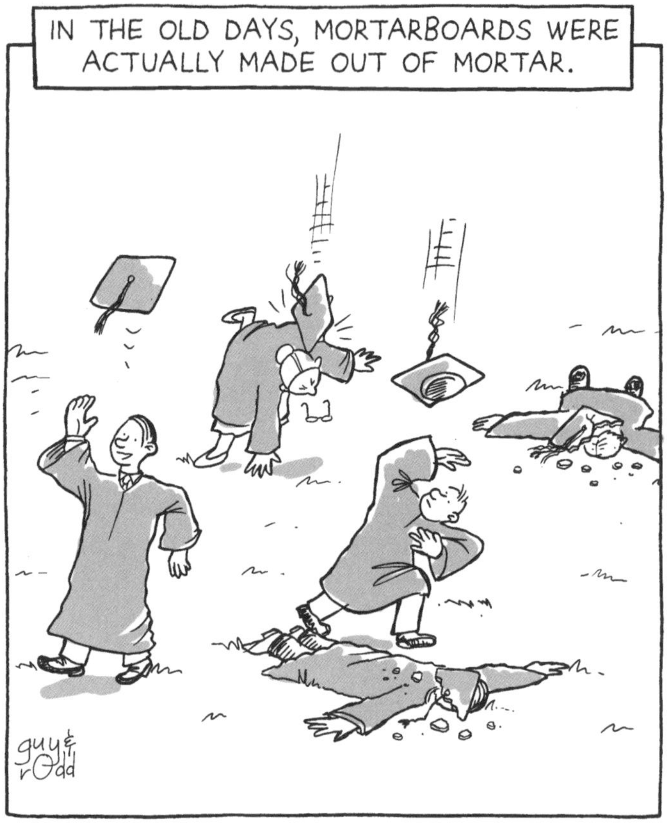
IN THE OLD DAYS, MORTARBOARDS WERE ACTUALLY MADE OUT OF MORTAR.
guy & rodd

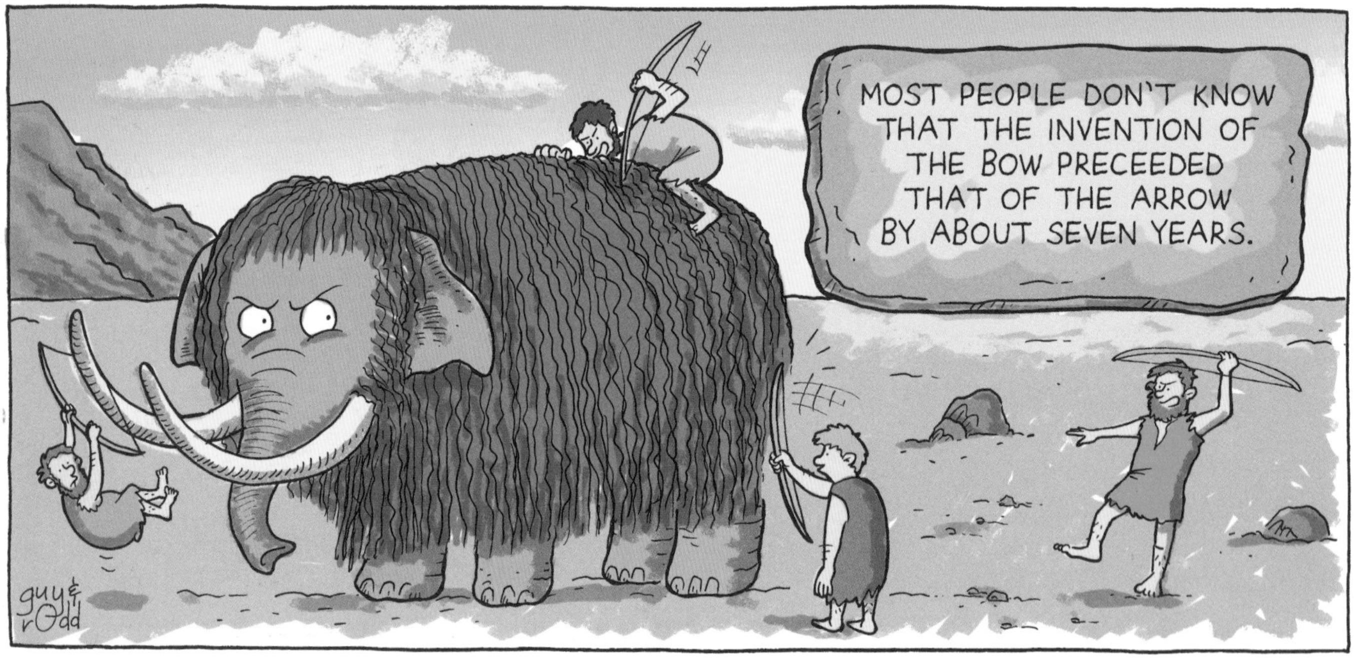
MOST PEOPLE DON'T KNOW THAT THE INVENTION OF THE BOW PRECEEDED THAT OF THE ARROW BY ABOUT SEVEN YEARS.
guy & rodd

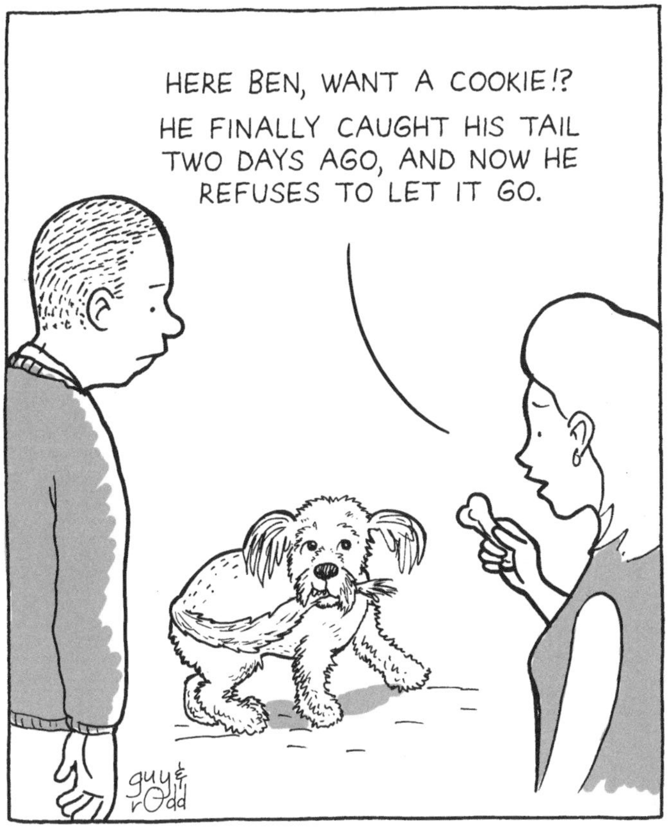
HERE BEN, WANT A COOKIE!?
HE FINALLY CAUGHT HIS TAIL TWO DAYS AGO, AND NOW HE REFUSES TO LET IT GO.
guy & rOdd

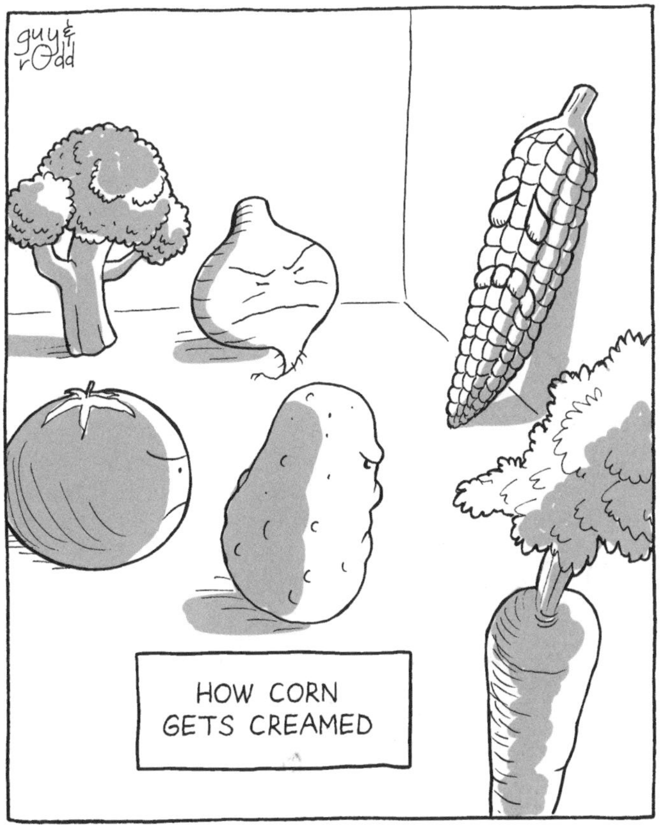
guy & rOdd
HOW CORN GETS CREAMED

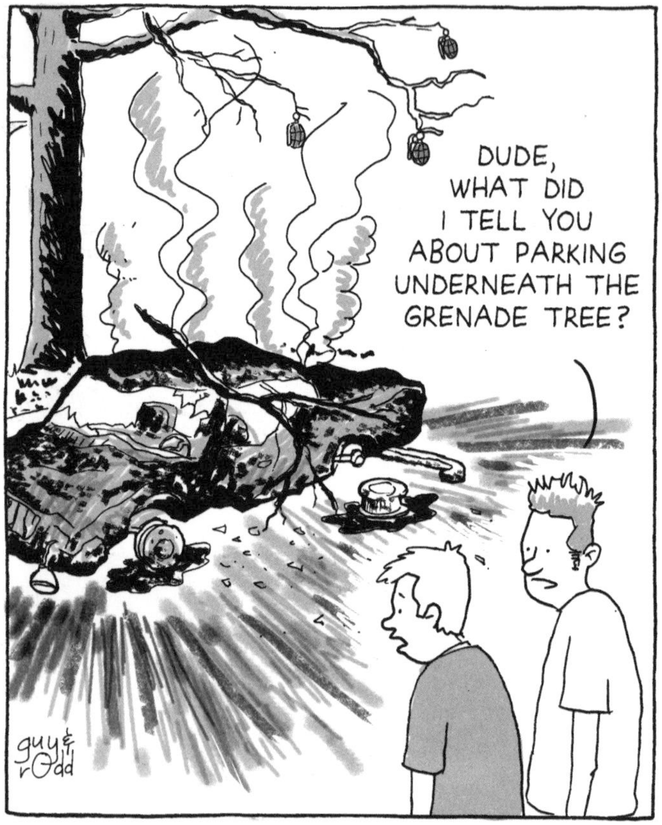
DUDE, WHAT DID I TELL YOU ABOUT PARKING UNDERNEATH THE GRENADE TREE?
guy & rOdd

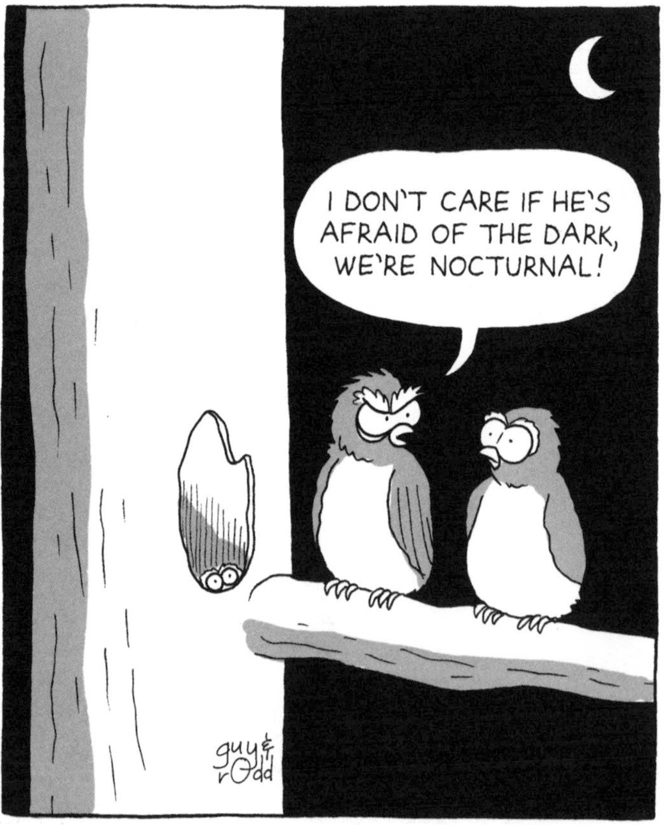
I DON'T CARE IF HE'S AFRAID OF THE DARK, WE'RE NOCTURNAL!
guy & rOdd

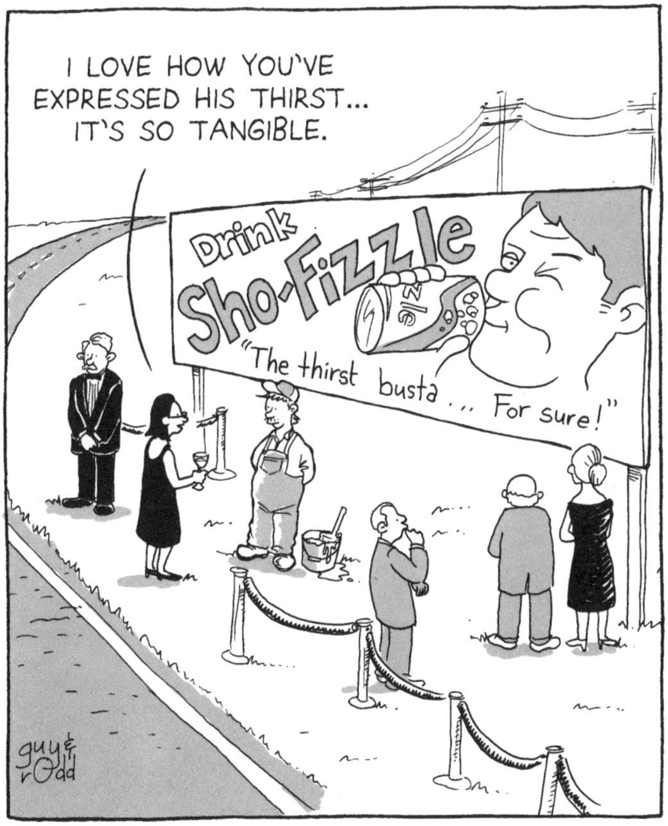
I LOVE HOW YOU'VE EXPRESSED HIS THIRST... IT'S SO TANGIBLE.
Drink Sho-Fizzle
"The thirst busta... For sure!"
guy & rOdd

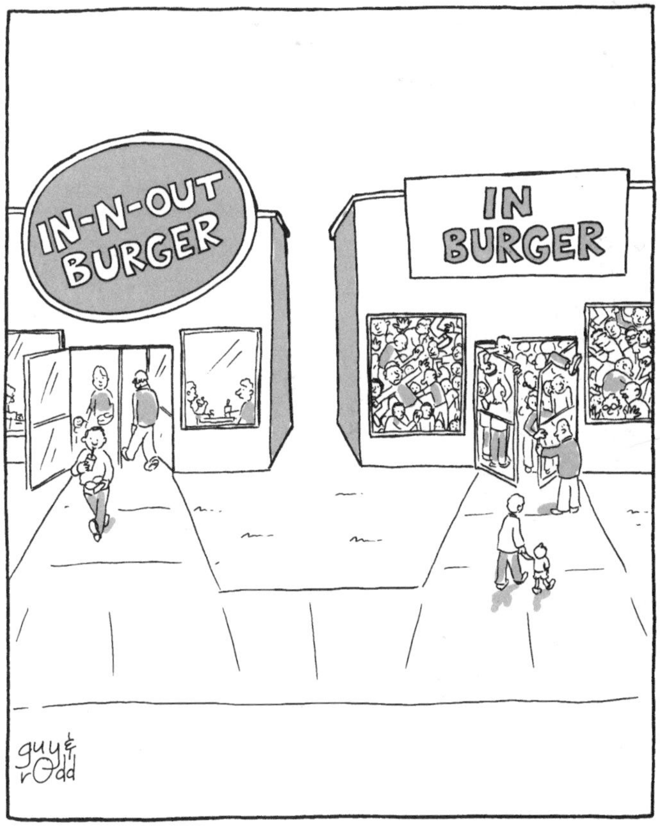
IN-N-OUT BURGER
IN BURGER
guy & rOdd

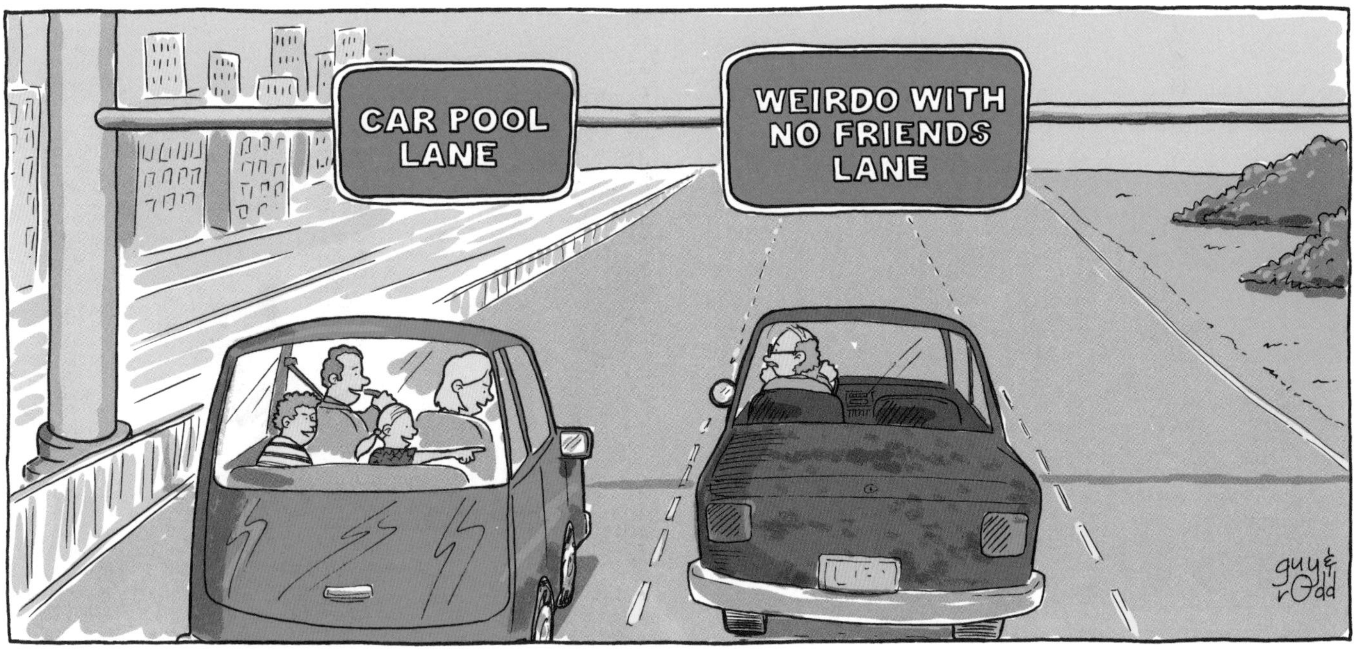
CAR POOL LANE
WEIRDO WITH NO FRIENDS LANE
guy & rOdd

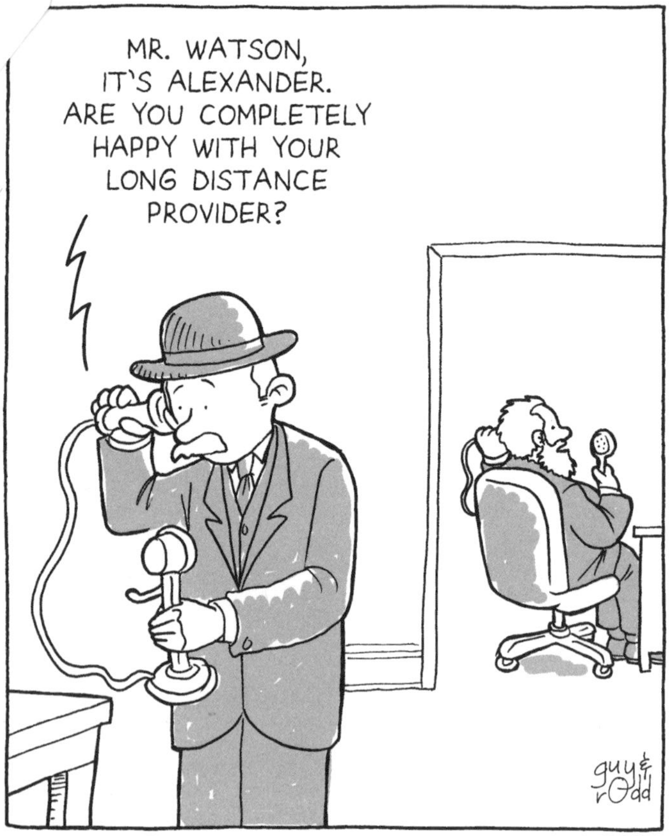
MR. WATSON, IT'S ALEXANDER. ARE YOU COMPLETELY HAPPY WITH YOUR LONG DISTANCE PROVIDER?
guy & rOdd

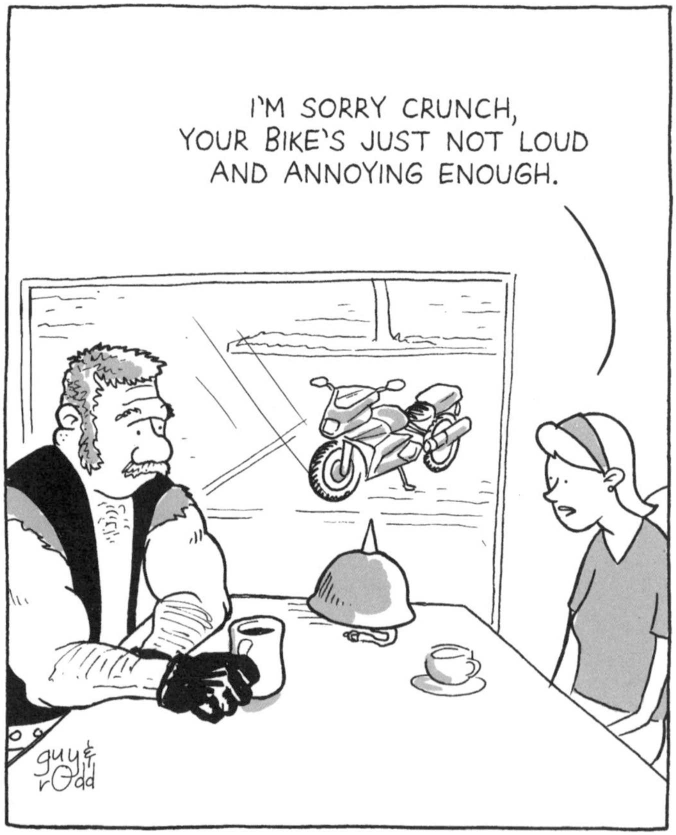
I'M SORRY CRUNCH, YOUR BIKE'S JUST NOT LOUD AND ANNOYING ENOUGH.
guy & rOdd

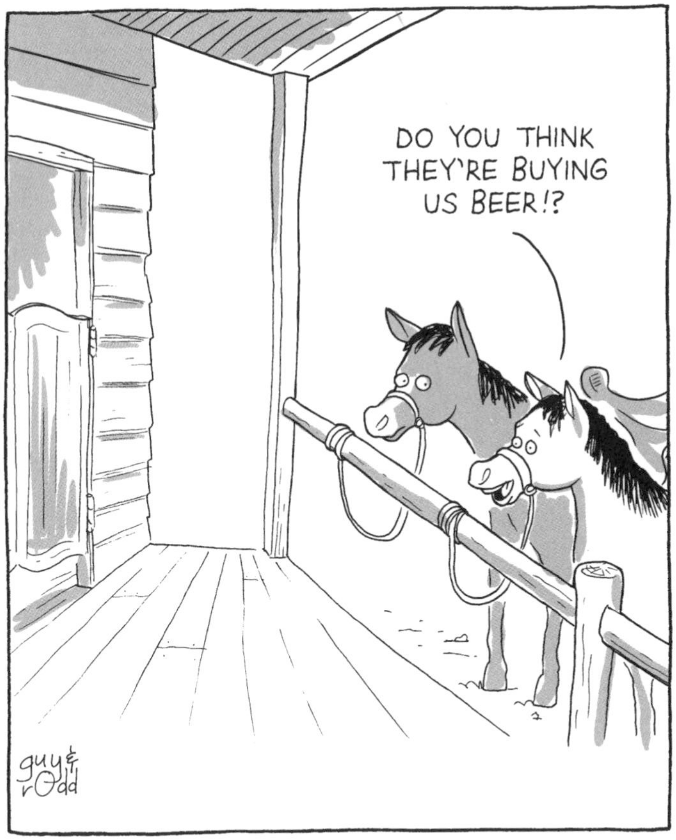
DO YOU THINK THEY'RE BUYING US BEER!?
guy & rOdd

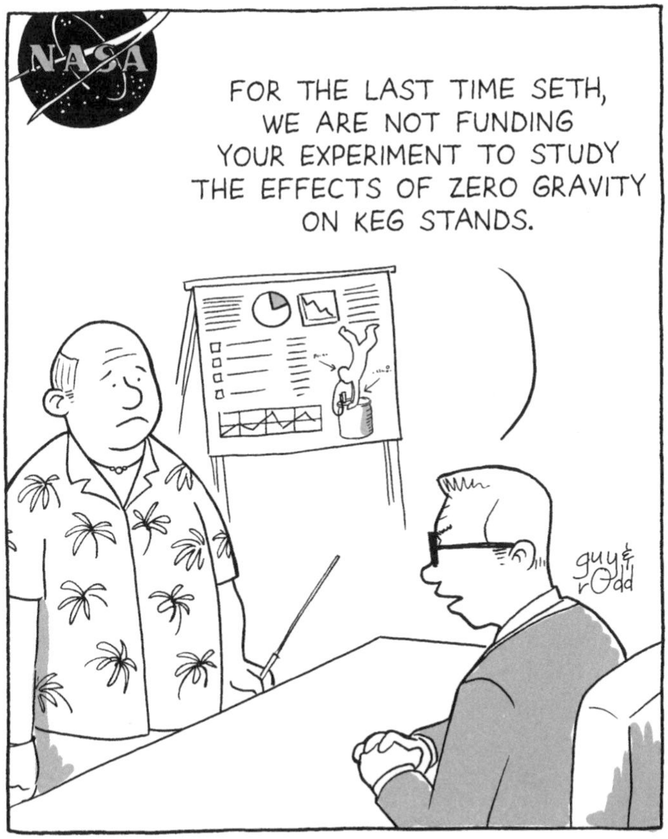
NASA
FOR THE LAST TIME SETH, WE ARE NOT FUNDING YOUR EXPERIMENT TO STUDY THE EFFECTS OF ZERO GRAVITY ON KEG STANDS.
guy & rOdd

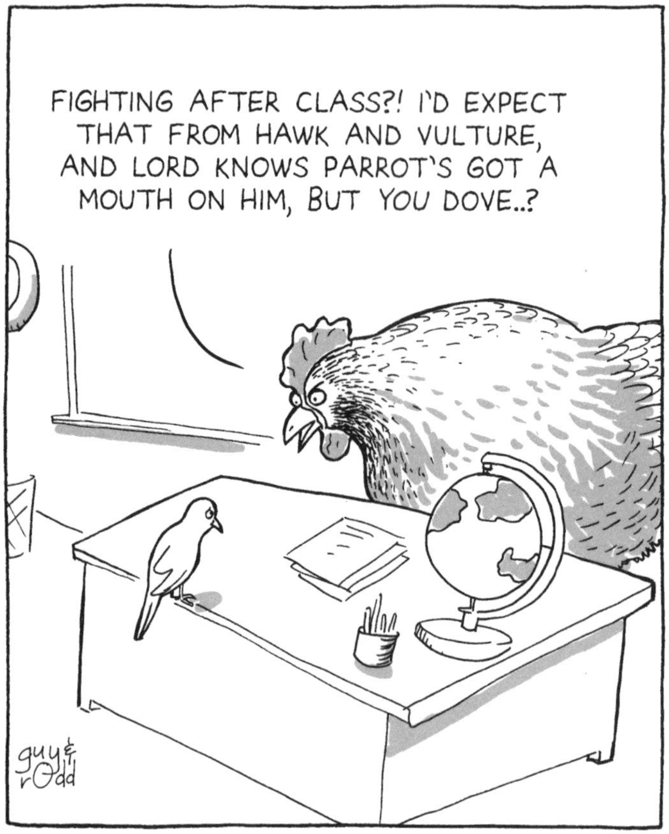
FIGHTING AFTER CLASS?! I'D EXPECT THAT FROM HAWK AND VULTURE, AND LORD KNOWS PARROT'S GOT A MOUTH ON HIM, BUT YOU DOVE..?
guy & rOdd

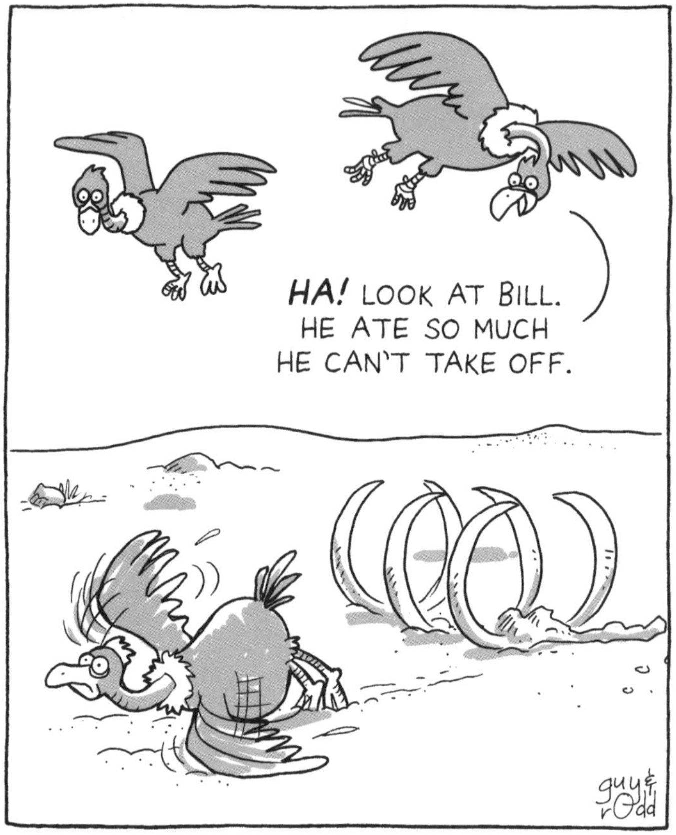
HA! LOOK AT BILL. HE ATE SO MUCH HE CAN'T TAKE OFF.
guy & rOdd

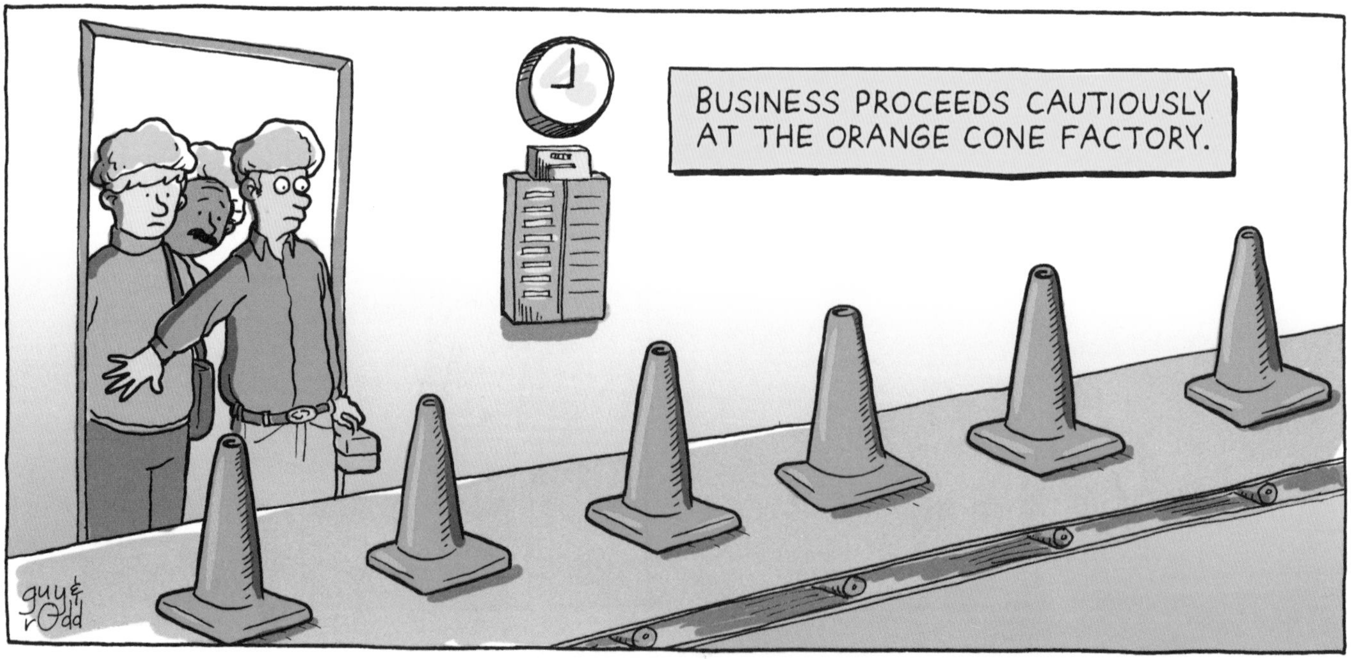
BUSINESS PROCEEDS CAUTIOUSLY AT THE ORANGE CONE FACTORY.
guy & rOdd